Awakening Nature's Healing Intelligence

Healing Intelligence

EXPANDING AYURVEDA

THROUGH

THE MAHARISHI

VEDIC APPROACH TO HEALTH

Hari Sharma, M.D., FRCPC

LOTUS

Cover art: Paul Bond, Art & Soul Design
Illustrations: Linda Suurkula
Design & Page Layout: Carola Höchst-Teague

First Edition, 1997

Printed in the United States of America
Library of Congress
Awakening Nature's Healing Intelligence includes bibliographical references.
ISBN 0-914955-35-7

Published by: Lotus Press, P.O. Box 325, Twin Lakes, Wisconsin 53181

Also by Hari Sharma

FREEDOM FROM DISEASE:
HOW TO CONTROL FREE RADICALS,
A MAJOR CAUSE OF AGING AND DISEASE
1993

DEDICATED TO HIS HOLINESS MAHARISHI MAHESH YOGI

ACKNOWLEDGMENTS

I wish to express my deepest appreciation to Maharishi Mahesh Yogi for sharing his unparalleled insights into the wisdom of the ancient Vedas. His deep understanding of the intimate connection between the fine fabrics of consciousness and the health of the physiology combined with the ancient knowledge of Ayurveda has made it possible for him to create a complete health care system that goes far and above simply fixing symptoms of disease.

Next, I would like to thank my family, whose love and support are a constant source of comfort and happiness in all my activities.

I would like to express my gratitude to the distinguished Ayurvedic Vaidyas who generously shared their vast knowledge with me. In particular, I wish to thank Brihaspati Dev Triguna, Balraj Maharshi, Jaya Ramanuja Raju, and Manohar Palakurthi. I would also like to thank the many doctors and researchers who worked with me to explore the countless potentials of this natural approach to health and make it generally available; in particular, Leslie Davis, Roger Chalmers, George Janssen, Michael Jensen, Michael and Susan Dillbeck, Chris Clark, and Barry Charles.

In the planning and preparation of this book, I have received much help for which I am extremely grateful. A special thanks goes to Eva Herriott for her expert editorial assistance. I also appreciate the assistance provided by Ellen Kauffman in the late stages of manuscript preparation and the graphic design provided by Linda Suurkula. In addition, I have been blessed with valuable advice, ideas, and comments from a number of people, including Scott Herriott, Steve Rector, Ken Walton, Jim Karpen, Jeff Golner, Sam James, Ken Chandler, David Orme-Johnson, Robert Oates, Geri McFadden, and Charlotte Bech.

A WORD TO THE WISE

This book presents a comprehensive natural health care system and discusses the underlying theory of this system, as well as research conducted on various modalities of this health care system. With this knowledge in hand, it becomes very clear how the deficiencies of our current health care system can be corrected and how we as a society can become healthier and happier. However, those who read this book should not attempt to become medical experts on their own. Nothing in this book is meant to replace the advice of a physician. If you are ill, consult a physician. In the Resources section of this book, you will find a list of organizations you can contact to find medical doctors who have also received training in the natural health care system presented in this book. You can have the best of both worlds.

TABLE OF CONTENTS

INTRODUCTION

The field of medicine is undergoing dramatic changes that affect both our understanding of how disease originates and how it should be treated. The days of finding a cure for a particular illness simply by locating the agent that gave rise to it are long gone. The causes of disease are clearly multidimensional—stress, lifestyle, diet, personality factors, and genetic predisposition all interact with disease-causing agents in the emergence of disease. This is especially the case for the modern day scourges—the chronic, degenerative diseases which afflict a large percentage of individuals who seek a physician's help. Of special importance in this development is the increased appreciation of the role that mind and emotions play in the development of disease. It has become abundantly clear that disease cannot be understood or treated in isolation from the overall context of the individual who is suffering from it.

The multidimensional concept of disease is of recent origin; as a consequence, its therapeutic implications have not yet found their way into standard medical practice. Certainly, the search for more comprehensive therapeutic approaches is on. Open-minded medical practitioners are in hot pursuit of healing modalities that address not only physiological, but also psychological and social factors. Health professionals are experimenting with support groups, stress management, imagery and visualization, biofeedback, hypnosis, and other healing modalities in an effort to reduce pain, relieve tension, or slow the progression of chronic or even terminal disease. Since many alternative, or complementary, treatments are inherently holistic and multidimensional, they have become a center of interest.

These trends occur against the backdrop of what many view as a seriously ailing system of medicine. High-tech diagnostic methods, sophisticated surgical procedures, and high-priced drugs have driven health care costs through the ceiling. The U.S. in 1993 spent almost 14 percent of the gross domestic product on health care—about 2.5 billion dollars *per day*.[1] At the current rate of health expenditure growth, this number is projected to increase to 4.7 billion dollars per day by the year 2000.[2] Yet, health outcomes have not improved in step with expenditures. Total mortality rates for most diseases have remained unchanged for the last 30 years.[3] The U.S. has greater infant mortality than most industrialized countries and ranks behind in life expectancy as well.[4] Despite the marvelous achievements of allopathic medicine in the treatment of acute trauma, critical care, and diagnostic technologies, successes in treating chronic degenerative diseases have been few and far between. A 1996 study showed that 90 million Americans had one or more chronic conditions in 1987, and over 45 percent of noninstitutionalized Americans had one or more chronic conditions.[5] The direct health care costs for this segment of the population accounted for three fourths of U.S. health care expenditures. Total costs for people with chronic conditions projected to 1990 was reported by the authors to be 659 billion dollars.[6] Under the current medical system, physicians' best efforts at treating chronic illnesses often fall short of the mark, and in many instances worsen the patient's health status. Up to 40 percent of people undergoing medical care experience negative side effects from drugs.[7] Obviously, the allopathic system of health care has grave deficiencies which must be addressed. Americans have grown discontent with the course of this medical system. A 1988 survey showed that 89 percent of Americans interviewed want a change in both the direction and structure of the U.S. health care system.[8]

It came as a shock to many mainstream physicians when a survey in the *New England Journal of Medicine* revealed that roughly one in three of their patients was using alternative treatments in addition to the conventional care provided by the physician.[9] And seven out of ten of these did not inform their physician that they were doing so. Americans, the survey estimated, are spending well over ten billion dollars out of their own pockets annually on unconventional therapies.

Together, these developments could well lead to a dramatic shift in the practice of medicine. Perhaps the most significant indication of changing times came in 1992 when the National Institutes of Health established the Office of Alternative Medicine. Its purpose is to encourage research on alternative therapies and to help integrate those found to be effective into mainstream medical practice.

In spite of the growing interest in complementary treatments, however, many health professionals fail to realize that most natural therapies operate within a theoretical framework that is incompatible with the mechanistic, reductionist approach of allopathic medicine. Allopathic therapies center around the treatment of specific symptoms, assuming that the component entities of the body can be successfully treated in isolation from their overall context. Systems of natural health, on the other hand, aim at enlivening the body's own healing resources, an approach that is most effective when applied in the earlier stages of the disease process. If we simply apply alternative techniques as if they are magic bullets in the conventional symptom-treating, fix-it approach of allopathic medicine, we will not realize the full value of natural therapies. These treatments cannot be assessed for their full effectiveness unless considered in the multifactorial context in which they are meant to function.[10]

In no instance is this so evident as in the case of the traditional system of health care from India—Ayurveda—which has enjoyed increasing popularity in the West over the last decade. Dating back more than 5,000 years, it is the oldest system of traditional medicine still in use. Its influence can be seen in ancient Greek medicine and the Hippocratic tradition where allopathic medicine has its roots. Ayurveda includes a wide range of clinical and pharmacological procedures relevant to the prevention and treatment of disease. Treatments embrace such diverse areas as internal medicine; eye, ear, throat, and mouth disease; surgery; toxicology;

pediatrics; fertility; nutrition; meditation; massage and rejuvenation ther-apy; and herbal mixtures. The ancient Ayurvedic texts deal with subjects whose importance has gained recognition within allopathic medicine only within the last 100 years, such as the sterilization of medical and surgical instruments, and dietetics. In addition, a number of modern surgical tech-niques are described in detail in Ayurveda.[11]

In spite of the widespread interest in Ayurveda, the full range of its approach to healing is still poorly understood. Ayurvedic therapies are part of a comprehensive model of health and disease which emphasizes the importance not only of physiological, but also psychological, socio-eco-logical, and spiritual factors in the development of illness. All too often, only partial aspects of the Ayurvedic knowledge are put to use. The most simplistic level of application draws on the Ayurvedic *materia medica*—its vast body of knowledge regarding healing herbs—to prescribe herbal mix-tures for various diseases. A more sophisticated level of usage focuses on balancing the three Ayurvedic physiological principles, which is consid-ered fundamental to health. While this approach certainly employs a wider range of the Ayurvedic wisdom, it still leaves out the most powerful healing connection of all. In the Ayurvedic framework, disease is ulti-mately understood to be rooted not merely in the physiology, but in con-sciousness itself. Therefore, the most effective and powerful methods of healing are those that operate at this fundamental level of existence.

This level of healing has been the focal point of the revival of Ayurve-da undertaken since the early 1980s by Maharishi Mahesh Yogi, who also brought the Transcendental Meditation® technique to the West. During the British colonization of India, much of the ancient Vedic knowledge, including Ayurveda, became fragmented, scattered, and obscured. By gathering together experts in a number of diverse aspects of Ayurveda and pooling their knowledge into one comprehensive system, Maharishi has restored many of the lost dimensions of the Ayurvedic knowledge. Even more significantly, he has highlighted how the Ayurvedic knowledge only reaches its full potential in the complete context of consciousness, mind, body, behavior, and environment. This reformulation and restoration of Ayurveda in its completeness is known as the Maharishi Ayur-Veda® health program.

Maharishi has also cast the broad spectrum of Vedic Literature into a systematic and comprehensive understanding, which brings an expansive but practical grasp of the Vedic wisdom into the reach of anyone. His uniquely profound insight is that health care cannot be complete, holistic, and truly effective without incorporating relevant approaches from the whole range of Vedic Literature. All parts of the Vedic knowledge contain valuable insights into enhancing all facets of human life. Ultimately, everything we do and experience in life is related to health—mind, behavior, lifestyle, environment, the architectural and interior design of our homes and workplaces, and the 'cosmic counterparts,' i.e. sun, moon, planets, and solar and lunar constellations, all produce influences to which our physiology must adapt. This broader and more complete form of health care is referred to as the Maharishi Vedic Approach to Health℠, in honor of the significant contributions Maharishi has made to this field of knowledge.

Moreover, associating Maharishi's name with the many aspects of the Vedic Literature upon which he has cast new light is a mark of quality. It signals the time, energy, and profound insights Maharishi has brought to bear on enlivening many 'lost' facets of the Vedic knowledge. This is critical, because in today's society, when a technique for enhancing human life is found to be effective, dozens of appallingly incomplete clones spring up overnight. For example, I know of a massage practitioner who, after taking a weekend course on the principles of Ayurveda, bought a steam bath unit and started offering the Ayurvedic purification treatment *panchakarma* as part of his practice. Certainly, panchakarma treatment does include oil massage and steam therapy, but these are just part of the many treatments of panchakarma, each of which is designed to work synergetically to achieve a specific therapeutic aim. These treatments should never be administered indiscriminately and in isolation, but only after a careful assessment of the individual's physiological imbalances and overall health status. Such half-baked health care practices are one of the main challenges that the fledgling field of natural health care must address.

In the West, a number of allopathic doctors have taken supplementary training in the Maharishi Vedic Approach to Health program, and are working together with visiting Indian *vaidyas*, expert Ayurvedic doctors, who have come to the U.S. to lend their expertise to their Western colleagues. This system of health care has gained widespread popularity in the U.S., Europe, Russia, Japan, South America, and in India itself. Of special interest to many people have been the programs offered for preventing or treating a wide range of chronic diseases—disorders with which allopathic medicine has had little success.

The focus of this comprehensive system of natural health care is on the underlying wholeness of existence and the structuring dynamics of intelligence that give rise to the human physiology. Disease is viewed as the result of a breakdown in the delicate balance of the coordinating intelligence that rules the functioning of the body. This breakdown occurs on a level deeper than organs, tissues, or cells—it results from the disconnection of intelligence from its source in wholeness. This concept of wholeness derives from the Vedic tradition and parallels modern physics' discovery of the unified source of reality beyond the subatomic level. The insubstantial nature of material creation—as identified by both Vedic science and modern physics—cannot be ignored if we are to have a complete model of the human body and the nature of health and disease. As the only system of health care that provides a model for integrating this understanding of the deepest nature of reality with our current understanding of health and disease, the Maharishi Vedic Approach to Health has much to offer.

Whereas allopathic medicine focuses on the diseased part of the body, the Maharishi Vedic Approach to Health treats the *whole* person in the context of all aspects of individual life: consciousness, physiology, behavior, and environment. It aims to "avert the danger that has not yet arisen," by making the maintenance of physical and psychological well-being a key focus of therapeutic approaches, rather than relying on the crisis management that constitutes 90 percent of allopathic medicine. The main contribution of this system of natural health care, however, lies in its restoration of the complete Vedic understanding of the importance of consciousness and the mind in nurturing and bringing fulfillment to all areas of life. The Maharishi Vedic Approach to Health is about balance—providing the guidelines for maintaining a balanced psychophysiology, routine, and lifestyle. But most of all, it is about inner discovery, about realizing that as health unfolds, so does vitality, happiness, and the many other positive attributes we all seek. In this context, prevention or treatment becomes a process of enrichment and spontaneous unfoldment of the very best of all life's wonderful possibilities. The Maharishi Vedic Approach to Health is truly a multidimensional system of health care. It approaches health from its most basic level—the interface of consciousness, mind, and body—and also contains a large cache of techniques for addressing the more expressed levels of health—on the level of the physiology, behavior, and environment.

Chapter One

HEALTH AS BALANCE

My friend Larry is a successful commodities trader and living proof of how far you can get with a healthy share of determination. Bringing to his job a bachelor's degree from an unknown Arkansas college, Larry[12] nevertheless advanced faster than any of his ivy league peers.

His secret? Larry lives and breathes for his job—or rather, for what it brings him. Comfort and security for his family, a five-bedroom home in a posh area of town, vacations in Hawaii, skiing in Aspen—in short, the good life. Larry is determined that his kids are going to grow up having everything they need. They won't be working their way through college as Larry did.

What's wrong with this picture? Nothing, at first glance—but take a closer look.

Trying to stay ahead of the game, Larry works long hours and rarely gets to bed on time. He relies on coffee to perk him up in the morning and get him through the long weary hours of the afternoon. When the going gets tough, as it often does, he eats lunch in his office, biting away at a sandwich between phone calls. He comes home from work so tense that his kids have learned not to go near their otherwise good-natured Dad until he has had plenty of time to unwind.

Lately, Larry has been feeling more tired and irritable than usual. He tosses and turns at night, sometimes waking up at 3:00 am before an especially demanding workday, unable to get back to sleep. He has developed a tendency towards stomach acidity, and he goes through a bottle of

Tylenol much faster than he used to. Yet, at his last physical, his doctor told Larry not to worry, assuring him that by all measures he is in excellent physical shape. Larry should be—he is only 31.

Larry realizes that his long, pressured work hours probably have something to do with his fatigue and crankiness. Even on weekends, he worries about matters related to his job. However, there really isn't much to be done about it—in his job, pressure is the name of the game. "And, at 200,000 dollars a year, who can complain?" he quips, whenever the subject comes up. "Besides, at the rate I'm going, I can retire at 60. I'm simply working to build a brighter future."

Larry is right, he is working to build a future. But is it going to be brighter?

Unknown to Larry, his daily routine and the constant pressure he feels from his job is getting to him. Externally, his body is functioning fine, with a few minor imperfections that by all medical standards are nothing to worry about. Internally, however, his body is in a state of constant disarray.

When Larry gets a call and learns that his biggest trades yesterday are now on the wrong side of the market, his physiology kicks into crisis mode. Neurotransmitters and hormones gush from his sympathetic nervous system, jolting Larry's heart into action, pumping blood to his muscles and brain up to five times faster than when he rests. Major arteries contract, increasing his blood pressure and putting strain on the delicate points where his blood vessels branch into smaller vessels and capillaries. Because Larry goes through this process day after day, the smooth inner lining of the blood vessels has started to tear and scar, making them more susceptible to the accumulation of deposits of fats, starches, and calcium that we know as atherosclerosis. In the long run, Larry is putting himself at risk for a wide assortment of serious diseases, including coronary heart disease, myocardial ischemia, angina pectoris, stroke, and a painful condition of the legs and feet known as intermittent claudication.

At the same time as his heart jumps into overdrive, Larry's body is frantically releasing energy supplies to meet the crisis at hand. This certainly would be helpful if Larry could flee to happier places, but it is not what his current situation demands. The body uses energy just to release the stored fuel, and because this mechanism is constantly triggered, Larry has started to tire faster—hence the fatigue he has been complaining about lately. Even worse, the cascade of biochemical processes that is involved in mobilizing extra energy could, over time, put Larry at greater risk for developing adult-onset diabetes—a condition nearly epidemic among Americans over the age of 60.

As if this weren't enough, when Larry's body mobilizes its energy reserves, it stops expending energy on processes that aren't useful in an emergency situation. His stomach halts its contractions and no longer releases the enzymes and digestive acids needed to break down food; the peristaltic movement of Larry's small intestine grinds to a halt, preventing nutrients from being absorbed. The long-term effects could be any of various digestive disorders, including constipation, ulcers, chronic diarrhea, colitis, and irritable bowel syndrome.

The chronic pressure that Larry experiences is also likely to impair his immune system functioning, putting him at increased risk for immune-related disorders such as respiratory infections, rheumatoid arthritis, and cancer.[13]

The Meaning of Health

Is Larry in good health? From the point of view of my Western training, I would have to say, yes—sort of. From the point of view of my Ayurvedic knowledge—absolutely not. Although Larry is not yet showing any signs of disease, he is working hard to lay the foundation for chronic health problems which, unless checked in time, are likely to manifest some five, ten, or 15 years down the road. There is no telling whether Larry will develop any of the afflictions listed above. He may come down with a totally different ailment when he is, say, 65. Or he may retire to Florida at 60 and live happily ever after—or at least until his 80s or 90s. Or, he may drop dead from a massive heart attack at age 54, with no warning at all.

The variability in individuals' responses to external pressures or poor lifestyle habits is so great that it is impossible to predict which of two people—all other things equal—will develop health problems, and which will not. What we *can* say is that Larry's physiology is already starting to show signs of poor adaptation to the demands placed on it—and that should be a cause for alarm. Although Larry and his doctor may think he is in good health, he is not.

What *does* it mean to be healthy? It is a deceptively simple question. Most of us would say that being healthy simply means not being sick. In Western culture, people are generally regarded as healthy if they don't show any obvious signs of disease. This understanding is not only common among laypeople, it dominates the approach to prevention and treatment of disease and also most of the research efforts within the medical field. Medical studies measure health in terms of mortality, morbidity, number of yearly doctor visits, and number of missed work days. Allopathic medicine simply has no method of measuring positive states of health. Current health rating scales focus exclusively on the absence of disability and disease.[14]

Health is much more than the mere absence of disease. It is a state of complete balance on the level of body, mind, and consciousness; a state of optimum happiness, an integrated state of emotional balance and well-being, psychological flexibility, and energy. It is an active state of self-realization, where individuals live and breathe their full potential. In this model, health and disease form two ends of a continuum, with complete balance on one end and extreme physiological imbalance, manifesting as disease and disability, on the other end. In a state of complete balance, an individual possesses tremendous resistance against environmental assaults. This person's physiology is flexible and able to adapt and recover easily from environmental challenges. Psychologically, he or she is able to cope with daily stressors and remain balanced even in the face of serious adversity.

As the body goes out of balance, the individual's general resistance is impaired, and he or she will start to move toward the middle of the health-disease continuum, experiencing the minor ailments of which Larry is complaining: digestive problems, headaches, bleeding gums, insomnia, leg cramps, vague aches and pains, fatigue, irritability, mood swings, depression, etc. These are the typical complaints of the so-called 'worried well,' a term physicians have coined for the large group of patients who do not exhibit any diagnosable symptoms of disease.

Health   Disease

FIGURE 1. THE HEALTH-DISEASE CONTINUUM
Health is more than the absence of disease. There is a wide range between disease and health where a person can be considered neither well, nor really sick. The health status of most people in today's society falls somewhere within the two points marked on the continuum.

Diagnosable illness results from increasing imbalances on the 'micro-level' of physiological functioning. These are most often caused by the ongoing biochemical drama that Larry, as well as the majority of people in our society, are exposed to on a daily basis. As we saw above, if repeated over time these subtle imbalances gradually lead to a breakdown of 'macro-level' physiological processes and the emergence of what we call disease. In other words, long before diagnosable symptoms appear, there exist detectable preconditions for disease. The Ayurvedic concept of preconditions encompasses the Western notion of disease risk factors, such as hypertension and high cholesterol, but goes much further. According to Ayurveda, diseases progress through six stages of development. The first stage is the *accumulation* of imbalances in the physiology. The second stage is *aggravation*, which occurs when imbalances have accumulated to the point where they are predisposed to spread. If the imbalances are not corrected at this point, the third stage of the disease process begins to occur; this is *dissemination*, the actual spreading of imbalances through tissues and organs. With their *localization* in certain tissues or organs in the fourth stage, imbalances will start to cause subtle subclinical impairment. In the fifth stage, this impairment reaches the point of *manifestation*, when actual symptoms appear. The sixth and final stage of the disease process consists of the *disruption* of physiological functions, which, if not checked, will progress to the point of impairment, disability, or death.

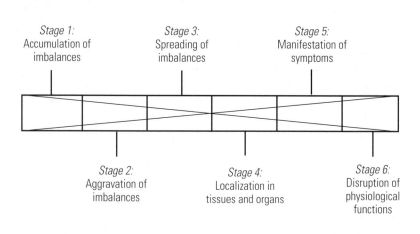

FIGURE 2. THE SIX STAGES OF DISEASE.
In the development of disease, the earlier imbalances are addressed, the easier it is to restore the body to health.

In other words, the concept of disease in allopathic medicine does not appear in the Ayurvedic model of disease until stages five and six. This apparently simple divergence between the two models of health gives rise to significant differences in their approach to both prevention and treatment. When Larry's doctor declared him in good health after his last physical, it was because Larry's blood pressure was normal, his blood sugar and cholesterol levels within acceptable range, and his blood and urine analyses normal. If Larry had insisted, his doctor might have ordered more sophisticated tests, yet none of those tests would have given the doctor any further clues to the source of Larry's complaints. The imbalances in Larry's physiology are still *subclinical*. They have not reached the level where they produce clinical signs of dysfunction detectable by the diagnostic methods of allopathic medicine. Larry will therefore have to wait another five or ten years—until he develops a health problem or a recognized risk factor for one—before he will get the attention of the medical establishment.

A Stitch in Time

As long as health and disease are viewed as a dichotomy in which a person is either healthy or sick, then certainly the bulk of health care efforts must focus on treating illness after symptoms of disease become manifest. However, if health and disease are seen to exist along a continuum of physiological balance and imbalance, then the focus of health care efforts must be on neutralizing or removing factors that cause the slide toward the disease-end of the continuum.

"A wise person, desirous of his own well-being, should take recourse to the appropriate therapies before the occurrence of the diseases or even while the diseases are in their primary stage of manifestation," wrote Charaka more than 5,000 years ago in *Charaka Samhita*, the major text-book of Ayurveda.[15] Charaka is making a simple point that has profound implications. If we wait until a disease manifests as symptoms, not only will we have to suffer the pain and misery of illness, but it will also be more difficult to reverse the physiological processes that have long since gone awry. In view of the illnesses with which we as a society are faced today, this is of special importance. Larry is working around the clock to create a future like that of more than 36 million[16] other Americans suffering from chronic diseases such as adult-onset diabetes; autoimmune disorders;

gastrointestinal diseases such as ulcer, Crohn's disease, or colitis; thyroid disorders; hypertension with its concomitant risk of cardiovascular disease and stroke; osteoporosis; impotence; and chronic impairment of the immune system, which increases susceptibility to various diseases including AIDS and cancer. These are the so-called degenerative diseases—the scourges of our modern age. They are chronic conditions that typically emerge in the later stages of life, after years of wear and tear on the body. They are also diseases that allopathic medicine can do very little about. When it comes to chronic diseases, high-tech diagnostic methods, drugs, and sophisticated surgical procedures provide little more than symptomatic relief, if that. And not uncommonly, the side effects associated with these treatments are themselves debilitating, and in the long run create more problems than they solve.

Ironically, chronic degenerative diseases are often avoidable. The three biggest killers of our time—heart disease, cancer, and stroke—which together are responsible for about two thirds of all deaths per year,[17] do not develop from inescapable external threats to the physiology. They derive from a mixture of physiological, psychological, behavioral, and social factors. This appears to also be the case for many of the other chronic diseases which afflict our population.[18]

Piecemeal Prevention

So what are Larry's choices? Well, he could get a boring desk job in a quiet office. However, that wouldn't be much of a solution, since Larry would be so frustrated there that he really wouldn't gain any ground with his health—intense negative emotions put the body under stress as well.

Unfortunately, under the practices of the current medical system, his other options are few. Larry could adopt a low-fat diet for the rest of his life to reduce his chances of developing heart disease, a disease that kills more people than cancer and stroke combined. However, even if he eliminated all the known risk factors for heart disease, he still would not be totally covered, since standard physiological risk factors for heart disease predict only a small minority of cases.[19] And Larry would still be at risk for the many other chronic diseases his lifestyle and its constant stress could cause.

Even if Larry develops the signals that trigger active medical interventions, he will still not be in a good position. Let's visit Larry ten years from now. By that time, his rollercoaster ride over the relentless heaves and pitches of shorts and longs, options and futures has taken its toll. Larry is no longer just fatigued and irritable, he is overweight, and has heartburn and high blood pressure. And although he eats a cholesterol-lowering diet, his cholesterol count is way too high. Due to fatigue, his job performance has begun to suffer, reducing his income and raising his frustration and blood pressure still further. Deciding that Larry is at risk of developing heart disease, his doctor has put him on a cholesterol-lowering drug and medication to lower his blood pressure. The cholesterol-lowering drug disturbs his digestion still further, causing vague nausea, constipation, and flatulence. By current medical practices, Larry will now be on blood pressure and cholesterol-lowering drugs for the rest of his life.

What is wrong with this scenario? From an Ayurvedic point of view—a lot.

Let's consider just one aspect of Larry's medical problems—his high cholesterol level. Certainly, a high level of cholesterol is associated with atherosclerosis. However, that does not necessarily mean that very low levels of cholesterol are good. We cannot live without cholesterol. It constitutes an important part of cell membranes and is needed for the synthesis of a large number of hormones. It is also used for the generation of bile, which is necessary for the absorption of fat-soluble vitamins, such as vitamins A, D, E, and K. Although low levels of cholesterol are associated with a decreased incidence of heart attack, studies have also linked low cholesterol to an increase, by as much as one third, in overall mortality from other causes, such as lung cancer, respiratory disease, digestive disease, trauma, stroke, accidents, and suicide.[20] As a consequence, there is an ongoing controversy in the medical community about the widespread use of cholesterol-lowering interventions, especially drugs. Many researchers feel the safety of using these drugs is far from firmly established. And this is without even considering the potentially harmful side effects of cholesterol-lowering medications. In the case of one widely-used drug, patients must have blood tests done at least twice a year to ensure that their liver function remains unaffected by the drug.[21]

This is just one example of how focusing on one or two factors, without due consideration to the full context in which they occur, often creates more problems than it solves. Medicine's 'risk factor' approach to prevention is replete with such instances. As Dr. Geoffrey Rose comments in a *British Medical Journal* article, when a preventive measure, instead of removing a supposed cause of disease, adds an unnatural factor, ". . the end result is to increase biological abnormality by an even further removal from those conditions to which we are genetically adapted. . . . Long-term safety cannot be assured, and quite possibly harm may outweigh benefit."[22]

The allopathic approach to prevention also encompasses a number of safe and effective measures, such as smoking cessation, exercising, adopting a healthy diet, etc. These approaches seek to restore biological normality through natural means. In practice, however, few physicians attempt to implement these. Larry has about one chance in three that his doctor will ask him about his dietary habits as part of the consultation, or incorporate recent findings on the role of nutrition in his recommendations to Larry.[23] Although some of today's most prevalent risk factors, such as hypertension, cholesterol, and obesity, are known to be highly responsive to dietary modifications, only half of the physicians in the U.S. give dietary advice as a treatment recommendation for these conditions.[24] This is not surprising when one looks at what is taught in medical schools. Out of 129 medical schools in the U.S., only 29 have a required course in nutrition.[25] Similarly, general skills needed for health promotion, such as risk assessment and methods for initiating behavior and lifestyle changes, are rarely taught in medical schools. Because the focus of the medical system is on intervention, even preventive efforts take on the character of interventive methods, such as popping a pill to decrease the cholesterol level or lower the blood pressure.

In this chapter, I have spent some time discussing the consequences of adopting a partial approach to prevention, because it provides an excellent illustration of the theme of this book: Prevention and treatment can be very complicated if you try to manipulate single elements in a highly complex system without consideration of the complete context in which they occur. It can be comparatively much more simple if one aims at balancing the body and augmenting its own healing processes. This, in a nutshell, is the focus of the Maharishi Vedic Approach to Health.

Chapter Two

THE BODY'S HEALING INTELLIGENCE

Dean (name has been changed) is a writer and lecturer based in Colorado with a 50-hour work week and a frenzied lifestyle not unlike Larry's. Over the years, his hectic travel schedule and intense job demands had taken their toll. He was beleaguered by a cough that wouldn't go away, and suffered from frequent flu, low energy, and heart palpitations. Being of a more insistent nature than Larry, he had a number of tests run to find out what was going on. However, neither the cardiologist nor the pulmonary specialist were able to diagnose his symptoms. He wasn't clinically sick, yet his whole system was flashing red lights. On top of it all, Dean saw his cholesterol level increase from 231 to 245 over a nine-month period in spite of the fact that he followed a strict, low-fat diet to bring it down. Dean tried various alternative approaches, but he didn't get any better. At a friend's suggestion, he decided to consult with a doctor trained in the Maharishi Vedic Approach to Health.

Along with other diagnostic procedures, the physician used the ancient art of *nadi vigyan*, or pulse diagnosis, to get a sense of the state of Dean's physiology. Because the blood flows through every single part of the body, a trained practitioner can feel any obstruction or imbalance in any part of the body in the pulse. Through the pulse, the physician assessed not only the condition of bodily organs, but also the interaction and balance of different parts of the mind-body system. Based on the distribution of imbalances in Dean's body, he then recommended an array of interventions targeted to Dean's specific needs. These included 'customized' diet and lifestyle recommendations, herbal mixtures and purification procedures to facilitate the correction of imbalances, and consciousness-based techniques to enliven the health-supporting balanced functioning of mind and emotions.

To Dean's surprise, the doctor never focused specifically on treating any of Dean's symptoms. He didn't target his high cholesterol or set out to get rid of his cough, heart palpitations, or low energy level. He simply put him on a multidimensional health care regimen designed according to the principles of the Maharishi Vedic Approach to Health. Yet, after a short while Dean had noticeable improvements. His cough and heart palpitations disappeared. His digestion improved and he felt better than he had for decades. When his previous doctor did a cholesterol test, they were both surprised to find it had dropped from 245 to 191.

Dean's story is a good illustration of how dramatic the results can be when you focus on correcting the underlying cause of health problems— the accumulated imbalances in the body—rather than trying to treat specific symptoms. Symptoms that appear very different on the surface often have a common underlying cause and will therefore disappear when this cause is removed.

Focusing on individual risk factors for disease is like trying to plug holes in a leaking dam. Preventive efforts are far more effective when they focus on removing the underlying physiological imbalances and increasing the individual's general resistance to disease. This means not only augmenting the body's resistance resources, but also boosting the individual's psychological capacity for handling environmental challenges.

According to the Ayurvedic tradition, there are three types of resistance. Our *constitutional strength* is determined by our genetic makeup; it exists from birth. Our *temporal strength* is based on our age—there is a natural tendency for bodily strength to diminish with age. Our *acquired strength* is the end result of the mental and physiological habits we have. A cacophony of biological, psychological, and social influences—each in itself contributing an insignificant amount of disorder—*over time* may weaken the body's resistance resources and make it more susceptible to disease. We often contribute to this process ourselves through the foods we eat, the lifestyle we adopt, the feelings and thoughts we entertain. If our daily habits tax our physiology, and our mind is under constant stress, our acquired strength will naturally be low.

Choosing to augment our acquired strength opens a new range of possibilities for maintaining and improving health. All the health habits which in allopathic practice are considered potential negative risk factors—habits of diet and exercise, habits of emotions, thought, and behavior—can be reversed and harnessed to boost the physiology into greater health and well-being. Even genetic predisposition and old age are not necessarily final determinants of disease. As we grow older and begin to lose some of our strength and flexibility, we do have to be more alert to maintain health habits that will support balanced physiological functioning and maximize our acquired strength, but within these limitations it is possible for most people to stay perfectly well. And, being genetically predisposed to heart disease, for example, does not mean that one will die of a heart attack or even develop heart disease. It *does* mean that if the body becomes more and more out of balance, the area that is genetically weak will be the link in the chain that breaks down.

Judy (name has been changed), who is now in her late 30s, is a good example of just how much one can achieve by enhancing one's acquired strength, even in the face of poor odds. Judy has had preliminary symptoms of multiple sclerosis (MS) on and off since she was 21. In 1989 she developed optic neuritis, a disease that is often a precursor of full-fledged MS. Instead of just giving up and letting the disease run its course, however, Judy decided to use a health regimen prescribed by a physician trained in the Maharishi Vedic Approach to Health and customized to her condition. By following it, she has managed to stay remarkably well in the face of an otherwise crippling disease. She has not been cured of MS, but the treatment modalities she has followed have allowed Judy to remain in reasonably good health. She has not required hospitalization nor needed steroids to avert some of the more severe complications of MS. She has even stayed well enough to continue her demanding job.

A Network of Self-Organizing Intelligence

The healing modalities employed in the Maharishi Vedic Approach to Health aim at something more profound than simply improving immune functioning and acquired strength, as useful as that may be. Overcoming established disease, preventing the development of new disease, and promoting graceful aging all amount to the same thing—adopting health measures that strengthen, balance, and enliven the underlying self-organizing, self-healing intelligence of the body. That self-organizing intelligence is the fundamental essence, the regulating homeostatic principle integral to all physiological functioning.

"Nature heals and the doctor sends the bill," Mark Twain once remarked. His comment is a wry observation of a simple fact that is all too often ignored. The body has a remarkable ability to heal itself. In fact, an estimated 90 to 95 percent of the ailments that people consult their physician about are self-terminating—they would resolve on their own even if the patient did not seek a doctor's help.[26]

The human immune system encompasses about one trillion (10^{12}) white blood cells (the soldiers of the immune system) and 100 million trillion (10^{20}) antibodies (molecules produced to destroy invading agents). In just the past few minutes, your body has produced about one million billion new antibody molecules—each one of them designed to locate and eliminate one specific type of foreign intruder. Yet, white blood cells and antibodies are just one line of defense in a full-fledged army which involves genes, neurotransmitters, hormones, glands, organs, and even the central nervous system. The logistics of organizing the billions and trillions of processes that comprise the body's healing system are of mind-boggling proportions. Yet, when functioning in balance, all parts of this army march together in one precisely orchestrated, harmonious wholeness.

The human body at its most palpable level consists of the external manifestations that we can all observe—sense organs, limbs, trunk, shoulders, skin, hair, etc. The internal aspect of the body consists of systems—the musculoskeletal system, the circulatory system, the lymphatic system, the respiratory system, the digestive system, the excretory system, etc. Systems are comprised of organs, glands, and other components. Organs and other structures are formed by various tissues, which in turn are constituted of more than a quadrillion singularly differentiated cells that comprise the human body. Every single physiological parameter, be it heart rate, blood pressure, hormone levels, or electrolyte balance results from immensely complicated processes. Each part of the body is constantly adjusting to the needs of the physiology as dictated by current conditions in the inner and outer environment. At the same time, every physiological function fluctuates biorhythmically with its own frequency and amplitude. The values of some bodily parameters vary dramatically during a normal 24-hour period. In other words, what we see as our stable unchanging physiology is, in reality, a constantly changing, dynamic network of interacting processes. The functioning of all systems, all organs, all cells is correlated with the overall needs of the whole system at any given moment. Our body is a constantly changing flow of chemical and electrical interactions interwoven in a network of phenomenal complexity.

What is the common theme, the red thread that binds all these individual elements together and creates a coherently functioning human body? What is the element responsible for maintaining equilibrium in the face of a constantly fluctuating internal and external environment?

The only word that adequately describes the ingeniously coordinated complexity of the human body is *intelligence*. Intelligence, in the Vedic framework, is that which gives direction to change. It is the source of order in physiological functioning, the unseen force that aligns the functioning of the parts to the system as a whole, giving a specific direction to biological activity, which in turn gives rise to the specific expressions of biological function or structure. Every point in the body is a focus point of a vast, self-organizing intelligence, constantly coordinating, rebuilding, maintaining, and renewing. A grand and detailed blueprint of hierarchical intelligence generates the order and purpose of even the minutest of physiological processes. Without an underlying, integrating intelligence, the exquisite coordination between the innumerable macro- and micro-level entities of the body would be inconceivable.

The concept of the body as a network of intelligence is central in the Maharishi Vedic Approach to Health. Health is viewed as the dynamic, carefully-tuned equilibrium of all the elements in this network. Disease emerges from the loss of balance, which in turn results from a loss in the full expression of intelligence in the body. The gradual breakdown of coordination, order, and function of micro-level processes will, over time, give rise to dysfunction of macro-level physiological processes. Healing and prevention must therefore consist of efforts to restore and maintain order by enlivening the body's inherent intelligence.

Healing efforts that focus on enhancing the body's own healing intelligence constitute a universal theme in all systems of natural health care. Even in the ancient Hippocratic tradition of the Greeks, from which allopathic medicine is derived, the sophisticated healing intelligence of the body played a central role. It was referred to as *vis medicatrix naturae*—the healing power of nature. The ancient Greek physicians were keenly aware that treatment and prevention must seek to strengthen this healing intelligence rather than impeding it.

Allopathic medicine, however, has long since departed from this feature of the Hippocratic tradition. As the late Norman Cousins noted, it is one of the great paradoxes of medical science that it has almost no awareness of the body's own healing system and the potential it holds for our health care efforts. "Less is known and taught about the healing system than about any of the other internal forces that govern human existence," he wrote. There is a great deal of focus on the immune system in medical schools, but the healing system is much more than simply the functions of the immune system. The body's healing system is immensely comprehensive, with a wide range of 'tools' at its disposal—it precisely diagnoses problems, then musters the necessary resources for repairing and regenerating the diseased part of the body.

This divergence in focus is not just a casual rhetorical difference. It is the main feature that sets systems of natural health care apart from allopathic medicine. When we forget it is the body and not the doctor that heals disease, we shift the balance of health care efforts toward outside, high-tech interventions. Yet, when genuine healing—not symptom management—occurs, it is brought about by the body itself. At best, doctors provide the prerequisite condition for this to happen, helping the body overcome demands that might otherwise prove too great for the compromised healing system to manage. Doctors may administer an antibiotic, for example, which delays the spread of bacteria long enough to enable the body's own healing forces to catch up, or they may align broken bones to ensure they grow together in the right way. In far too many cases, however, the treatments that are recommended by doctors do little but manage symptoms. Administering powerful drugs for migraines, anxiety, or depression, or treating rashes with cortisone cream may produce short-term relief, but these treatments do not in any way aid the body in overcoming the problem at its root.

This brings us to the crux of the matter. When we completely ignore the body's own self-healing abilities, our treatment efforts may actually impede the healing process, while offering only short-term relief. Drugs, for example, most often add a harmful element to an already imbalanced system, delaying or hampering the body's ability to restore the needed balance. Some drugs, for example, affect the absorption of vitamins and minerals—nutrients the body needs in the restoration process. Others create reactions so severe they prolong disease. According to some studies, up to one third of hospitalized patients have a drug reaction, almost doubling the length of their stay.[27]

Why the lack of conscious cooperation with the body's own regenerative powers? Why has medicine developed its characteristic reliance on drugs, technology, and invasive procedures? What is the source of the body's tremendous self-regulating intelligence, and how can this potent source of healing be enlivened?

To answer these questions, we shall first look at how the basic assumptions of allopathic medicine developed. We shall then take a look at what triggers the healing intelligence of the body and at some fascinating biological puzzles that demonstrate the power and range of nature's healing intelligence. We will also see how modern physics holds lessons for medicine we cannot afford to ignore. We will then explore the concept of nature's self-organizing, self-regulating intelligence as it is laid out in the Maharishi Vedic Approach to Health, and see how we can best harness this powerful healing force in our health care efforts.

Chapter Three

THE PROBLEMS OF A PARADIGM

The advances of allopathic medicine within the past 100 years have been spectacular. The end of the 19th century saw the emergence of anesthetics, immunization, X-rays, and the discovery that many diseases are caused by microscopic agents. These landmark developments were but harbingers of the medical advances of the 20th century. The ability to transplant vital organs, such as the kidney, liver, and heart from one person to another has saved hundreds of thousands of lives. The development of more than 100 artificial body parts has eased the plight of millions of people with otherwise crippling disabilities. Allopathic medicine has gained the ability to manufacture human biochemicals, such as insulin, interferon, and clot-dissolving enzymes; it has developed synthetic substitutes for skin, blood, and veins; its use of radioactive isotopes allows researchers to chart biosynthetic processes and the degradation of biochemicals within the body. Diagnostic methods such as the CAT scan and MRI enable us to form a precise picture of the internal components of a patient's body. Researchers have penetrated the deepest secrets of the cell, have probed the blueprint of the physiology—DNA—and traced diseases to defective genes or chromosomes. And the medical profession stands poised for what many consider its greatest *tour de force* of all time—the mapping of the human genome.

In its wake, however, allopathic medicine has churned up a multitude of problems. As a result of the widespread use of antibiotics, we now face new virulent strains of bacteria that are unresponsive to all known treatments. Another drawback of pharmaceuticals is the possibility of side effects from the drugs, which may be as bad or worse than the problem being treated. Up to 40 percent of people undergoing medical care experience side effects from drugs.[28] Such effects may be nothing more than mild discomfort such as fatigue, dizziness, or sensitivity to sunlight, but far too often they manifest as muscle disorders, diseases of the liver, damage to the kidneys or brain, bone decay, etc.[29] Some 20 to 40 percent of side effects involve the gastrointestinal tract, resulting in intestinal hemorrhage, ulceration of the bowel, and other disorders.[30]

Surgical techniques have grown more sophisticated and more widely used, yet many highly invasive surgical procedures result in complications and even death. Unnecessary operations numbering in the millions are performed each year, resulting in more than 10,000 unnecessary deaths.[31]

"We have gotten to a point in medicine where it is somehow considered radical or an ordeal to ask people to stop smoking and manage stress better and walk and eat a healthful diet," notes physician and author Dean Ornish. "And it is considered conservative to saw people open and bypass their arteries or to slip balloons inside their arteries and squish them, or to put them on powerful drugs for the rest of their lives."[32]

Medicine—traditionally that most human and compassionate of all professions—has grown into a trillion dollar technological enterprise. Two and a half billion dollars are spent every day on Americans' health—most of it going to high-tech crisis management, in many cases in the last six months of patients' lives. An estimated 425 billion dollars was spent in 1990 on direct health care costs for persons with chronic conditions.[33] About 16 billion dollars are spent annually on surgical procedures, almost half of which have to be redone within five years. The expense associated with drug toxicity that arises during hospitalization runs up a three billion dollar tab per year. And neither doctors nor patients are happy about this whole situation. Almost nine out of ten Americans express dissatisfaction with the direction and structure of the U.S. health care system.[34] And one survey showed that nearly 40 percent of doctors are so disenchanted with their career that they would change professions if they were able to make a career choice again.[55]

How did medicine end up like this? Most of the problems with allopathic medicine can be traced to inherent limitations in the conceptual framework—and hence the body of knowledge—upon which this practice of medicine is based. In the early 1960s, the physicist and science historian Thomas Kuhn pointed out the immense, yet unseen influence that our underlying assumptions have on scientific inquiry. Kuhn used the term 'paradigm' to denote the implicit model we hold of the nature of reality or some part of reality. A paradigm is a set of assumptions about the nature of the world around us; it is an internally consistent conceptual framework that forms the basis of all efforts to expand our knowledge. A paradigm will specify which phenomena our universe contains and—as importantly— which it does not. It delimits which problems we consider for study, and which we don't. This underlying conceptual framework determines the methods we use to gain knowledge, and the standards we set for what represents acceptable solutions to the problems we set out to solve.

Paradigms form the subtle, unseen framework that influences our perception and shapes our entire reality. We are generally not aware of the extent to which our perceptions and thoughts are formed by the predominant paradigm of our culture. Only when a new theory runs against the grain of current thinking do we become aware of the underlying assumptions we take for granted. If I told you that researchers had discovered the sun does move around the earth after all, you would think I was decidedly demented. Yet, Copernicus faced this same situation in the beginning of the 16th century, when he introduced the idea that the earth revolves around the sun. In the heresy-conscious Europe of those days such an idea was dangerous to even voice, and it took almost 30 years before Copernicus agreed to commit his theory to print. A paradigm changes only when too many observations accumulate that are inconsistent with it. Such observations are known as anomalies—conceptual irregularities that simply cannot be explained within the framework of the predominant paradigm.

When this happens, a scientific revolution takes place in which scientists start to look at the world in a radically different way. Paradigm shifts can lead to profound changes in our perception of reality. As Kuhn puts it, "What are ducks in the scientist's world before the revolution are rabbits afterwards."[36]

The Mechanistic Model of the Human Body

Knowledge plays a pivotal role in shaping the conditions of human life. The knowledge we have at our disposal forms the basis of our actions, and consequently the basis of the results of those actions and the ensuing fulfillment we derive. To the extent that our knowledge and understanding of a given phenomenon is correct and complete, the actions based on this knowledge will bring the desired results. To the extent that our knowledge and understanding is incorrect—or incomplete—the actions based on this knowledge will bring unforeseen and often undesired results. This is the problem faced by allopathic medicine—its prevailing world view is based on an underlying set of incorrect and incomplete assumptions that exert an unseen, far-reaching, disruptive influence on all areas of the practice of medicine.

Allopathic medicine has its philosophical roots in a sweeping paradigm shift that took place in Europe from the mid-16th century to the 18th century, a 200-year period known as the Age of Reason. During this period, mankind's ideas about the nature of the universe and methods of gaining knowledge changed radically. A key player in this development was the 17th century philosopher René Descartes, whose ideas laid the foundation for many of the assumptions that later scientific efforts, including allopathic medicine, came to be based upon. Before Descartes, most philosophers had subscribed to a view of the material world that dated back to the ancient Greek philosopher Aristotle. Emphasizing the holistic harmony found in the universe, the Aristotelian 'teleology' attributed the orderly, cooperative, and purposeful functioning of the parts of living organisms to their subordination to an inherent plan or final goal. This organizing theme was considered a perfect 'idea,' a blueprint which 'organized' the collective behavior of all elements of an organism, and 'guided' the orderly and systematic development and behavior of the organism. The concept of *vis medicatrix naturae* —the healing power of nature—fitted neatly into this teleological world view, because this curative power was considered the execution of the initial blueprint seeking to maintain the body in accord with its original design.

Descartes ousted all such teleological principles from the material world and postulated that the behavior of material objects could be explained solely with reference to mechanical, mathematical laws. From this developed the notion of the human body as a purely physical entity, an apparatus functioning according to mechanistic processes, not much different than a clock. In the centuries that followed, people became convinced that human and animal bodies are merely wonderfully complex machines. People even went so far as to construct machines copying animals and animal behavior, thinking it would only be a matter of time until advances in knowledge made it possible to create a complete replica of an animal.

The same conception of the human body continues in a less inflated form to this day. Although researchers are daunted by the complexity of the human body, the notion is still prevalent that it would, at least in principle, be possible to manufacture an artificial human being by piecing together artificially engineered body parts.[37] Admittedly, this is a logical conclusion when living systems are considered as purely physico-chemical mechanisms.

The conceptual transformation initiated by Descartes and other influential thinkers took place over a period of more than 200 years. As the mechanistic paradigm took shape, traditional wisdom about the nature of health and disease was discarded. Out went the concept of health as inner balance, a concept the medical profession had inherited from Hippocrates. This concept invoked elements beyond the mechanistic model of the body and, in addition, was entirely unprovable. Out went the notions forwarded by Galen—the early Greek physician who had influenced the practice of medicine in Europe for fourteen centuries—that personality and emotions play a causal role in more than half of patients' complaints. Out went the concept of *vis medicatrix naturae*, the healing power of nature, which formed one of the guiding precepts of early medicine. It could neither be proven nor disproven, and it simply did not fit into the emerging model of the body as a machine. A machine cannot heal itself.

The Reductionist Approach to Scientific Inquiry

Descartes also helped lay the foundation for modern scientific inquiry by breaking with the unsystematic means of gaining knowledge that characterized medieval science. To gain precise knowledge, Descartes wrote, we must "divide each of the difficulties into as many parts as possible and as might be necessary for its adequate solution."[38] A few decades later, Sir Isaac Newton introduced the idea that the universe is a giant clockwork, whose functioning can be reduced to individual mechanical principles. With this, the foundation had been laid for the emergence of the reductionist approach to gaining knowledge. According to this approach, all objects, including biological entities, consist of individual components and are ultimately reducible to these. Consequently, the way to understand anything, be it the eye of a beetle, the hardness of a rock, or the functioning of the entire human physiology, is through the study of the constituent parts of the system.

The reductionist approach to gaining knowledge combined well with the empirical tradition of drawing scientific conclusions only on the basis of evidence, another of Sir Isaac Newton's major philosophical contributions. By dividing multiplex objects of study into their fundamental parts and studying the contributions of these parts to the overall object, it became possible to collect meaningful and reliable evidence. The systematic collection of micro-level pieces of knowledge to characterize the nature and reality of macro-level objects, became the hallmark of rational scientific inquiry.

The mechanistic, reductionist approach to scientific inquiry that held sway over the following centuries fostered remarkable results. It gave man a potent framework for probing the depths of the cosmos around and inside him, allowing him to advance his knowledge of the material world with greater speed, accuracy, and power than ever before. It eventually launched the Industrial Revolution, piloted us into the skies, and took the first man to the moon. It gave us the telephone, the computer, and the ability to instantly access people and information on the other side of the globe. It also brought us dangerously polluted oceans, a hole in the ozone layer, global warming, and the atomic bomb.

Insufficient Assumptions, Insufficient Treatments

The mechanistic, reductionist approach to medical analysis has shaped many of the defining characteristics of scientific medicine. One assumption that dominated research for the better part of a century was the Theory of Specific Etiology. According to this theory, each disease can be traced to one root cause. The theory originated at the end of the last century with the work of Louis Pasteur, who discovered the connection between microorganisms and disease. This finding resonated well with the reductionist concept of disease as an externally induced, isolated, mechanical breakdown. Implicit in the specific etiology theory is the concept that when a disease has one cause, then treatment can be effected by one factor, the so-called 'magic bullet'—an antibiotic or other drug that eradicates the disease at its root without harming the patient. In recent decades, more and more evidence has forced the realization that diseases are of multi-causal nature. Illness results from the interplay between 'external' physical factors and 'internal' psychological, social, or behavioral factors. This understanding, however, has not yet succeeded in changing our prevailing approach to the treatment of disease, which largely remains unimodal. Our therapeutic and research efforts are still dominated by the search for the one magic drug, the one wonder treatment that will take care of the problem at hand.

The isolation of active ingredients for use as drugs is another example of what sometimes happens when we mistake the knowledge of one causal factor for knowledge of the whole system. In the early 1800s, the young German chemist F. Serturner succeeded in isolating morphine, the active ingredient in opium. With Serturner's discovery of morphine, researchers came to believe the isolated active ingredient created the total effect of the plant. Once the active principle was located, all other ingredients in the plant were labelled 'inactive.'

Serturner's finding signalled the beginning of Western pharmacology. Today, approximately 75 percent of Western drugs employ an active ingredient derived from plants, but taken in isolation from the plant itself.[39] However, the ability to produce drugs which are biochemically characterized and reproducible in mass quantities—and patentable—may not be the best thing for the patient after all. Medicinal plants are a mixture of phytochemicals, and it frequently is the interaction of these and not the effect of individual ingredients, that creates the healing benefits of herbs. Isolating the 'active principle' eliminates other substances that might have a protective effect. The result can be a drug that is more toxic than the original plant. For example, two drugs commonly used to treat heart problems—digoxin and digitoxin—are derived from plants of the genus Digitalis, including the foxglove plant. Traditionally used by herbalists to slow and strengthen the heart, foxglove in its complete form contains a compound that induces nausea and vomiting if the plant is given in too great a dose. Digoxin and digitoxin do not contain this compound, however, and consequently can be taken in excessive doses, causing irregular heartbeat and death.[40]

Levels of Causality

An additional limitation of the reductionist method arises from the inherent difficulty of taking into account all the causal relationships that may be involved in a given phenomenon. Researchers in different areas tend to focus on different levels of causality, and bridging their disciplines is made difficult by differences in the language, concepts, and goals of scientists in different fields. The specialization that goes hand in hand with reductionist methods is a double-edged sword. On the one hand, it allows for greater efficiency in gaining knowledge; on the other hand, as it is often said, specialization involves knowing more and more about less and less. Much too often, the big picture is lost.

If we focus on only one cause-and-effect relationship, overlooking deeper causal relationships, we may take actions that do not accomplish what we set out to achieve, and we might even create more problems than we solve. For example, surgeons perform coronary bypass surgery to remove the most obvious cause of severe angina pectoris pain—the clogged blood vessels leading to the heart. However, since the factors that caused the vessels to clog are not addressed by this procedure, about half the blood vessels clog up again within five years.[11] For the majority of people who undergo it, the operation does little more to increase their long-term survival rate than medicinal treatment.[12] Angioplasty, another commonly used procedure in coronary heart disease, expands clogged arteries with the help of a tiny balloon. This procedure also needs to be redone, within as little as six months, because the treated arteries become clogged again.[13]

The human body is so multifarious that it is difficult, if not impossible, to identify all factors and all levels of causality involved in any given phenomenon. Returning to the example of cholesterol, we have seen how altering the level of one isolated physiological factor can give rise to a host of other problems. Why would lowering cholesterol with drugs decrease the incidence of heart disease, but increase overall mortality from all other causes of death? Because we haven't considered the context in which high cholesterol occurs and all the levels of causality involved. Identifying one apparent level of causation still leaves a host of other questions unanswered. Does high cholesterol cause heart disease or is it simply a condition often associated with the disease? It is well-known that the body has an amazing capacity for regulating cholesterol levels independent of our dietary intake. Is high cholesterol an indication of a deeper imbalance? And what about those people who develop heart disease even though they don't have high cholesterol? Perhaps it is not cholesterol *per se*, but its interaction with other factors, that is mainly responsible for the clogging of arteries that leads to heart disease.

Research over the past decade has made it clear that this appears to be the case. We now know the oxidation of fat molecules is a major factor in initiating atherosclerosis.[44] The 'bad' component of cholesterol, low density lipoprotein (LDL), appears to be especially susceptible to oxidation. However, even after identifying the mechanisms whereby oxidized LDL damages the blood vessels, we are still left with unanswered questions. What are all the events that cause fat molecules, especially LDL, to be oxidized? And what are all the inducers of these events? The potential levels of causality are so numerous they may well outweigh our methodological capacity for exploring them, no matter how sophisticated and high-tech our research methods become.

In celebrating our success in charting the parts, we often forget the questions that have not been answered or not even asked. As our knowledge of physiological structures has enabled us to undertake ever more invasive treatments and procedures, the consequences of what we don't know become greater and greater. The more invasive our treatments, the more damage is wrought by violating physiological laws of nature we do not take into consideration or are not aware of.

All of this would perhaps be less disturbing if medicine were celebrating grand achievements in the eradication of important diseases. However, the victory of allopathic medicine over disease is not as overwhelming as we might prefer to believe. It is true that life expectancy in the U.S. has increased from 49 years at the turn of the century to 75 years in 1990. It is generally agreed, however, that this increase has resulted from improved hygiene, public sanitation improvements, better housing, better nutrition, and an associated increase in resistance to disease. The development of specific therapeutic interventions has had little impact on overall life expectancy.[45] In addition, total mortality rates for most diseases have remained largely unchanged for the past 30 years. In spite of having one of the most technologically advanced medical systems in the world, the U.S. ranks behind most industrialized nations in infant mortality. For life expectancy, we come in 22nd in the world for men, 16th for women. And although the incidence of coronary heart disease in the U.S. is on the decline, having peaked in 1963,[46] it would be very difficult to attribute this to improvements in medical technologies. Despite a declining incidence, heart disease remains the largest killer, responsible for one of every three deaths.

In today's society, chronic degenerative diseases occur in almost epidemic proportions. The three major killers—heart disease, cancer, and stroke—together account for approximately two thirds of all deaths in the U.S. One quarter of the U.S. population suffers from high blood pressure, a known risk factor for heart disease and stroke.[47] And the age-adjusted mortality rates for cancer are still rising, although we have spent more than 20 billion dollars on research over the past two decades.[48]

Our knowledge of the human body and our medical technologies have never been more extensive. The capabilities of allopathic medicine to handle medical crises and emergencies is supreme. However, when it comes to effectively managing one of the biggest medical problems today—chronic disease—more than three decades of intensive research have produced few concrete results. In spite of immense expenditures, the knowledge gained has not generated substantial advances in our repertoire of *effective* treatments for many chronic diseases.

The late Lewis Thomas, a renowned medical scientist, categorized modern high-tech treatments as 'halfway technologies.' He used this term to denote therapies that are applied after the fact to compensate for the disabling effects of diseases whose course of development medicine has little power to control. Halfway technologies, according to Thomas, are such interventions as transplantations of the heart, kidney, liver, and other organs; a large percentage of cancer treatments—including surgery, radiation, and chemotherapy; and the costly technologies for managing the end stages of coronary heart disease. "The media tend to present each new procedure as though it represented a breakthrough and therapeutic triumph, instead of the makeshift that it really is," writes Thomas. "In fact, this level of technology is, by its nature, at the same time highly sophisticated and profoundly primitive. It is the kind of thing that one must continue to do *until there is a genuine understanding of the mechanics involved in disease.*"[49] [emphasis added]

Due to their multifactorial nature, chronic diseases are especially inaccessible from the vantage point of a medical framework that focuses mainly on single causes and single cures. The reductionist paradigm has proved to be of limited value in managing the complexities of the human physiology. Dividing a composite phenomenon into its component parts and trying to deal with each one in isolation backfires, when dealing with a highly complex system comprised of an interwoven network of delicately tuned processes. Treating a problem at its surface level without addressing underlying causes most often results in short-term benefits, while generating deeper, more complicated imbalances. Limited knowledge produces limited results. An incomplete and inaccurate model of the body generates incomplete and flawed treatments.

Chapter Four

WHOLENESS, PLASTICITY AND THE GHOST IN THE MACHINE

As we have seen, most of the differences between the practices of allopathic medicine and the Maharishi Vedic Approach to Health can be traced to the divergent assumptions upon which they are based. The concept of disease in allopathic medicine is largely dichotomous—you are either sick or not sick. Conversely, in the Maharishi Vedic Approach to Health, health and disease exist along a continuum of physiological balance and imbalance. The emphasis of allopathic medicine is on fixing the dysfunctional parts of the system. The main focus of the Maharishi Vedic Approach to Health is stimulating the body's self-healing intelligence to restore and maintain balance, preferably long before symptoms of disease appear.

As I noted in the last chapter, the mechanistic model on which allopathic medicine is based leaves no room for the notion of an innate intelligence. Yet, a medical model that regards the body as simply the sum total of the interaction of physico-chemical processes is hard pressed to account for the forces of the body and mind that do not fit into the current scientific framework. As the late medical researcher René Dubos put it, "I have always felt that the only trouble with scientific medicine is that it is not scientific enough. Modern medicine will become really scientific only when physicians and their patients have learned to manage the forces of the body and the mind that operate in *vis medicatrix naturae*."[50] In this chapter, we will survey some of the physiological phenomena that are relevant to understanding the self-regulating, self-regenerating intelligence of the body.

One of the most intriguing manifestations of the body's potent self-healing capabilities is found in the placebo response. The placebo effect is the mysterious alliance between a mind that believes in the efficacy of a given treatment and a body that calls into play its healing forces to fulfil the expectations of the mind. Most of us equate a placebo with an inert sugar pill, which will relieve pain if a person believes it to be a potent drug. But placebo effects range much further than that. In addition to pain, such ailments as cough, hay fever, mood changes, angina pectoris, migraine headaches, seasickness, anxiety, dermatitis, rheumatoid arthritis, peptic ulcers, allergies, acne, multiple sclerosis, diabetes, and depression have been shown to improve with placebo interventions alone.[51,52] As many as 60 to 70 percent of patients given nothing but a placebo improve.[53] The mere belief that one is receiving an efficacious treatment can trigger healing in all parts of the body—organs, tissues, bone structures, glands, etc. The placebo response can even influence the impact of real drugs, altering their effect depending on the type of instructions patients are given. Placebos can trigger the same physiological patterns as active medications—mimicking the time-effect curves and peak, cumulative, and carry-over effects of the drug patients believe they are receiving.[54] Blood pressure, heart rate, and self-perceptions of relaxation and activation can be altered with a placebo.[55] Even functions such as reaction time, grip strength, and short-term rote memory can be manipulated through the placebo response.

Surgery can also produce considerable placebo effects. In the 1950s, a widely heralded surgical procedure used for relieving the pain of angina pectoris, was discovered to be a fluke when a group of doctors put the procedure to a test. They performed the complete surgical procedure on one group of patients, and simply opened the chest of the other group, then sewed it back together again. Such an experiment would not make it past a Human Subjects Review Committee today, but it yielded unambiguous results. The second group of patients, believing they had undergone the full surgery, experienced as much relief from the pain of angina pectoris as the first.[56] As far as current treatments for heart disease, some researchers have even suggested that much of the relief patients experience after coronary bypass surgery may be due to a similar placebo effect. Some patients report continued benefits even when all the grafts have clogged up and are rendered ineffective.[57]

The placebo effect provides a powerful illustration of both the body's self-healing and self-regulating capabilities. Ironically, within allopathic medicine, researchers consider the placebo effect a nuisance—a whimsical phenomenon that can obscure the results of the 'real' medical treatment unless it is controlled for. "The healing process has been relegated to the position of a disturbing effect," writes Dr. Norman Sartorius of the World Health Organization. "[It has been] summed up under the name of 'placebo,' equated to some kind of noise in the system that has to be eliminated before the 'real' treatment, the action of the magic pill, can be assessed." Instead, he notes, we ought to regard the nonspecific factors that produce the placebo effect as *the key* to our understanding of health and healing. Drugs and other 'non-placebos' are, in reality, simply adjuncts to the treatment process. The real source of healing derives from the body's own regenerative powers.[58]

The processes that bring about placebo effects are varied and extensive. There is no single placebo effect with a single mechanism, but numerous effects mediated through countless physiological pathways.[59] Placebo effects, however, share one common feature. Belief—or what can be called 'a stable state of knowing'— is the crucial factor that triggers the physiological response. "Within placebo-mediated healing, knowing and healing are directly linked," notes M.D. Sullivan. "A shift in beliefs is itself therapeutic. Knowing is itself healing."[60] The effects of a drug may be altered if instructions are changed, hence changing the patient's expectations. The impact of a drug is likewise modified if the drug is secretly administered.[61] If both the doctor and the patient have a strong belief that a specific treatment will work, it is almost twice as likely to produce results—even if it later turns out to be ineffective.[62]

Interestingly enough, the expectations or beliefs that mediate placebo effects can also result in unfavorable physiological changes. In one study, a group of people given a placebo instead of a chemotherapy drug experienced as much nausea as the group given the actual drug. In fact, one third of the patients in the placebo group lost their hair! In another study, seven of ten people who were told their head was exposed to a (nonexistent) electric current, developed headaches.[63] This effect has been dubbed the 'nocebo' effect, and it has been evident in many other contexts. Drowsiness, nervousness, constipation, and insomnia are just a few of the conditions created by the nocebo effect. Such results again underline how a certain belief can trigger global physiological responses.

As testimony to the potency of the body's self-regulating intelligence, the placebo effect is tantalizing on three counts. It illustrates the tremendous range of the body's self-regenerative capabilities; it bears witness to the enormous plasticity and malleability of the human body; and it brings to light the power wielded by the human mind in shaping this plasticity and in triggering the healing responses of the body.

Physicians and nurses are familiar with many other phenomena which demonstrate that the body possesses an uncanny plasticity, which in some way is mediated by the mind. A commonly cited example involves multiple personality disorder, a psychological condition in which a person appears to be inhabited by distinctly different personalities. Inexplicably, shifts from one personality to another are often accompanied by dramatic physiological changes. Gait, gestures, and voice may change; a person may need eye glasses in one personality, but not in another. In one well-known case, one of the multiple personalities of a boy with almost a dozen personalities, was allergic to orange juice. If the boy drank orange juice in any of the other personalities, he was fine. If he shifted to the allergic personality before the juice was fully digested, he broke out in a rash![64]

A happier example of the body's plasticity is found in spontaneous remissions—those rare instances in which a person recovers from an otherwise terminal illness. There is no apparent reason—in the form of an effective medical treatment—for the recovery. In fact, in about 20 percent of these cases, there is no medical intervention at all. In another 20 percent of cases, the medical procedure involved is not one that can effect a cure. In the following example, a purely diagnostic procedure appears to have triggered a remission from cancer. In 1947, a 59-year old man was admitted to George Washington University Hospital complaining of persistent weight loss and a chronic cough. His X-rays showed clear indications of lung cancer. When his chest was opened to take a biopsy, his doctors determined the malignant growth was inoperable and simply closed his chest again. Laboratory tests confirmed the tumor was malignant. The patient was monitored regularly with X-rays after his biopsy. Much to his doctors' surprise, the tumor proceeded to shrink. Thinking they had made a diagnostic error, they performed repeated tests, which confirmed the original diagnosis. Yet, five years later the patient was in excellent health, the lesion in his right lung almost gone.[65]

Spontaneous remissions live a shadow existence at the fringes of the medical domain. They have been studied very little, and practitioners who report such cases are often accused of having made a diagnostic mistake. In spite of risking such ridicule, doctors have reported instances of spontaneous remission in more than 3,500 papers appearing in 830 different journals in 20 languages.[66] What triggers a spontaneous remission? We know very little about it. In some instances, the remission has been linked to an infection which brought about a high fever. In some cases of cancer remission, innocuous medical events—such as a partial surgery, or the administration of an ineffectual drug in which the patient has special confidence—appear to trigger the remission. In other cases, the cancer involved is one that simply is more liable to regress.

Several researchers have suggested that many spontaneous remissions are triggered by the mind. In some cases, such as the gentleman with lung cancer, a diagnostic procedure may elicit a placebo response that mobilizes the body's self-healing system to rid itself of cancer. In other cases, it appears that a dramatic change in a person's outlook on life is a key factor. An "existential shift" is how the Dutch researcher, Dr. Marco de Vries describes it.[67] Such a dramatic shift in outlook may result from the occurrence of major events in life, for instance marriage, birth of a child or grandchild, or religious conversion.[68]

The Ghost in the Machine

The placebo effect, multiple personality disorder, and spontaneous remissions give us important clues about "the forces that operate in *vis medicatrix naturae*." One of the things they teach is that to understand the nature of the body's self-healing intelligence, we must understand the nature of the mind and the relationship between the mind and body. When belief, or what we might term 'a stable state of knowing' is involved, the mind appears unreasonably capable of shaping physiological outcomes. Yet, in trying to understand the mechanics that turn 'knowing' into healing, we once again run up against the limitations of the underlying theoretical model of allopathic medicine.

The relationship between mind and body is an age-old puzzle. For centuries, the practice of medicine has been influenced by yet another conceptual heritage from Descartes—the *dualist* notion of mind and body. Descartes viewed mind and body as two separate substances: *res cogitans* is a thinking substance which is unextended and indivisible, and *res extensa* denotes all the physical substances, which have extension in space, i.e. they can be measured and analyzed, and which exist independently of *res cogitans*. In this model, the human body functions completely independently of the mind. The human body, wrote Descartes, is a machine made up of bones, sinews, veins, blood, and skin, and fitted together "in such a way that even if there were no mind in it, it would still carry out all the operations that . . . do not depend upon the command of the will, nor therefore, on the mind."[69]

Although he considered mind and body as two separate essences, Descartes did not deny their ability to interact. The translation of a mental impulse into a physiological action is so commonplace that we don't even think about it. If you decide to reach for a glass of water, your arm extends automatically and your hand grips the glass. Yet, from the point of view of the dualist model, this is an inexplicable phenomenon. How can a non-physical substance influence a totally separate physical substance? Descartes proposed that mind and body interact through the small part of the brain known as the pineal gland, but he neglected to answer the question of how the non-physical mind acts on the pineal gland.

In spite of its obvious shortcomings, variations of the dualist notion of mind and body influenced the practice of medicine in the centuries after Descartes. As we saw in Chapter Three, early Greek physicians emphasized that some patients' complaints had their root in mental factors, but after Descartes the mind was denied a role in the disease process. Cartesian dualism influenced the biomedical model which is still commonly accepted today. According to this model, physical disorders are afflictions brought about by a disruption of physiological processes, which in turn may result from bacterial or viral infection, biochemical imbalances, injury, etc. The mind is not a contributing factor.

The dualist model of mind and body had too many deficiencies to remain unchallenged, and many alternative models have since been proposed. In our century, the scientific community has come to regard the mind as a product of the interaction of matter. In this materialist model, mental events are explained with reference to purely physical principles—a thought is the end result of the complex interaction of neurophysiological processes. "[Y]our joys and your sorrows, your memories and your ambitions, your sense of personal identity and free will, are in fact no more than the behavior of a vast assembly of nerve cells and their associated molecules," says scientist Francis Crick, who shared a Nobel prize for discovering the structure of DNA.[70] But if the mind is simply an outgrowth of physiological factors, again there is no apparent reason why it should play a role in the disease process. How could something pervasively influence that of which it is but a product?

Yet, the link between mental factors and the development of disease has been impossible to ignore. Researchers like Dr. Hans Selye, who introduced the stress concept, and Franz Alexander, who introduced the notion of psychosomatic disease, were among the early pioneers who tried to identify the mechanisms through which mental factors might lead to physiological disease. In the last 20 years, these attempts have been spearheaded by researchers in the multidisciplinary field of psychoneuroimmunology. This exciting new field of research focuses on the interplay of psychosocial actions, brain processes, and the immune system.

Almost everywhere they have looked, researchers have found a smoking gun linking psychological factors with disease. If a randomly selected group of people are all exposed to the same infectious agent, such as a cold virus or streptococci bacteria, as few as one fifth of them may actually develop symptoms of infection. Heart disease appears to be more prevalent among individuals who have a high degree of anger, hostility, and cynicism.[71] Depression, feelings of hopelessness, or repressed negative emotions may predispose a person to cancer.[72] People with a pessimistic explanatory style, who tend to blame themselves for negative events and perceive the effects of these events as durable and pervasive, experience poorer health when they reach middle age.[73] Social isolation appears to be especially marring; it is involved in the development of a whole range of diseases, including heart disease, cancer, depression, and arthritis.

In other words, environmental stressors are not the only factors that influence health. Internal 'stress,' in the form of negative emotions or feelings of loneliness, plays a role as well. Simply being in good psychological health may provide the best protection of all against disease. A 40-year prospective study provided substantial evidence that positive mental health may delay the typical midlife decline in physiological health.[74] In this study, only four percent of men in good mental health acquired a chronic disease or died before the age of 53, in contrast to poorly adjusted males, more than one third of whom developed a chronic disease or died. The mind, in other words, not only exerts a short-term influence on our health, but also a long-term influence.

Researchers in the field of psychoneuroimmunology have been successful in identifying some of the pathways through which mental factors exert an influence on the body. The brain and the immune system are now known to interact in a number of ways. Many biochemicals considered to be the mediators of the nervous system form extensive communication highways throughout the immune system as well. Immune system cells have receptor sites for neuropeptides and neurotransmitters, the main messengers of the brain, and immune system cells can secrete many of these biochemicals themselves. In addition, various organs, especially the lymphoid organs and the gastrointestinal tract, are wired extensively with noradrenergic autonomic nerve fibers, allowing them to participate in the complex symphony of neurohumoral communication. Thus, the immune system is not an independent entity as previously assumed; the autonomic nervous system plays a significant role in orchestrating its functioning.

Because the messengers of the mind, the neuropeptides, are found so extensively throughout the body, many researchers are now suggesting we should not so much talk of a body and a mind, as of a 'bodymind.' Says psychoneuroimmunologist Margaret Kemeny, "From my own viewpoint, the mind and the body are two manifestations of the same process. Even to say they are 'interconnected' is improper, because they are two parts of one whole."[75]

Whether we consider the mind as the result of brain activity or as an integral part of a bodymind network, however, one of the most basic questions remains. We know more than ever about how psychological processes might translate into immune responses and, in the long run, possibly disease states. Yet how do these global, holistic responses come about in the first place? The body reacts instantaneously to mental impulses. Some people are able to increase the hand's skin temperature by imagining their hand is being stimulated by a heat source. Simply putting your attention on a finger in expectation of a slight touch results in an increased blood flow to the areas of the brain that detect touch in that finger. In other words, attention alone is enough to activate a specific pattern of brain activity. The increased blood flow is a sign that the neurons in that area are increasing their firing activity.[76]

How does the simple shift of attention to the finger cause the appropriate brain cells to fire? What coordinating intelligence translates the mental impulse into physical neuronal activity? If we consider the mind a 'byproduct' of brain activity, how does this 'byproduct' turn around and suddenly influence the brain? If we consider the mind a separate substance, how does it reach into the physical world and manipulate the electrochemical processes of the brain? If we conceive of the bodymind as a complex interwoven network, "two parts of the same whole," what coordinates the activity of this whole?

The organization of the human body is a logistical nightmare. The body is comprised of more than a quadrillion cells, each of which has a specialized function. The cells, in turn, are formed of proteins, lipids, carbohydrates, nucleic acids, water, and trace minerals, all of which are constituted of atoms of many of the elements that make up everything else in the universe—hydrogen, carbon, nitrogen, iron, etc. And these atoms, ironically, are comprised mostly of empty space. All components and functions of the body—from the nitrogen atoms of an amino acid, to the catalytic enzymes of a cell, to the carefully calibrated firing of selected groups of the brain's 10^{12} neurons—are, at every moment, single voices in a finely orchestrated, harmonious symphony. They change instantaneously and globally in response to external or internal stimuli.

What holds together the untold multitude of oxygen, hydrogen, carbon, and nitrogen atoms, and transforms them into a coherently functioning human body? How can global coherent changes in the body be induced instantaneously? How can a mental impulse of fear or joy in a split second trigger the collective, coordinated activity of billions of neurons, neurotransmitters, and immune system cells throughout the entire body?

Although we know more than ever before about the intermediate steps in this holistic response, we must be careful not to mistake the *mechanics* of a phenomenon for its source. Knowing that impulses from the brain are communicated to the immune system through hormonal and neuropeptide messengers still tells us nothing about the coordinating intelligence that initiates this communication.

Many researchers maintain that such questions remain unanswered because we don't yet know enough about all the physiological processes involved. The complexity of the human body is so vast it will take several decades, or even centuries, before we know if this position is right or wrong. Yet one is left to wonder. Are we approaching these questions in the most useful way? The expressions of the body's self-regulating, self-healing intelligence go beyond what could be expected from a passive, mechanically-functioning end product of metabolic processes and biochemical interactions. The influence of the mind on physiological functioning goes far beyond what can be expected from an entity that is nothing itself but a product of that very functioning.

The human body is an effervescent entity, a functional wholeness, a pulsating, fluctuating, ever-changing, ever-regenerating collection of atoms. From atoms to molecules to cells to tissues to organs, the body is a dynamic fluctuating network—the expression, it seems, of an elaborate pattern of intelligence. If we don't concern ourselves with the nature and source of this wholeness, we leave out one of the most important questions of all.

Chapter Five

GREATER THAN THE SUM
OF THE PARTS

The self-healing properties of the body are just one attribute of the immense physiological intelligence that coordinates all aspects of bodily functioning. Intelligence is that unseen factor that gives direction to change, aligning the functioning of the parts of the body to the whole in a purposeful manner. As the British physicist Paul Davies expresses it, "The mystery of life . . . lies not so much in the nature of the forces that act on the individual molecules that make up an organism, but in how the whole assemblage operates collectively in a coherent and cooperative fashion."[77] A vast self-organizing intelligence 'reigns' over atoms, molecules, cells, tissues, organs, and organ systems, compelling them to operate in a collective and cooperative manner. This intelligence is self-regulating, adjusting from instant to instant the activity of the countless elements of the body, in accord with demands of the internal and external environments. It is self-regenerative, inducing broken bones to mend and wounds to heal, and orchestrating the constant renewal of all organs and structures of the body. It is self-reproducing, in nine months creating a living, sentient being of immense complexity from a single fertilized cell.

As we consider life on a global scale, it becomes obvious that the biosphere is a marvel of ingeniously organized multiplicity. Each stage of biological organization features increasingly complex organisms, each displaying greater self-organizing capabilities and more refined faculties. Organisms are multifarious, intricate, and sophisticated structures, so much so that we cannot claim to have full knowledge of even the most elementary of them. Our most advanced supercomputers are ludicrously primitive compared to the inexhaustible complexity of living systems.

The cell, the smallest functional unit of living systems, is an excellent case in point. It is nothing but a 'bag of chemicals,' yet its organizational ingenuity is awe-inspiring. It is far more complex in structure and function than the biochemicals of which it is comprised. The various functions of the cell include maintenance, defense, synthesis of cell products such as proteins, carbohydrates and lipids, and cell division. To derive energy to perform these functions, the cell takes in nutrients, which are also used as building blocks in the synthesis of proteins. The cell is a miniature society, complete with governing body (the DNA), power plants to fill the cell's energy needs, manufacturing centers for cell maintenance and cell products, and infrastructure, communication, and defense systems. Yet, the cell is more like a process than an entity. Cells are dynamic conglomerates of ceaseless bioelectric and biochemical operations. The rate of activity within a living cell challenges comprehension—speed up an aerial view of the traffic in New York City one million times, and you'll have a sense of the incredible velocity of cell functioning.

Each individual aspect of the cell is a master feat of organizational complexity. Consider, for example, the mitochondria, the power stations that generate 90 percent of the energy used by the cell. Each one of the quadrillion (10^{15}) cells in the body has hundreds, sometimes thousands of mitochondria. Each mitochondrion in turn averages 100,000 electron transport chains, the molecular energy plants of the mitochondrion. In other words, this aspect of the body's energy production system alone involves the activity of a hundred billion trillion entities.

Each electron transport chain consists of 15 to 20 precisely sequenced enzymes, arranged on the mitochondrial membrane in the order of the reaction steps they catalyze. Their internal bioelectric dynamics cause an electron deposited at the beginning of the chain to move down the entire lineup of enzymes. Much as the flow of a waterfall turns a turbine to create electricity, the flow of electrons down the chain converts adenosine diphosphate (ADP) into adenosine triphosphate (ATP), the universal energy-transfer molecule of the cells. Without the electron transport chain, the cell could still split a glucose molecule for energy, but it would yield only two molecules of ATP. By using the electron transport chain, an additional 36 ATP molecules can be produced. This system's efficiency level is quite high—it recovers about five times as much of the available energy as a typical gasoline engine.

The cell, as we noted, is the smallest unit of life. The simplest independently living system is a bacterial cell, an organism whose functioning is no less complex than that of a human cell. How did this basic unit of life appear? We don't know for sure. However, there is no shortage of theories about how the random interaction of chemicals in the 'primordial soup' gave rise first to amino acids, then nucleic acids, proteins, and eventually living systems. Under the right conditions, it has been shown, the four major classes of small organic molecules found in cells will form: amino acids, nucleotides, fatty acids, and carbohydrates.

After that it gets more complicated. If one adopts a purely mechanistic view of the origin of life, some researchers argue, there are improbable odds against the spontaneous appearance of systems more complex and ordered than amino acids. Living systems use some 2,000 functioning enzymes, each of which is composed of several hundred amino acids. In his book *Origins*,[78] Robert Shapiro calculates the odds for the spontaneous development of a simple bacterium such as *E. coli*, using an argument developed by astronomers Fred Hoyle and N.C. Wickramasinghe. The odds that some 20 existing amino acids would accidentally group together into one functional enzyme consisting of some 200 amino acids is about one in 20^{200}. When the author allows for the fact that more than one amino acid sequence might be able to catalyze a given reaction, the probability becomes one in 10^{20}. However, to create a bacterium, not just a single enzyme, but some 2,000 functioning enzymes are needed. The odds against this compute to one chance in $10^{40,000}$. To fully appreciate the magnitude of this number, consider the fact that the total number of hydrogen atoms in the universe is around 10^{60}. As several authors have remarked, these odds are comparable to the odds of a tornado touching down on a junkyard and creating a Boeing 747.

The paradox of biological complexity is that there are many more ways in which a system can be disordered than it can be ordered. In other words, the more orderly the system, the greater the number of disorderly arrangements that are possible for that system; thus, the odds against randomly generated order increase exponentially with the order of the system. There is no evolutionary advantage in increased complexity. Highly ordered biological units are vulnerable to even the minutest changes. Most biological units are so finely tuned that it takes very little to destroy their properties. In many cases, if just one small part is not in place, the properties of the whole entity are disrupted or impaired. An alteration of just one amino acid in the 200+ polypeptide chain of an enzyme, for example, or even just a change in its position, can make the enzyme nonfunctional. In proteins other than enzymes, such a change may cause the protein to function differently and be unable to fulfill its physiological role properly.

"The main reason why the origin of life is such a puzzle is because the spontaneous appearance of such elaborate and organized complexity seems so improbable," writes physicist Paul Davies. "[Scientists have] succeeded in generating some of the building blocks of life. However, the level of complexity of a real organism is enormously greater than that of mere amino acids. Furthermore, it is not just a matter of degree. Simply achieving a high level of complexity per se will not do. The complexity needed involves certain specific chemical forms and reactions: a random complex network of reactions is unlikely to yield life."[79]

Once life has been established, the accepted explanation for biological change is that the genetic pool of organisms undergoes random variation, and those changes that enhance the organism's ability to survive are retained. The evolutionary development we observe in fossil records is caused by this process of natural selection, which ensures that only the fittest organisms will survive. The theory of natural selection provides a mechanistic explanation of nature's creative, apparently purposeful power. Natural selection is viewed as a 'tinkerer' that has pieced together, over millions of years, increasingly sophisticated life forms by retaining the useful changes and discarding the rest.

Biologists working within the framework of the relatively new sciences of complexity, have started to question whether the theory of natural selection provides a complete account of the evolution of immense order that has occurred over billions of years in our biosphere. "Science has left us as unaccountably improbable accidents against the cold, immense backdrop of space and time," writes biologist Stuart Kauffman of the Santa Fe Institute. "Thirty years of research have convinced me that this dominant view of biology is incomplete. . . . [N]atural selection is important, but it has not labored alone to craft the fine architectures of the biosphere, from cell to organism to ecosystem. Another source—self-organization—is the root source of order."[80]

As we shall see later in this chapter, a number of biologists are voicing similar views to those of Kauffman, emphasizing the importance of exploring the role the self-organizing dynamics of organisms have played in the emergence of the vast variety of structures in our biosphere.

Attributes of Intelligence

The order and intelligence expressed in the biosphere is strikingly displayed in the self-regulating, self-regenerative, and self-reproducing properties of living organisms. The ability to regulate, regenerate, and reproduce themselves is precisely what distinguishes living organisms from inanimate systems. Healing is but one expression of this three-fold ability, which in many cases takes on such magnificent expressions it is hard to imagine how it could be explained within a framework that views organisms as purely mechanistically interacting entities.

As an example, the self-regulating and self-regenerative properties of many species include the ability to recreate themselves when they have been mutilated. If the embryo of a frog is divided when it is still in the two-cell state, two complete, albeit smaller frogs will be produced.[81] If one cell of a sea urchin embryo in the two-cell stage is destroyed, a complete sea urchin still develops.[82] A flatworm cut into several pieces regenerates into several complete worms. In the plant kingdom, a branch of a willow tree under the appropriate conditions will grow into a whole new tree. And almost every single cell of a carrot can regenerate into a whole plant; in this case, each cell has become differentiated, yet somehow it retains its ability to reproduce the entire organism.

Remarkable regenerative abilities are also present in more complex organisms such as vertebrates. Research has shown, for example, that when the lens is removed from a newt's eye, a new lens grows from the edge of the iris—though in normal embryonic growth the lens develops from the skin. It is hard to explain this by referring to natural selection alone, since this type of mutilation would never happen accidentally in nature.[83] The Xenopus frog possesses similar remarkable abilities. If the frog's eye is surgically rotated by 180 degrees while the frog is still in the embryonic state, at birth the visual information fed by that eye will obviously be rotated. Uncannily, however, the visual system immediately starts to compensate by altering its functional connections in such a way that the input to the visual center of the frog's brain remains congruent, and the frog retains its sight.[84] The central nervous system of organisms has a tremendous ability to rewire itself as its needs change. However, given the prevailing explanatory models, it is hard to understand how organisms could have the ability to adapt to changes they could not have been exposed to during the normal course of evolution.

If development is engineered simply by the information stored in the genetic material, how is it possible for an organism to compensate for the disruption of the physico-chemical pattern that orchestrates its functioning and growth? How is it possible for these organisms to adapt effectively to external challenges to which its species could never have been exposed in nature? It is difficult to account for the self-organizing, holistic properties of living systems by simply referring to organisms as chunks of matter structured by the information stored in the DNA, the long strands of nucleic acids thought to contain the biological blueprint of living systems.

The *self-reproducing* properties of living systems are also puzzling within in the traditional biological framework of understanding. Over the course of nine months, billions of inanimate, randomly fluctuating atoms somehow get organized to ultimately form a living person. In spite of our immense knowledge of the development of the human embryo, the fundamental features of this process remain an enigma.

The fertilized egg enters the uterus three days after fertilization. By this time, it has already cleaved many times and has become an embryonic cell mass clustered in a small ball. The outer layer of cells burrows into the uterine lining and becomes the extra-embryonic material, i.e. the placenta, etc., that supports the fetus before birth. The inner cell mass gives rise to the fetus itself. The cell mass first divides into three basic structures—the ectoderm, mesoderm, and endoderm—and these in turn develop into substructures from which the various parts of the body are formed. From the ectoderm arise the nervous system (spinal cord, brain, and nerve cells) and the skin, hair, nails, and teeth. From the mesoderm spring the circulatory system (heart, arteries, and veins), kidneys, digestive organs, part of the lungs, skeletal bones, and muscles. The endoderm develops into the inner lining of the respiratory system and digestive tube, and together with the mesoderm forms the digestive glands. After less than two months, all structures have taken form. The fetus weighs only two grams, yet the development during the following seven months consists almost exclusively of the growth of already established structures.

The process of development involves two fundamental processes—cell differentiation and the development of form. The zygote in the course of nine months undergoes about 50 rounds of cell division and the original single cell eventually gives rise to 256 different cell types, all of which are specialized for different functions. Biologists have long been trying to chart how this magnificent organizational feat is engineered by genetic information residing in the DNA. We know the building blocks for embryo formation are produced through cell division and transcription of the DNA code by messenger RNA. So far so good. A number of features of the developmental process, however, are not accounted for by referring to proteins and their interactions. How do cells specialize for their formative tasks? When the fertilized egg begins to divide, each of the resulting cells (a few cell types excepted) contains the *entire* pool of genetic information—i.e. some 100,000 genes. How does a given cell know which part of the global DNA plan to implement? How do the various cell types know which genes to express?

When one operates with a purely mechanistic view of the DNA, a number of questions are left unanswered. The DNA is a tiny molecule, yet it supposedly engineers the temporal and spatial arrangement of billions of cells spread across regions comparatively as large to this molecule as the solar system is to us. What is the mechanism that causes some cells to develop into neurons, others to compose hair follicles, and yet others to form the smooth inner lining of the blood vessels? How does an organism determine when a sufficient number of cells have been created for the formation of a specific organ? How do parts of the organism, such as the arm and leg, which contain identical cell types (i.e. muscle cells and connective tissue cells) develop into different shapes?

"[The genetic] instructions . . . can determine the molecular composition of a developing organism at any moment in its development, but they are insufficient to explain the processes that lead to a heart, a nervous system, a limb, or any other organ of the body. . . ." maintains biologist Brian Goodwin. "[K]nowing the molecular composition of something is not, in general, sufficient to determine its form. . . ."[85]

These are some of the riddles biologists are still grappling with. One proposed explanation is that the organism's development is guided by physico-chemical patterns. These provide positional information, which causes a particular part of the cell's genetic program to be switched on or off. This theory of 'gene switching' may give us deeper insight into the mechanisms involved in the generation of biological forms, but it still does not tell us how this 'pattern-maker' is made to execute the global plan that results in the embryo. What is the mechanism that enables some genes to be active while others are suppressed? How can we account for *the pattern* in which the genes are switched on and off?

The conditions to which each developmental step is exposed are so varied and require so many ad hoc adjustments that they cannot have been anticipated through the process of natural evolution alone. The same is true for many expressions of the self-regulating and self-regenerative properties of living systems. It is hard to escape the conclusion that intelligence—the alignment of parts to the whole in a purposeful manner—is a dominating feature of organisms at every level of biological functioning. A self-organizing, holistic dynamism coordinates and unites the activity of billions of parts into coherent, precisely functioning wholes.

Wholeness and Intelligence

There is an old tale about an Asian monk, who got into an argument with a king about what constituted the essence of the king's chariot. As the debate heated up, the monk removed the horses from the king's chariot, asking the king whether the horses were the chariot. The king shook his head no. The monk proceeded to remove the wheels of the chariot, asking the king whether the wheels were the chariot. The king again said no. The monk then detached the bars of the chariot and one by one all other removable parts, each time asking the king whether that particular part was the chariot. Each time the king replied no. Eventually, only the chassis was left. "This chassis," the monk asked, "is it the chariot, O king?" The king, of course, could do nothing but shake his head no.

What then, is the essence of the chariot?

It is, we might say, the whole that emerges from, and is more than, the assembly of the parts. The appearance of higher-order wholes with higher-order properties is a pervasive feature in the organization of the universe. Take the simple example of two randomly fluctuating hydrogen atoms, which combine with one oxygen atom to form water. Water has characteristics that are dramatically different from the properties of its hydrogen and oxygen atoms. It is a liquid, it freezes at zero degrees Celsius and boils at 100 degrees Celsius, and is an excellent solvent. These are so-called emergent properties of water. Emergence is present in holistically functioning systems whose properties are different from those of its constituents. The phenomenon is summed up in the old saying, 'the whole is greater than the sum of its parts.'

Emergence is a universal phenomenon encountered in all areas of science. It is precisely due to this feature that we can talk about distinct layers of physiological and biological organization. Subatomic particles bound together by strong and weak nuclear forces and electronic forces form a new unit—the atom; atoms clustering together form various new units—the molecular building blocks of animate and inanimate matter.

In living systems the phenomenon of emergence is most striking, because in many cases the whole seems to take on a life of its own—gaining new properties, taking on regulatory roles, and orchestrating the activity at lower levels of organization. The human physiology can be described in terms of innumerable layers of 'emergent wholenesses' nested within each other. Individual parts are hierarchically organized, subordinate to and functioning within layers of interrelated systems that are themselves functioning within and subordinate to even more inclusive systems, and so on. Carbon, hydrogen, oxygen, and nitrogen atoms cluster together to form amino acids, which have dramatically different properties than their constituent atoms. Amino acids join together in polypeptide chains to form proteins, each with its own higher-order function. The protein may be hemoglobin, which transports oxygen in red blood cells, or the keratin of a hair strand, or the ptyalin enzyme that initiates sugar digestion in the mouth, or insulin, which regulates the blood sugar level. At every level of the physiology, something more is at play than the sum of the individual components. Whether molecules, cells, tissues, organs, or organ systems, each forms a wholeness in and of itself, and each combines with other units to produce greater wholenesses with entirely new emergent features and functions. And at every step, each emergent entity contributes to the harmonious functioning of the whole physiology.

Emergence is one of the most pervasive characteristics of the organization of living systems. From the perspective of a purely mechanistic understanding of living systems, it is also one of the most puzzling. First of all, emergent systems are so holistically coordinated it is hard to conceive how they could have developed through a stepwise compilation of mutational changes over the course of evolution. Darwin believed that small hereditary changes, gradually tinkered together through the process of natural selection, add up to the large-scale differences we observe between species. However, most complex behaviors or functions call for *many* mutational changes before they reach their level of usefulness. A spider's web does not serve much purpose until it has reached its full complexity—a few rudimentary strands would capture no prey. A limited repertoire of the dance movements used by the honey bee to communicate the location of food would give information too imprecise to be of any use.[86] How could a specific mutational change, useful only in the context of a fully functioning system, have been favored?

Secondly, the phenomenon of emergence is at odds with the reductionist assumption that we can eventually understand the whole system by simply studying its component parts. Emergence is an expression of a pervasive nonlinearity in the organization of the biosphere. In living systems, the whole is not simply equal to the sum of the parts—it is more than the sum of its parts. Because most biological systems function in a nonlinear way, the fact that you can get from whole to parts does not imply the ability to get back from parts to whole. The behavior of large, complex assemblies of biological units cannot be understood as a simple extrapolation of the properties of these units. We can start from the units of living systems, such as the cell and the DNA, and show their activities derive from chemical laws which in turn derive from the laws of physics. However, as many researchers have pointed out, if we start from the elementary laws and try to proceed to the biological system as a whole, we run into difficulties. New 'laws' as if emerge at each hierarchical level. These laws can be traced back to the laws of physics and chemistry, but it is not possible to work in the other direction and derive them from the laws of physics and chemistry, since they depend upon the specific organization of the constituent components of the biological entity.

"The idea that all can be reduced to the spare concepts of physics and chemistry . . . [is] untenable," writes physicist Alwyn Scott of the University of Arizona, "because each level of the hierarchy is dynamically independent of its neighbors. Dynamic independence—in turn—arises from nonlinearity, which induces the emergence of new and qualitatively different atomistic entities at each level."[87]

Thus, in spite of its considerable success, the reductionist approach to scientific inquiry has left us with a vacuum—we know more than ever about the fine details of the many-faceted structures of living organisms, but we are unable to build a theory of the whole. As J. Cohen and I. Stewart put it, "The reductionist Tree of Everything is insufficient: There are huge gaps in its explanations. We think that DNA controls biological development, but we don't know how; we think that appropriately arranged neural networks generate consciousness, but we don't know how. We can see what's at the bottom of the reductionist funnels, but not how it rises to the top."[88] When we seek to understand the world around us using reductionist methods, we are like a fisherman who probes the ocean with a one-inch mesh and concludes that there are no fish smaller than an inch in the ocean. If we look only at parts, while ignoring the most salient organizing principle of the human nervous system and of all living systems, we ignore the most important clue to understanding living systems.

How do organisms get from the "disparate scramble of molecular activities"[89] to the integrated systemic order of a cell, an organ, or a human body? This is a key question faced by biologists and physiologists in all areas of research. Physicist-philosopher H.H. Pattee expressed this conundrum succinctly more than 25 years ago in a remark that is still relevant: "If there is to be any theory of general biology, it must explain the origin and operation . . . of the hierarchical constraints which harness matter to perform coherent functions. The problem is universal and characteristic of all living matter. It occurs at every level of biological organization, from the molecule to the brain. It is the central problem of the origin of life, when aggregations of matter obeying only elementary physical laws first began to constrain individual molecules to a functional, collective behaviour. It is the central problem of development where collections of cells control the growth of the genetic expression of individual cells. It is the central problem of biological evolution in which groups of cells form larger and larger organisations by generating hierarchical constraints on subgroups. It is the central problem of the brain where there appears to be an unlimited possibility for new hierarchical levels of description. These are all problems of hierarchical organisation. . . . [H]ierarchical control is the essential and distinguishing characteristic of life."[90]

Our knowledge will not be complete until we understand how individual atoms, ruled by the laws of physics and responding to the purely *local forces* produced by adjacent atoms, can act in a 'macro-determined'—i.e. cooperative, organized, and purposeful—manner. Instead of ignoring the apparent macro-determined development present in living systems, we need to address the question of how, at every step of evolution, holistic systems with properties greater than the sum of their parts can emerge.

The macro-determined behavior displayed by living systems is at odds with the traditional biological understanding that organisms are solely mechanically interacting systems. As we saw in Chapter Three, the metaphor invoked in the mechanistic model of living systems is that of a clock, in which preexisting parts are assembled into a functional unity. Not all scientists are comfortable with this model. Especially within the past decade, researchers working within the sciences of complexity have made a strong case that the mechanistic picture is incomplete—there are important and distinctive types of order that emerge *from the interaction of the component parts* of holistic systems. As biologist Brian Goodwin puts it, "[T]he parts of an organism—leaves, roots, flowers, limbs, eyes, heart, brain—are not made independently and then assembled, as in a machine, but arise as a result of interactions within the developing organism. . . . [O]rganisms are not molecular machines. They are functional and structural unities resulting from a self-organizing, self-generating dynamic."[91]

Biology has become too narrowly focused on genes and their products, Goodwin asserts. Organisms are irreducible entities, as fundamental as the molecules of which they are made. Along with many other researchers working within the emerging sciences of complexity, Goodwin advocates a shift in focus from the properties of the component parts of systems, to the ways in which the parts are related to one another. "[M]olecular composition is not sufficient to specify properties such as the dynamic patterns of excitable media or the forms of organisms that emerge from these patterns," notes Goodwin. "We must understand also *the relational order* between molecular constituents, the way they are organized in space and how they interact with one another in time, which requires a description in terms of fields and their properties. Fields are fundamental in physics, and it turns out that they are equally fundamental in biology. It is from their properties that the capacity of organisms to make wholes out of parts arises."[92] [emphasis added]

The properties of the component parts cannot be ignored, since they determine a number of important features of a holistic system. However, the patterns of dynamic interaction in such a system cannot be predicted from isolated knowledge of the components alone. The interaction of the components, in and of itself, creates characteristic types of order. This shift in emphasis from the parts to the *relational* order of the parts of holistic systems, highlights the dynamic interrelation that exists between the whole and its parts.

Within this emerging model, spontaneous self-organization is viewed as the source of the magnificent order we observe in the architecture of the biosphere. "The order of the biological world, I have come to believe, is not merely tinkered, but arises naturally and spontaneously because of these principles of self-organization—laws of complexity that we are just beginning to uncover and understand," writes biologist Stuart Kauffman.[93] He continues, "Laws of complexity spontaneously generate much of the order of the natural world. It is only then that selection comes into play, further molding and refining. Such veins of spontaneous order have not been entirely unknown, yet they are just beginning to emerge as powerful new clues to the origins and evolution of life. We have all known that simple physical systems exhibit spontaneous order: an oil droplet in water forms a sphere; snowflakes exhibit their evanescent sixfold symmetry. What is new is that the range of spontaneous order is enormously greater than we have supposed. Profound order is being discovered in large, complex, and apparently random systems. I believe that this emergent order underlies not only the origin of life itself, but much of the order seen in organisms today."[94] Given the known physical and biochemical parameters of the interactions between a specific holistic system and the environment, Kauffman and others seek to show, the distinctive features of self-organization and order that we observe in living systems will arise spontaneously.

Footprints of Intelligence

The phenomenon of emergence holds valuable clues to a deeper understanding of nature's intelligence. It provides a significant indication that the explanatory models of a reductionist, mechanistic science are incomplete. If we take a step back and look at the scenario in a broader perspective, we can say that the phenomenon of emergence, wherever it appears, leaves the footprint of nature's intelligence, telling us something important about the characteristics of this intelligence. Emergence is an expression of the whole-making tendency at all levels of organization of the universe. As Maharishi puts it, evolution is a progressive development of wholes in stages of increasing sophistication and complexity. The range of the evolution of life is from the wholeness of the single-celled amoeba, one of the most primitive life forms, to the wholeness of the immensely complex human physiology. The range of the evolution of the universe is from the wholeness of the atom to the wholeness of galaxies.[95]

As we shall see in later chapters, the body's self-organizing intelligence can be viewed as an expression of the structuring dynamics of this wholeness. In his restoration of the Vedic knowledge, Maharishi has shown how the *internal dynamics* of this immanent wholeness orchestrate the body's countless bioelectrical interactions and biochemical processes into harmoniously interacting layers of structure and function.

The self-regenerative and self-reproducing characteristics of organisms are emergent properties of life. The expressions of the body's healing intelligence are expressions of the internal dynamics of wholeness, restoring or maintaining the coordinated, harmonious functioning of the human physiology. Therefore, if disease is present, our first concern should not be so much with the diseased parts, as with how wholeness can be reenlivened. This approach takes health and healing back to its root meaning. The words 'to heal' and 'health' derive from the old English word 'hāl', which means 'whole.' Healing in its deepest sense is restoring wholeness, bringing the physiology back to a fully integrated state of functioning. Health is the full expression of the self-organizing wholeness that constitutes the dynamics of the human physiology. Healing is reviving wholeness at the level of every unit embedded within the totality of the physiology. To understand healing, therefore, we must first understand the dynamic principle of wholeness, of which nature's healing, self-organizing intelligence is an expression.

Chapter Six

VARIATIONS ON A THEME

In seeking to understand nature's healing intelligence, we must understand the holistic source of the expressions of this intelligence. Emergence, or whole-making, as we saw in the last chapter, is a fundamental organizing principle of living systems. In this chapter we shall explore the evidence that wholeness itself may be the most fundamental property of our universe. This conclusion is one toward which modern physics has been moving since the beginning of this century, with the development first of quantum theory and later of unified field theories.

Quantum theory, developed during the first 30 years of this century, presented a dramatically new model of the subatomic world. It is safe to say that, perhaps with the exception of Einstein's theory of relativity, no theory of physics has ever had more profound ramifications. Quantum theory undermined the Newtonian model of a predictable, automatically functioning, clockwork universe. Even more significantly, quantum theory compelled physicists to reconsider their notions of the very nature of reality. Werner Heisenberg, one of the founders of quantum theory, characterized it as "a real break in the structure of modern science."[96]

The quantum world is a paradoxical, nonmaterial non-world whose properties are hard to account for by invoking the concepts and characteristics of our familiar world. At the deeper levels of existence, physicists did not find the minute building blocks of matter that they had expected to find. Instead, matter evaporated into a world of probabilities, of nonexistent entities displaying only tendencies to exist. Take for example the atom, which ever since the ancient Greeks has been considered the ultimate building block of the universe, the smallest unit of material creation. According to quantum theory, atoms are anything but well-behaved, solid building blocks. They take on completely different properties depending upon whether or not they are being observed and upon the experimental context in which they are being observed. When observed, atoms display the particle-like properties we associate with matter. When not observed, however, they do not behave like particles; they can only be represented by a mathematical formula called the atom's wave function. The wave function is not really an atom in the classical sense of a particle; it represents *a probability* of the atom being present in one specific portion of space rather than another. In other words, when not observed, the tiny units of material creation exist only as probability patterns. They are semireal vibrating possibilities, mere fluctuations of existence with no apparent actuality of their own. As physicist Nick Herbert remarks, in its mathematical representation the unobserved atom "is everywhere and nowhere at the same time."[97]

At the same time as the building blocks of matter evaporated, wholeness emerged as an intrinsic feature of reality at the subatomic level of existence. Many of the apparently diverse paradoxical phenomena of the quantum world bespeak the holistic nature of existence. As we journey into the infinitesimal realms of the quantum world, we must take leave of our classical notions of autonomous parts whose interactions are clear-cut and entirely predictable. "By getting to smaller and smaller units," Werner Heisenberg explains, "we do not come to fundamental units, or indivisible units, but we do come to a point where division has no meaning."

Quantum entities may exhibit the characteristics of particles, but these are mere abstractions or idealizations—they have no independent properties and appear only through their interplay with other systems. No longer is it possible to view the fundamental reality of the world as consisting of elemental parts. No longer can we defend the notion of physical systems simply being different arrangements of basic building blocks. The world is not an aggregation of separate things; rather, the fundamental reality is a web of relations between parts of a unified whole. "Isolated material particles are abstractions," said Niels Bohr, "their properties being definable and observable only through their interaction with other systems."[98]

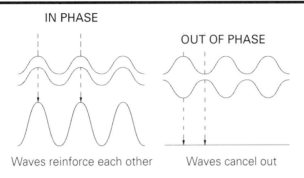

IN PHASE

OUT OF PHASE

Waves reinforce each other   Waves cancel out

FIGURE 1A. THE WAVE-PARTICLE DUALITY
One of the experiments that most strikingly demonstrates the wave-particle nature of atoms is Young's famous two-slit experiment. The experiment skillfully makes use of the interference properties of waves. When two waves meet together, the wave crests and troughs in phase with each other reinforce each other, whereas wave crests and troughs not in phase will cancel each other out.

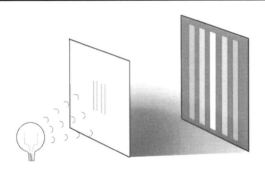

FIGURE 1B.
Photons, the elementary constituents of light, have both particle and wave-like properties. When a light source illuminates the two slits in the front screen, the photons passing through interfere with each other and in some cases reinforce each other (lighter stripes) and in other cases cancel each other out (dark stripes).

Close examination of the photographic plate behind the front screen reveals that the interference pattern is really a collection of tiny dots, each dot recording the absorption of a single photon of light. If we turn the light down so that only one photon arrives at the photographic plate at a time, the pattern of dots that eventually gets collected is still the same, indicating that each photon somehow went through both slits at the same time. In other words, the photon behaves like a wave when it is travelling and behaves like a particle when it registers on the photographic plate.

The Quantum Theme: Resonant Modes of Undifferentiated Wholeness

Variation One: Space and Time Transcendence

In the beginning days of quantum mechanics, physicists fervently debated the meaning of the 'fuzzy,' undefinable, acausal picture of the subatomic world that quantum theory painted. One of the central arguments was between Niels Bohr and Albert Einstein, who disagreed heatedly on the implications of quantum theory. Einstein could not accept the random, observer-dependent picture of reality that quantum theory presented. He felt that the quantum mechanical description of the world appeared so strange only because quantum theory was incomplete. In a famous 1935 paper, Einstein together with physicists Boris Podolsky and Nathan Rosen proposed a thought experiment which could present evidence for his position.

As I noted above, a quantum entity, such as an electron, does not appear to have any definite attributes until it is observed. When unobserved, the electron's momentum and its position in space, for example, remain in a state of limbo and can only be described as a probability pattern. Only when a specific experimental setup collapses the wave function of the electron is it observable as a distinct 'particle.' Furthermore, according to the principle known as Heisenberg's Uncertainty Principle, we cannot with complete accuracy determine *both* the electron's position and momentum as we can in the case of 'normal' objects. We can determine either its momentum through space or its position in space, but not both at the same time. Measuring one attribute accurately blurs the value of the other.

The thought experiment proposed by the trio—since known as the EPR paradox—involved taking advantage of a property known as phase entanglement to bypass Heisenberg's Uncertainty Principle. Once two particles have interacted, they become 'phase-entangled,' or correlated, and they remain so no matter how far apart they may be. This enables the momentum of electron One to be calculated by subtracting the momentum of electron Two from the total momentum of the phase-entangled wave system. An analogous calculation can be done to determine the position of electron One from a measurement on the position of electron Two. In this way, argued Einstein, Podolsky, and Rosen, it is possible to determine *both* the position and momentum of electron One. Now, imagine that electron Two is so far away from electron One at the time the measurement is performed, that an influence from electron Two would no longer be able to reach electron One even at the speed of light (Einstein's theory of relativity rules out the possibility of signalling faster than the speed of light). The measurement of electron Two can therefore not affect electron One. In other words, the position or momentum values of electron One must in principle be independently accessible and exist independently of electron Two. The reason we cannot predict them, maintained Einstein, is simply because quantum theory is incomplete.

However, the EPR thought experiment backfired in the sense that there is an alternate explanation, as Niels Bohr was quick to point out. The paradox of Einstein, Podolsky, and Rosen was based on the assumption of locality—that objects exist independently and any interaction between them is mediated through space-time. Einstein was assuming that the measurement of the position or momentum of electron Two did not affect electron One because they were too widely separated to interact via local signals. However, said Bohr, what if the two electrons are actually connected in a *nonlocal* manner? What if they have become like *one single wave system*, in which an observation of one electron's attributes immediately influences the attributes of the other—even though they may be too far apart to interact through conventional forces?

What Einstein, Podolsky, and Rosen had really demonstrated, argued Bohr, was that particles cannot be understood as separate micro-entities, but only as parts in a macroscopic context. They are inseparable parts of the same quantum system. Therefore, no physical transmission is needed to account for the particles' interrelated behavior. The two particles form a whole, no matter how far apart they may be.

The Einstein-Bohr debate remained unresolved for more than 30 years. Not until then were physicists able to design an experiment to determine which was the correct interpretation. A crucial step on the way came in 1965 when the Scottish physicist John Bell formulated a mathematical theorem. This theorem specified the theoretical limits on the degree to which the measurement of dynamic attributes of a particle, such as position and momentum, should be correlated if reality is local.

Bell's theorem is based on two assumptions that are compatible with classical physics: first, the behavior of quantum particles is determined by inherent, objectively existing properties, and second, their influence upon each other is localized, i.e. they cannot exert an instantaneous influence on each other when they are not in the same location. Based on these two assumptions, Bell predicted the degree of correlation that should occur between two attribute-correlated particles in a given measurement situation. If Einstein was right—and quantum particles are 'normal' particles which possess a local, objective reality that is not accounted for by quantum theory—the correlation of the particles would stay within the limits demarcated by Bell's theorem. If Bohr was right—and quantum particles possess no such thing as a local, objective reality—the opposite would hold true.

In 1972, the American physicists John Clauser and Stuart Freedman designed the first experiment to attempt to determine who held the right interpretation—Einstein or Bohr. The outcome might well have turned Einstein in his grave. Bohr had been right all along. The results of a more refined experiment conducted in 1982 by the French physicist Alain Aspect further supported Bohr's position. Aspect was able to demonstrate definitively that although there is no possibility of signalling between the two electrons, a change in the measurement of electron One still influences the outcome of the measurement of electron Two.

So, what does all this mean? It means that, on the quantum level there is no such thing as a purely local cause. The quantum world is replete with nonlocal, *unmediated* influences. Quantum entities that may be galaxies apart are linked instantaneously without any signal passing between them. There is no way of explaining this phenomenon within the framework of Newtonian physics. According to Einstein's theory of relativity, no message can travel superluminally, faster than light; it simply is not possible—nothing 'real' can move that fast. The results of the EPR experiments force us to discard the notion of a reality with purely local causes, one of the pillars of Newtonian physics.

What, then, can we put in its stead? One school of thought has adopted the position that Bell's theorem clearly shows reality is nonlocal. If we consider electrons as separate particles, it is very difficult to understand how two particles can be instantly correlated across vast distances. However, if we simply consider the particles as part of a larger wholeness, these difficulties disappear. "A universe that displays local phenomena built upon a *non-local reality* is the only sort of world consistent with known facts and Bell's proof," notes physicist Nick Herbert.[99]

"[This] property of 'nonlocality' has sweeping implications," writes Paul Davies. "We can think of the Universe as a vast network of interacting particles, and each linkage binds the participating particles into a single quantum system. In some sense the entire Universe can be regarded as a single quantum system. . . . [T]here is a strong holistic flavor to the quantum description of the Universe."[100]

Before Bell's theorem, the property of phase entanglement showed up only in the mathematics, and it was possible to relegate it to the category of theoretical artifacts. Now, those days are over. If we want to operate within the notion of 'reality,' we must adopt a concept involving a far more subtle and holistic order in the universe. "The violation of separability seems to imply that in some sense all these objects constitute an indivisible whole," concludes Bernard d'Espagnat in an article on Bell's theorem.[101] "[T]he inseparable quantum interconnectedness of the whole universe is the fundamental reality," echoes the late British physicist David Bohm, a strong proponent of the concept that the universe is an undifferentiated wholeness.[102]

The property of nonlocality illustrates that the quantum wholeness exists beyond the confines of *spatial* separation. Other findings have demonstrated that this wholeness transcends not only our notions of space but of time as well. Our usual concept of *time* has little meaning on the quantum level.

Remember, whether we observe a quantum entity as a wave or a particle depends entirely upon our experimental setup. In a famous experiment known as the 'delayed-choice experiment,' physicist Caroll Alley and colleagues were able to show that the decision of whether to measure the wave or particle aspect of, for example, a photon, can be delayed until—from a classical perspective at least—the photon is already 'committed' to appearing as either one or the other form of expression. Simply speaking, in the experimental setup the photon can travel by one of two paths and appear as a particle; or it can—by virtue of a phenomenon known as superposition—travel by both paths and appear as a wave by causing wave interference with itself. The crucial feature of the delayed-choice experiment is that the decision of whether the photon will travel by one route or by both routes can be delayed until almost all its travel has *already* taken place. In other words, from a classical perspective the experimenter as if determines which path(s) the photon travelled in the past!

Part of the reason it is so difficult to understand the properties of the quantum world is that our concepts and words derive from a purely classical view of the world. When we say the photon travels by one route or both, this is only an approximation to the actual situation, created by our habitual notions of time and space. Before our observation, nothing, or 'no-thing'—in our usual sense of the word—exists. We may call it an 'abstract quantum wave function,' a 'probability distribution,' a 'subatomic particle,' or a 'world of potentia,' but whatever term we use only approximates the quantum reality. The quantum world is a wholeness that lies beyond the bounds of our space-time, object-referential reality, and beyond the concepts we have developed to understand and describe that reality.

"If we're ever going to find an element of nature that explains space and time, we surely have to find something that is deeper than space and time—something that itself has no localization in space and time," explains John Wheeler. "The amazing feature of the elementary quantum phenomenon . . . is exactly this. It is indeed something of a pure knowledge-theoretical character, *an atom of information which has no localization* in between the point of entry and the point of registration. This is the significance of the delayed-choice experiment."[103] [emphasis added]

However, it is not only Bell's theorem and the delayed-choice experiment that paint the quantum picture of an 'unbroken wholeness' that lies beyond space and time. A second and even more powerful variation on the theme of quantum oneness can be found in quantum field theory.

Variation Two: Quantum Field Theory

The concept of fields was introduced in the middle of the 19th century by physicist Michael Farraday, who used it as a tool to describe the action of physical forces, such as gravity and electromagnetism, on physical bodies. Fields, Farraday argued, are the media through which these forces exert their effects on physical bodies. Like other media with which we are more familiar—for example, water—fields can sustain wavelike action.

In quantum field theory, the concept of fields is applied to quantum physics to provide a framework for understanding elementary particles. Quantum field theory extends the notion of classical field theory about how to create waves, and thereby provides a mechanism for depicting how the waves that describe matter can be created. It does so in a way that unifies particles and forces by describing them as waves of the same underlying field. Quantum fields are present everywhere in space, and they are different from classical fields in a number of respects. For example, whereas the energy levels of a classical field can be continuous, those of the quantum field are discrete, or 'quantized.' According to quantum field theory, what we perceive as particles are not material entities, but quantized expressions, or discrete states of excitation, of their respective underlying quantum field. It is the discreteness in energy levels that gives rise to the granular, particle-like structure of matter, which has led to the notion that reality is composed of elemental particles.

Quantum field theory presents a picture of reality very different from that posited by the classical Newtonian view of billiard balls acting on billiard balls. It demonstrates that the difference between the macroscopic world and the microscopic world is not only quantitative, it is also profoundly qualitative. At the quantum level there are no 'things.' Elementary particles have no existence as 'objects' in any sense of the word; they are nothing but discrete states of excitation of their underlying quantum field.

The quantum field concept provides one step toward unification of the multiplex world of elementary particles, reducing them to simple concentrated expressions of underlying quantum fields. Quantum fields, however, not only account for the *particle* aspect of matter, but also for the fundamental *force*s that act on physical bodies. Particles are just one state of activity of the field; the field can sustain other forms of activity as well, producing configurations that, unlike particles, are unstable, do not propagate, and do not possess well-defined energy. These transient modes of activity are identical to the fundamental forces which transfer energy and momentum from one particle to another. The field also has a third mode of activity, the ground state or least excited state of activity. This is also called the vacuum state, since it corresponds to the state of no particles. It is not, however, an inert dormant state of the field, but a lively field of continuous fluctuations. These fluctuations are purely quantum mechanical activity which is present continuously, not only in the vacuum state but in the excited states of the field as well.

Quantum field theory provides the unification of two such previously unrelated concepts as particles and fundamental forces. The picture of reality presented by quantum field theory is one of a continuous, lively, but undifferentiated field present everywhere in space. Any appearance of discontinuity results from the field's particle-like, granular expression.

The elementary particles that become the 'building blocks' of what we know as 'reality,' are mere epiphenomena; the field alone exists. Forces and matter, the two fundamental elements of Newtonian physics, merge into a dynamic pattern of continuously changing field configurations. "We may therefore regard matter as being constituted by the regions of space in which the field is extremely intense. . . ." wrote Albert Einstein. "There is no place in this new kind of physics both for the field and matter, for the field is the only reality."[104]

Quantum theory and quantum field theory have therefore undermined one of the oldest assumptions of Western science. The notion that the universe is ultimately constituted of pieces of matter has turned out to be a myth, as the physicist Paul Davies points out: "The matter myth is built on the fiction that the physical Universe consists of nothing but a collection of inert particles pulling and pushing each other like cogs in a deterministic machine. . . . Quantum physics especially pulls the rug out from under this simple mechanistic image. . . . When quantum mechanics is extended to encompass the field concept. . . .[e]ven the apparent solidity of ordinary matter melts away into a frolic of insubstantial patterns of energy. Quantum field theory creates an image of a Universe crisscrossed by a network of interactions that weave the cosmos into a unity."[105]

Each of the four fundamental forces of nature—gravity, electromagnetic force, and strong and weak nuclear forces—and the particles they affect are associated with different quantum fields. Physicists are confident that it will eventually be possible to formulate a 'unified field theory' which unites all four force fields and their associated particles into one unified description of nature. Already, three of the four fundamental forces—the electromagnetic force and the strong and weak nuclear forces—have been unified in what are known as grand unification theories. In the past decade, superstring theories have emerged as strong contenders for a model that also integrates gravity; the multiple variations of these theories are the first to cohesively account for the immense diversity of elemental particles and forces in nature.

Although the final formulation of a unified field theory has not yet been discovered, it is safe to say that in whatever form it eventually appears, it will enable us to understand all the elements of creation as nothing but resonant, vibrational modes of the same underlying field. Since everything in creation ultimately consists of particles and force fields, such a theory would also have relevance for phenomena studied within the areas of chemistry and biology. The 'stuff' of which the world is made would be described within the framework of this 'theory of everything.'

Some have characterized such a theory as the ultimate reductionist explanation of the universe. It would enable us to understand the fundamental law which gives rise to the structure of matter and controls the four forces of nature. Several physicists are of the opinion, however, that this would still be only half the story. A 'theory of everything' would provide us with a mathematical formula enabling us to reduce everything in creation to resonant modes of an underlying unified field. But the holistic and hierarchical organization of nature would not be explained within the framework of this theory. The theoretical physicist Murray Gell-Mann describes the concept of a 'theory of everything' as a "misleading characterization unless 'everything' is taken to mean only the description of the elementary particles and their interactions. The theory cannot, by itself, tell us all that is knowable about the universe and the matter it contains. Other kinds of information are needed as well."[106]

Variation Three: Cosmic Precision

The fundamental interconnectedness of the universe is also evidenced in the very rules that permit the manifestation of multiplicity from featureless simplicity. The very laws and constants that underlie the phenomena of the universe appear to be so sensitively attuned to one another that some scientists have characterized it as almost "too good to be true."[107]

The whole scientific enterprise rests on the ability to uncover patterns in nature, hidden regularities and cause-and-effect relationships that give rise to the specific expressions of creation. These are the laws of nature, expressions of the implicit order underpinning everything in the universe. The striking regularities we observe in nature, in the orbits of planets or the patterns and rhythms of atoms, are more than just an order projected onto nature by the human mind. They are objective regularities that can be mathematically modelled.

That we can uncover orderliness and regularities in the universe is itself a mystery. The universe could so easily have been completely featureless—or it could have been a totally chaotic affair without laws, or with laws that did not permit any stable states of matter to form. Even more significant is the fact that the laws of nature appear to be delicately tuned to encourage the emergence of the progressive complexity of the universe. The self-organization of matter and energy into increasingly sophisticated structures would not be possible if not for a series of *Cosmic Coincidences*, many of which are charted by astrophysicist John Gribbin and astronomer Martin Rees in their book by that name.[108] Combined with appropriate initial conditions, the hidden order embodied in the laws of nature is the source of the gradual formation of the multifarious forms in our universe. Structures arise from a disparate scramble of elementary particles as the result of 'processing' carried out according to carefully tuned, preexisting rules.

At all levels of organization, we see a hairline balance between the macroscopic and microscopic properties of the universe. The existence of stars, for example, is possible because of finely tuned conditions at the subatomic level of matter. Stars are born due to certain mechanical and thermodynamic properties of hydrogen gas combined with the force of gravity. Planets such as Earth are created because tiny subatomic particles known as neutrinos trigger a blast at the center of a massive dying star, causing the heavy elements from which planets are made to spread throughout the universe. Carbon, an element that is essential for the formation of life, could not have formed were it not for some very specific thermodynamic conditions occurring within the core of stars. And the list goes on and on.

A theme that has emerged in recent years within the field of biology is that greater organizational complexity may emerge spontaneously within physical and chemical systems, and this increased complexity greatly enhances the possibility that complex biochemical molecules will form. The self-organization of matter in this framework depends on the specificity of initial conditions and of laws of physics and chemistry, which appear to channel matter in a specific direction. Not any law or initial condition will do—in many cases even a small change would disallow life as we know it from coming into existence.

Commenting on this astounding cosmic precision, Paul Davies notes, "I think most physicists would agree that the emergence of complexity depends sensitively upon the specific details of the actual laws of physics that work in our actual universe. In other words, if I were to invite you to design a universe, to give one a set of laws and see how it works, the chances are you would not get the emergence of organized complexity—at least, not with anything like the efficiency that seems to work in the real universe. So this transition from simple to complex is not a generic feature of dynamical laws. It's a rather specific feature of the actual laws of the real universe. The central message, then, of the self-organizing universe is that laws that permit a spontaneously creative universe are very special in their form."[109]

This delicate interdependence can be viewed as another expression of the implicit wholeness of creation—the effortless precision that coordinates the large-scale structures of the cosmos with the minutest expressions of matter.

The Role of the Observer

Quantum theory undermines some of our most fundamental notions of reality. We might learn to live with the idea that the world at finer time and distance scales is vastly different from what we perceive at the level of everyday life, but quantum mechanics does not stop there. It profoundly implicates *us* in the shaping of the world in which we live.

Remember that before Newton, Descartes had divided the world into a domain of thoughts and a domain of material things—*res cogitans* and *res extensa*. This conceptual distinction resolved an ongoing battle with the church, by dividing the world into things of the mind, or spirit—the natural domain of the church—and things of the world. This distinction was especially valuable for physicians of that time, because they could now justify to the church that invasive medical procedures and dissection of the human body did not interfere with the domain of God, which was that of the spirit.

Descartes' partition of reality reflects the difference between subject and object, thoughts and things, mind and matter, that we all perceive in our daily lives. However, this separation of subject and object, observer and observed, was one of the first to crumble under the onslaught of quantum theory. As we have seen above, the reality of quantum entities is inextricably linked to the process of observation. The quantum reality takes shape in the process of measurement; what we know as the 'objective' world is born through the process of observation. Before observation, there are only fluctuating possibilities. The wave-particle duality represents complementary aspects of a quantum entity's characteristics and behavior. What causes it to 'collapse' into a specific expression is the process of observation. Likewise, the influence of the observer is made prominent by Heisenberg's uncertainty principle. The more precisely we locate one aspect of a quantum particle, for example an electron's momentum, the greater the uncertainty that exists around its paired attribute, in this case the electron's position.

When not observed, an electron exists as a wave function, a superposition of several physically inequivalent states. Between observations, the wave function is spread out, not restricted to a specific location. The moment an observation is made, however, the wave function collapses and the electron's mode of existence is transformed from a nonspecific state of limbo to a single, concrete reality. This seems absurd if we think of the quantum world as a world of separate objects. However, it makes sense if we reverse our concept of reality at this level from one in which parts are primary, to a reality in which wholeness is primary. Reality at the quantum level can be conceptualized as a seamless whole that is differentiated in the process of measurement. "In order to measure such a system, one is obliged to break that wholeness," writes physicist Nick Herbert, "to cut open the apple of knowledge as it were. How we make that necessary cut determines in part how that system will appear to our eyes. But unobserved the system has no cuts at all, and is, in a sense, indescribable by conventional means."[110]

The apparent influence of the observer is one of the greatest puzzles of quantum mechanics. What exactly is it about the process of measurement that causes the wholeness to 'break' into specific expressions? What causes the abrupt transition in the electron's mode of existence? The elementary quantum activity is only a phenomenon when it has been brought to a close by "an irreversible act of amplification," suggest physicists such as John Wheeler.[111] But what does this "irreversible act of amplification" consist of? What feature of the process of observation causes a wave function to shift from its world of probability fluctuations into the world of actuality? How does the interaction with an observer cause the electron to take on specific properties?

Central to resolving this issue is determining *where* the quantum wave collapses. When it enters the measuring apparatus? The measuring apparatus itself, however, is also fundamentally nothing but a quantum wave function—because of its complexity, a very elaborate and intricate one, but nonetheless it is essentially the sum total wave function of all its elementary particle constituents. Therefore, proposing that the quantum wave function collapses when it enters the measuring apparatus leads us into a sequence of infinite regress. Any quantum system is collapsed into a specific state when it is measured by a system outside itself—but then the larger system goes into a probability state and must be measured by another, larger system outside itself, and so on and so on.

This infinite regress is known as von Neumann's chain, named for the Hungarian mathematician John von Neumann, one of the brilliant minds of this century. Based on a detailed mathematical analysis of the problem, von Neumann concluded that the only link in the chain that is *qualitatively different* is consciousness. Only when a conscious individual is involved does the chain of infinite quantum limbo states turn into actuality. A small, prestigious group of physicists share von Neumann's interpretation, the most prominent of whom is Nobel laureate Eugene Wigner, who holds that the content of consciousness is an ultimate reality. "If one speaks of the wave function, its changes are coupled with the entering of impressions into our consciousness," writes Wigner. "If one formulates the laws of quantum mechanics in terms of probabilities of impressions, these are ipso facto the primary concepts with which one deals. . . . The principal argument is that thought processes and consciousness are the primary concepts, that our knowledge of the external world is the content of our consciousness and that the consciousness, therefore, cannot be denied. On the contrary, logically, the external world could be denied—though it is not very practical to do so."[112]

Lessons from Quantum Theory

We choose to ignore the lessons of the quantum world at our own peril. Science progresses as new findings force more precise models of reality. As we have seen in previous chapters, our choice of actions is decidedly linked to our understanding of the world. In the field of ecology, our failure to understand that every part of the biological chain is intertwined with the entire ecosystem has led to pervasive ecological disasters. In the field of medicine, our disregard of the body as a holistically functioning system has led to an emphasis on fixing broken parts, without consideration of the important context in which the malfunctioning parts occur.

In 20th century physics, the materialistic, mechanistic model of nature has come to be regarded as one of the founding myths of classical science. The world is not constituted of minute material building blocks. It is fundamentally an unbroken wholeness, of which the particles comprising our familiar, solid world of matter are but a by-product. Not only is the organization of the universe suffused with wholeness, as we saw in Chapter Five; the phenomena of the universe emerge from an undifferentiated wholeness beyond the boundaries of space and time.

In examining the nature of this wholeness, we find that our own consciousness appears to be inextricably linked to its specific expressions. As Sir James Jeans, one of the early quantum physicists noted, "[T]he universe begins to look more like a great thought than a great machine."[113] Physicists have been forced to turn physics around, and start with the whole instead of the parts. The findings of quantum physics strongly imply that we must turn around mind and matter as well. A central lesson of quantum mechanics is that consciousness is a far more important force in the universe than Western science has traditionally conceived it to be.

Chapter Seven

ONE SELF-EVOLVING CAUSE

L et us survey the terrain we have traversed thus far. We have seen that allopathic medicine fails to make conscious use of the body's healing intelligence in its treatment efforts, largely because the mechanistic model of the body leaves little room for the notion of an inherent biological intelligence. Yet, as we saw in Chapter Four, it is impossible to completely ignore the evidence for this tremendous self-organizing intelligence. The placebo effect, spontaneous remissions, and the uncanny plasticity of living systems are all difficult to account for within the rigid framework of the machine metaphor.

The common feature of the various manifestations of the body's intelligence is that they are holistic responses in which the body functions as a precisely coordinated system. The mind appears to play a pivotal role in mediating these holistic responses; in Chapter Four, we examined some of the evidence that the functioning of the body is closely linked to a person's experience of the world. In Chapter Five, we noted that wholeness emerges as a central organizing theme of the functional dynamics of all living systems. This organizing theme extends to the entire universe—the myriad diverse elements of the universe combine to form hierarchically organized wholenesses of ever-increasing size. With the development of quantum theory, it has become apparent that this cosmic display of 'wholenesses nested within wholenesses' emerges from an even greater unbroken wholeness beyond space and time—the unified field of superstring theories. And at the quantum level, mind, or the element of subjectivity, again stands out as somehow playing a pivotal role. In the same way as the functioning of the body is linked to the activity of our mind, at the quantum level the specific expressions of the 'observed' cannot be separated from the observer.

For more than 200 years, the Western materialist, mechanistic model of reality has been beleaguered by a number of persistent paradoxes. Philosophers and researchers operating within the traditional Western framework have been unable to produce an acceptable model for understanding the relationship between mind and body. No theory has adequately explained how the qualitatively different mental realm might emerge from the activity of the purely material structure of the body and, in turn, gain downward regulating control over this material structure. The varied display of intelligence in nature has proven equally difficult to account for. The seemingly magical aggregation of parts into self-organizing, holistically-functioning living systems, the increase in order and complexity during the course of evolution, and the organization of living systems in hierarchical layers of emergent wholes, pose serious challenges to a purely mechanistic understanding of living systems. On top of all this, the advent of quantum theory threw all traditional notions of the very nature of reality out the window. Understanding matter and accounting for the expressions of the intelligence that 'harnesses matter to perform coherent functions' has proven difficult, if not impossible, within the conceptual framework of Western science. A theory that presumes matter is primary and all living systems emerge from the random interaction of molecules and aggregates of molecules, has turned out to be too narrow to accommodate nature's plethora of marvels.

The basic postulates of the materialist, mechanistic paradigm are *assumptions* about the nature of reality, not assertions firmly based upon experimental data. Bearing this in mind, it is interesting to note that the paradoxes which have persistently beleaguered the Western paradigm can be resolved simply by changing these assumptions. If we turn the materialist, mechanistic model upside down, so to speak, a picture of the universe emerges which is devoid of the internal inconsistencies that weigh down the Western paradigm.

This becomes quite apparent when one studies the Vedic tradition of knowledge. The Vedas represent the oldest continuous tradition of knowledge in the world; for more than 5,000 years the Vedas have been passed down orally from generation to generation. The Vedic description of the deepest structure of reality in many ways parallels that of quantum physics. According to the Vedas, matter is a secondary expression of a more fundamental field of life; the basis of the differentiated universe is a timeless, undifferentiated state of unified wholeness. As you will recall, quantum field theory also describes elementary particles and forces of nature as passing configurations of a timeless, undifferentiated unified field. As Berkeley physicist Henry Stapp puts it, "[T]he fundamental process of Nature lies outside space-time . . . but generates events that can be located in space-time."[114]

The discoveries of quantum physics may be difficult to comprehend, since our everyday experience of the world is one of diversity and multiplicity, not unity and wholeness. However, the heritage bestowed on us by the Vedic seers makes it apparent that there is a level of experience in which the basic oneness of creation becomes evident. Quantum physicists are forced to rely on billion-dollar particle accelerators to gain knowledge of the finest structures of reality. The subtle insights recorded in the Vedas derive from the ancient Vedic seers' direct perception of the finest fabrics of reality at the most silent level of their awareness. Over time, much of the Vedic knowledge was obscured as the Vedic Literature became scattered and separated into different traditions and competing interpretations. Maharishi Mahesh Yogi's endeavors to reestablish the full potential of Ayurveda are just one part of his continuous efforts to restore the totality of this tremendous legacy of knowledge.

Modern man tends to regard Western civilization as the epitome of cultural and technological development, disregarding the exquisite monumental structures and brilliant intellectual legacies that ancient cultures have left us. The Egyptian pyramids, for example, are architectural wonders that a contemporary builder would be hard pressed to duplicate.

The monuments left us by the ancient Vedic seers are not tangible material structures; rather, they are found in their unprecedented insights into the nature and dynamics of human consciousness and the deepest structure of reality. Whereas Western science has mastered matter, the ancient Vedic seers mastered the realm of consciousness.

In the Vedic tradition, the deepest level of life is described as 'Being,' an unbounded field of wholeness, of pure existence, beyond the realm of space and time. Maharishi highlights the abstract nature of this field of Being in the following quote from his book *The Science of Being and Art of Living:*

> How can we distinguish existence from that which exists?
>
> Existence is abstract; that which exists is concrete. We may say that existence is life itself, while that which exists is the ever-changing phenomenal phase of the never-changing reality of existence. *Existence is the abstract aspect of life on which are built what we call the concrete phases of life* which encompass all aspects of the individual. . . . Existence, life, or Being is the unmanifested reality of all that exists, lives or is. Being is the ultimate reality of all that was, is, or will be.[115] [emphasis added]

The field of Being is the omnipresent, essential constituent of creation, the inexhaustible field of wholeness which lies beyond the forms and phenomena of 'relative' existence. The Vedic seers directly perceived this 'absolute' level of reality at that refined, settled level of awareness where the incessant murmur of mental activity stills and the mind merges with the deepest essence of its nature. To a person who is able to perceive this level of reality, Maharishi explains, the manifest expressions of the universe appear like ripples on the surface of a vast ocean of pure silence. All forms and phenomena ultimately have their basis in, and are nothing but expressions of, the same ever-present, immovable wholeness of pure existence. This wholeness is an unmanifest, transcendent reality, yet it also pervades everything. Note again a close parallel between the Vedic description of the deepest level of life and modern physics' current theories; according to the superstring theory, the unified field in its unitary transformation maintains its own nature even as it takes on specific expressions—the vibrational states we observe as elementary particles and forces.

Where quantum physics and Vedic science part ways is in their understanding of the *nature* of the underlying unified field. As we saw in Chapter Six, even though quantum theory forced physicists to relinquish the 'matter myth,' they have been unable to engender a viable alternative concept of the nature of reality. In contrast, the Vedic tradition of knowledge regards the existence of matter as *secondary* to the existence of consciousness. The essential characteristic of the primal 'substance' is its quality of awareness, or consciousness. As we shall see in a later chapter, it is this quality of pure awareness, or pure wakefulness, that induces the self-interacting dynamics which in turn generate the expression of the unmanifest field of existence into the manifest forms of that which exists. Our individual consciousness and mind are expressions of the one primordial consciousness; the forms and phenomena of the universe, including our physiology, emerge as increasingly more palpable expressions of the same abstract, underlying field of existence.

The quantum puzzles have impelled some physicists toward a similar understanding. The contemporary physicist Henry Stapp, for example, notes that quantum theory is consistent with a world whose primary constituent is 'mind stuff' and not matter. "In view of [the] uniformly idealike characteristics of the quantum-physical world, the proper answer to our question 'What sort of world do we live in?' would seem to be this: 'We live in an *idealike* world, not matterlike world.' The material aspects are exhausted in certain mathematical properties, and these mathematical features can be understood just as well (and in fact better) as characteristics of an evolving idealike structure. There is, in fact, in the quantum universe no natural place for matter. This conclusion, curiously, is the exact reverse of the circumstance that in the classical physical universe there was no natural place for mind."[116]

The Intangible Nature of Consciousness

To a Western-oriented mind, the notion that consciousness is a primal substance of the universe might at first seem unusual. It doesn't help that the term 'consciousness' is a rather nebulous concept in the English language. The term is used most commonly to refer to the quality of awareness or experience: we are *conscious of,* or *aware of,* the existence of *internal* processes, such as thoughts, emotions, and intellectual reasoning, as well as *external* objects and phenomena. Consciousness is also at times identified with the *faculties of the mind*, i.e. sensory perception, thinking, emotions, volition, etc. We may also refer to *states of consciousness*, such as the waking, dreaming, and sleeping states of consciousness. And finally, conscious experience is sometimes contrasted with subconscious mental processing. As we shall see below, understanding the full implications of the Vedic model of consciousness is made difficult by the fact that none of the Western connotations completely capture the Vedic notion of consciousness.

Western psychology has made only modest progress toward an understanding of the nature of human consciousness. The topic remained for a long time the disowned child of psychology. The behaviorist school of thought that dominated psychological thinking during the 1950s and early 60s insisted that behavior—being observable and measurable—was the only valid subject matter for objective psychological study. Behaviorists claimed that mental processes and consciousness were irrelevant to the study of psychology, arguing that human behavior can be understood as an automatic outcome of prior physical causes in interplay with environmental factors. So strong was the influence of behaviorism that scientists in the 1960s and even well into the 70s risked ridicule if they brought up words like 'conscious' or 'mental' at scientific gatherings.[117] "[A]n interest in the topic was usually taken as a sign of approaching senility," recalls the British Nobel laureate Francis Crick.[118]

Consciousness has now become an acceptable and widely pursued topic of study; yet researchers are still grappling with fundamental questions—simply reaching agreement on a definition of consciousness has proven a formidable task. The approaches for researching the topic are greatly varied. Some researchers are suggesting that consciousness is a quantum mechanical phenomenon; some have developed models based on bootstrap theory, some incorporate chaos theory. There are nearly as many theories of consciousness as there are researchers in the field.

Most theories and strategies for studying consciousness attempt to explain it in terms of basic brain processes, relating particular conscious experiences to particular patterns of neural activity. One of the major problems with these theories is known as the binding problem—how does the vast array of cortical centers involved in analyzing sensory data produce the unity of conscious experience? There is no single place where everything comes together, and no one has found physiological evidence for the existence of a 'central processing unit' that sorts and directs the flow of information through the brain. How then does the scattered firing of neurons turn into a unified perception? This problem is another variation on the theme we explored in Chapter Five: the uncanny manifestations of the functional wholeness present in the physiology. Explaining how the countless neuronal activities of the brain are coordinated and transformed into the perceiving, thinking, and feeling faculties of the mind, is as difficult as explaining how strands of nucleic acid in the DNA over a period of nine months orchestrate the development of the vast network of the human physiology.

For Western science, the quality of awareness, or experience, remains the most mysterious among the many connotations of consciousness. Conscious awareness is the most intimate feature of our existence, yet the hardest to explain. Our conscious experience has a fundamental unity to it. The mind may be like a street in rush hour traffic, crowded with sensory input, thoughts, plans, and emotions, yet a holistic element is always present. This is the property of awareness, which lies beyond the incessant activity of the mind. I experience the body as the specific 'form' I am in, and although it is part of me, it is not *me*, it is not the seat of my sense of self. In the same way as I distinquish between my body and my *self*, I can draw a clear distinction between the flow of thoughts and emotions through my mind and the *I* that experiences those thoughts and emotions. Our conscious awareness is like the unseen screen upon which the contents of our mind—whether external phenomena or internal mental processes—are projected. As the Scottish philosopher Thomas Reid once commented: "Whatever this self may be it is something which thinks, and deliberates, and resolves, and acts. . . . I am not thought, I am not action, I am not feeling; I am something that thinks, and acts. . . ."[119]

The very fact that there is awareness associated with our mental processes presents the greatest challenge of all to Western science.[120] Philosopher David Chalmers has characterized this as "the hard problem" of consciousness research. The *functions* of the mind can be studied and analyzed through reductionist methods, and most likely we will eventually have a clear picture of the specific neural mechanisms that bring them about. However, we still have no explanation of why these are accompanied by experience. As in the case of any input-output device, functional processes could conceivably take place equally well in the absence of experience.

If the only reality is material reality, why and how would an anomalous phenomenon like experience, a 'self with awareness,' arise? In theory, during the course of evolution we could have survived equally well as automatic nonconscious androids, highly sophisticated computers exhibiting sensory and cognitive faculties, but devoid of any conscious experience of these. What is the evolutionary benefit of conscious experience? Why should there be an 'I' who sees, hears, remembers, thinks, feels, and decides?

"At the end of the day," writes David Chalmers, one of the influential thinkers in the area of consciousness research, "for any physical process we specify there will be a question that the physical theory leaves unanswered: why should this process give rise to experience? For any such process, it remains conceptually coherent that it could be instantiated in the absence of experience. It follows that no mere account of the physical process will tell us why experience arises."[121] The jump from matter to conscious experience is profoundly qualitative. It involves a quantum leap in the ontological status of the organism, which cannot be accounted for within the framework of prevailing models.

A Continuum of Expression

Within the Vedic representation of reality, this question never arises. Whereas the unified field of superstring theories is an 'inert' field which forms the basis of particles and forces, in Vedic science the one self-evolving cause is a field of existence whose fundamental quality is its property of awareness, or consciousness.

The Vedic notion of consciousness is hard to capture in just a few words. Consciousness in the Vedic framework is essential experience devoid of thought, perception, volition, or any other object of awareness. It is a field of *pure wakefulness*, pure awareness. Consciousness in its pure form is like an empty screen upon which sensory input and thought processes are projected; it is transcendent, i.e. it lies beyond the world of forms and phenomena. Pure consciousness is purely self-referential; as Maharishi explains, "consciousness is that which is conscious of itself."[122] Pure consciousness is the unbounded, undifferentiated source of all that exists. Like ripples on the ocean, all the various forms of matter—indeed, everything in the universe—are the precipitated expressions of this unbounded ocean of pure existence. In the same way that waves on the ocean take every form from tiny ripples to giant waves, the sequential unfoldment of the field of pure existence proceeds from the less-precipitated, subtle, abstract levels of expression to the more-precipitated, gross, concrete expressions.

Mind and body emerge in the sequential unfoldment of the abstract, nonmaterial wholeness of pure consciousness. The refined, subtle levels of its manifestation are associated with the functioning of the mind; the different levels of functionality—ego, emotions, intellect, and senses—emerge as part of the sequential expression of this fundamental source of existence. The gross material expressions of the field of pure consciousness are associated with the body and other physical objects.

The Filter of Experience

If the basis of objective reality is a field of unmanifest abstract Being, then why, one might ask, don't we perceive it?

Maharishi explains that our nervous system is like a reflector through which the field of pure consciousness is mirrored. The nervous system functions as a filter or measuring apparatus that 'reads' the invisible reality according to the physiology's unique parameters. For most of us, the parameters on this measuring apparatus are set in such a way that our nervous system filters a very limited part of a much larger reality.

We know the world around us from the point of view of human beings with five senses; however, our senses give us a very limited representation of reality. We generally assume that the world 'out there' exists independently of our perception of it. This however is not the case—forms, colors, sounds, and tastes acquire their unique characteristics in the process of our perceiving them.

Let us use the term *phenomenal reality* to denote the ever-changing world of forms and phenomena around us, as opposed to the never-changing underlying field of unified existence. The specific appearances of phenomenal reality are predominantly a product of the functioning of our senses. What we perceive as blue, yellow, or red, is simply the perception of different frequencies of the spectrum of visible light, which itself is a highly limited range of the total spectrum of electromagnetic radiation. Though invisible to the human eye, the world is teeming with electromagnetic waves. Below the frequency range which our eyes can detect, lies an undulating mass of radio waves, television waves, microwaves, and infrared radiation. Above the frequency spectrum that our eyes can perceive, resides a volatile bundle of ultraviolet waves, X-rays, gamma rays, and cosmic rays.

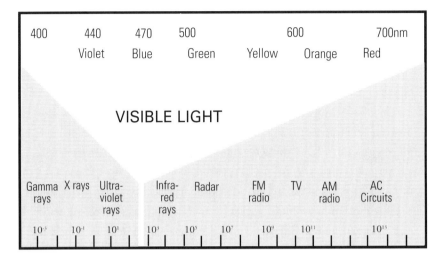

FIGURE 1. THE ELECTROMAGNETIC SPECTRUM.
What we perceive as light is only a small portion of the electromagnetic radiation emitted by electrically charged particles. Other organisms are sensitive to longer or shorter wavelengths of the electromagnetic spectrum and therefore inhabit a world of appearances quite different from ours. (Wavelengths in nanometers.)

From the vantage point of sensory perception alone, there is nothing very objective about objective reality. When we refer to the characteristics of a specific object—whether color, taste, smell, touch, or sound—we are actually describing *a specific, non-changing pattern of influence* upon our sense organs, rather than properties that can be ascribed to the external object.

There is a rare disorder of the senses known as synesthesia, which affects about one in 100,000 people. In those who have this disorder, the senses seem to be interlaced. These individuals can *feel* sounds and tastes, and *hear* colors. Instead of praising the sweet rich flavor of a rice pudding, for example, a person with a tactile perception of taste might make an analogy to familiar objects and characterize the taste as being of a pointed shape covered with little pricks. Synesthesia is a reminder that our senses tell us less about the actual properties of objects than about their effects upon our sense organs. In a way unknown to medical science, the nervous system of a person with synesthesia processes sensory input differently than it does in the 99,999 other people who do not have this disorder. The environment is filtered in a unique way, giving rise to a different phenomenal reality.

Many animals inhabit a phenomenal world vastly different from our own. Imagine what it is like to be a bat, navigating through dense, dark forests guided only by the echoes of high-pitched chirps. The bat has a keen sense of spatial relationships, adroitly dodging trees and zooming through openings in webs of branches not much wider than its wingspan. The bat is blind—yes, blind as a bat—yet it inhabits a phenomenal world rich in detail, but so different from ours that we cannot even begin to imagine what its world looks, or rather sounds, like.

The point is, different nervous systems reflect reality in different ways. Color, light, heat, even form and motion are apparent qualities that have their source in the way our nervous systems sense and process perceptual information. The phenomenal objects themselves are not much more than empty space, although they appear to be solid. If we consider them in terms of the atoms of which they are composed (for a moment considering only the particle aspect of the atom), the relative distance between the nucleus and electrons is vast. If we expanded an atom to the size of say, Lake Tahoe, the nucleus would be a small pebble in the middle of this huge lake. The electrons would be microscopic grains of sand at the shoreline, whirling around the nucleus at staggering speed. In an atom, one part in one million billion is matter—the rest is empty space. The apparent solidity of matter derives from a unique quantum mechanical feature, known as the Pauli exclusion principle, which prevents two electrons from occupying the same quantum mechanical state. In reality, however, the atoms in the chair in which you are sitting, and in every cell of your body, are essentially nonmaterial.

The objects of our experience possess as little stability as they do solidity. The atom is far from being a stationary entity—the protons and neutrons of the nucleus are whirling through space at 40,000 miles per second, and electrons swirl around the nucleus at even greater velocity. Objects are configurations of atoms in continual flux, constantly interchanging elementary particles with their environment. Everything in the universe is continuously being recreated. And if we look at the world from the viewpoint of quantum theory, even the elementary particles and forces cease to exist and become nothing but resonant modes of the underlying unified field.

Solidity and the specific characteristics of the world around us are a product of our mode of experiencing. Because we rely exclusively on the mode of knowing associated with sensory input, we experience only the limited version of reality that is filtered through our senses.

The Vedic seers knew long before the advent of modern science that the universe of our daily experience reflects the limitations of our sensory perception. At the same time, they realized there is a mode of knowing other than the transitory and unreliable input of sensory perception. Instead of looking outward to the world of phenomena, the Vedic seers turned their attention inward, and discovered in the deep silence of the meditative state the fundamental unity at the source of existence. This unity naturally involved both their own subjective existence and the objective existence around them. The most advanced of the Vedic seers were able to clearly 'perceive' and outline the mechanics through which the primordial state of unity is transformed into the diverse manifold expressions of the universe.

In Western society we refer to such subjective modes of knowing as intuition. The realizations of the Vedic seers, however, go beyond simple intuitive insight. They present a direct cognition of the finest fabrics of reality in that most settled state of awareness where individual consciousness merges with universal consciousness. Examples of such experiences of 'knowingness' are found in all cultures. Many great thinkers, from Plato to Plotinus and Augustine, from Leibniz to Hegel and Whitehead, report deriving inspiration from glimpses of a different, yet universal and unified domain of experience. Some scientists, including Kepler, Cantor, and Einstein might have achieved insights into the laws of nature from this experience. William James, the founder of American psychology, coined the term 'noetic' knowledge—from the Greek word 'nous'—to describe these states of insight into "depths of truth unplumbed by the discursive intellect."[123]

In the West, however, such experiences have been disparate and rare, because no systematic techniques for developing this 'subjective' mode of knowing have been available. The Vedic tradition, in contrast, contains a plethora of sophisticated methodologies that enable the individual to systematically develop the mind-body's ability to perceive and reflect finer levels of reality. Through these techniques, the Vedic seers refined their mind-body system to the degree where they were capable of experiencing the full potential of human existence. Maharishi uses an analogy of the sun reflecting off a glass to describe this process of gaining intimate, direct experience of the finest levels of reality. If the sun falls on a glass filled with muddy water, the rays of the sun will be partly absorbed and only a limited part of their range will be reflected. However, if the water in the glass gradually gets purified, the rays of the sun will be reflected in increasing values as the water gets purer. Through a number of Vedic consciousness-expanding practices, the ancient seers were able to perfect the functioning of their nervous system to the point where they could cognize the fine fabrics of the ultimate reality. It is illustrative that Sanskrit, the language of the Vedic Literature, contains more than half a dozen words for consciousness, reflecting the extraordinary degree to which the exploration of consciousness and its nature had developed in the ancient Vedic culture.

In his restoration of the Vedic knowledge, Maharishi has brought his own deep experience and profound insights into the inner workings of the ultimate reality to bear on the Vedic Literature. Before traveling to the West, Maharishi spent 12 years under the guiding influence of one of the greatest sages of modern India—Swami Brahmananda Saraswati—who for many years served as the Shankaracharya of Jyotir Math, a custodian of the Vedic tradition of knowledge. After the passing on of his Master, Maharishi spent a year in solitude and deep meditation in the Himalaya mountains. It was an impulse to share the blessings of the Vedic wisdom that finally brought him out of the Himalayas, initially to give a few talks in southern India. The response to his message was so great, however, that events soon propelled him to the West. As we shall see in Chapter Ten, it is part of Maharishi's great contribution that he has recovered many of the ancient Vedic technologies and made them generally available in the West.

Maharishi's revival of the ancient Vedic tradition of knowledge is referred to as Maharishi Vedic Science[SM]. As we shall see, although Maharishi Vedic Science derives from the ancient Vedic tradition, it is suffused with the spirit of modern science and it emphasizes the importance of empirical testing of the basic tenets of Vedic knowledge. As a result, extensive research has been conducted on the physiological and psychological correlates associated with direct experience of the fundamental field of existence—pure consciousness.

Resolving the Paradoxes of Western Thought

The Vedic representation of reality is internally consistent to an extent that the Western paradigm has never been. The paradoxes that weigh on the materialistic, mechanistic model do not even arise within the Vedic framework. In light of the Vedic knowledge, the question of how self-awareness or consciousness comes about is irrelevant. Individual expressions of consciousness are configurations of the same primordial field of existence, whose primary reality is its nature as pure consciousness.

In the same way, the questions that arise when we posit a duality of mind and body, or contend that consciousness is an epiphenomenon of matter, are irrelevant within the Vedic framework. The mind does not have to somehow reach into the physical world and create electrical forces that cause specific brain cells to fire. Mind and body are expressions of the same fundamental reality, so there will naturally be a reciprocal influence between them—whatever happens in the mind happens in the body, and vice versa. In Chapter Four, we saw this principle illustrated in the placebo effect, in the phenomenon of multiple personalities (and physiologies), and in spontaneous remissions, the 'mind-body mysteries' for which medical science has been hard pressed to find an explanation.

In the Vedic framework, there likewise is nothing mysterious about the fact that a shift occurring at a deep level of the mind—for example, the level of the ego or emotions—gives rise to a change in the sequential unfoldment of the body. Mind and body are expressions of the same underlying field of unity, and there is a continuity between the self, the mind, and the body. Mind and body are elements of the same continuously creative, recreative, and self-transformative wholeness. The mind-body relationship is a two-way street, yet the mind, being a subtler manifestation of the field of pure consciousness, is considered primary in this relationship. In other words, the influence of the mind in shaping the quality of the expression of the physiology, is greater than the influence of the body in shaping the quality of the expression of the mind. 'Deeper' levels of existence, being more primary manifestations in the sequential unfoldment of pure consciousness, and forming the foundation for subsequent, more expressed levels, are more powerful and influential than the subsequent levels formed from the primordial field of existence.

For a profound physiological change to take place, such as a shift from being allergic to orange juice to not being allergic, it must be preceded by a change at a fundamental level in the sequential unfoldment of the mind. Such a change cannot, for example, be produced by intellectual efforts on our part, because the intellect is a more expressed value of the field of existence. For fundamental physiological changes to take place, deeper levels of the mind must be involved. This is a principle that has tremendous implications for our healing efforts, and it forms the core of the Maharishi Vedic Approach to Health.

Chapter Eight

THE STRUCTURING DYNAMICS
OF INTELLIGENCE

A s we noted in the last chapter, our notion of reality is intimately linked to the structure and characteristics of the nervous system we inhabit. Human beings possess nervous systems that are largely similar to each other, so we have no problem agreeing on the main features of the phenomenal world around us. In reality, however, there is no green color 'out there,' no red, no yellow—what we perceive as colors are nothing but fluctuations of the underlying nonmaterial electromagnetic field. Beneath the phenomena of the universe, however, is an immense unified source of existence, a wholeness more vast than the sum of all the phenomena existing within it. A single cubic centimeter of empty space contains more energy than all the matter in the universe![124] As physicist David Bohm put it, "space, which has so much energy, is full rather than empty." According to Bohm, this tremendous immanent energy is evidence for an immeasurable hidden realm beneath the unfolded order of the universe.

If the source of creation is an unbroken wholeness, why do diversified values appear in the unity of this field of pure existence? How does the undifferentiated field give rise to the differentiations of the phenomenal world? And how does each value of expression gain its specificity?

According to the Vedas, the origin of all intelligent processes in nature can be traced to the structure and dynamism inherent within the field of pure existence. The same fundamental dynamism that causes diversity to appear within the unbounded field of unity also propels the evolution and functioning of specific forms and phenomena. Maharishi has laid out in exceptional detail the Vedic description of the inherent dynamism that precipitates the impulses from which the forms and phenomena of creation arise. The following description is based entirely on his deep insights into the subtle mechanics of the manifestation of diversity within the unbounded field of unity.

Maharishi explains that the relationship of unity and diversity within the nature of unity is generated and perpetuated by the very nature of unity itself. The essential feature of the pure, abstract field of unity is its property of awareness, which gives it the ability to be aware of its own existence. This simple process of pure consciousness knowing itself triggers a diversification within the structure of unity. As pure consciousness knows itself, it as if divides into a three-fold structure: the knower, the known, and the process of knowing that links the knower and known. This is purely a *conceptual division* that appears within the undifferentiated unity of pure existence. Consciousness is itself the observer, the observed, and the process of observing. It is the self-referral nature of consciousness that triggers this spontaneous diversification, *independent* of any external force.

The Sanskrit names for the features of this three-fold conceptual division are *Rishi, Devata,* and *Chhandas,* denoting respectively the aspect of knower, the dynamics of the process of knowing, and the known. In the Vedas, these three are called *triputi,* the triple group. Consciousness in its self-referral state is the unified state of Rishi, Devata, and Chhandas; this three-in-one structure of consciousness is referred to as the *Samhita* of Rishi, Devata, and Chhandas. The three-in-one structure of Samhita is the first 'warmed up' impulse of the creative intelligence that unfolds into the multifold manifestations of the universe.

The entire universe is the different permutations and combinations of consciousness knowing itself in its infinite range of possibilities. After the initial division of one into three, consciousness starts experiencing all the possible modes of itself knowing itself. In a stepwise progression, the original three interact an infinite number of times, assuming infinite degrees of shadings and complexities. All subjects and objects in the universe, along with the relationships between them, emerge as the passing configurations of unbounded pure consciousness knowing itself in its infinite range of possibilities.

The initial division of consciousness from one into three and back into one is an infinite oscillation between expansion and contraction—the expansion from unity into the diversity of knower, knowing, and known, and the contraction back toward unity, represented by Samhita. This contraction and expansion happens simultaneously, at infinite speed; consciousness is simultaneously one and three. This oscillation generates a whirl within the singularity of pure consciousness—the flat state of pure existence becomes endowed with a quality of *infinite dynamism*, which is the sprouting of creative intelligence within the nature of pure consciousness. As Maharishi explains,

> Infinity, fully awake to itself, is fully awake to its infinite value. At the same time, it is awake to its point value. In this we find the dynamism of infinity converging to a point and a point expanding to infinity. This [is the] infinite dynamism of the self-referral nature of pure consciousness.[125]

The infinite dynamism existing within the nature of pure consciousness is a ceaseless whirl from infinity to point and back to infinity, from wholeness to point and back to wholeness, from fullness to emptiness and back to fullness. This whirl generates a vibrational quality within the nature of pure consciousness, an eternal Hum, the sound of 'warmed up' pure consciousness ready to sprout into the manifestations of the universe. As consciousness knows itself in progressively more differentiated modes, additional vibrational qualities are generated. Each mode of consciousness knowing itself has a specific vibrational quality associated with it. All the expressions of creation—material or nonmaterial—are ultimately nothing but these specific vibrational frequencies. As we have seen, quantum physics describes the finer levels of reality in terms of frequencies and waves; subatomic entities are actually insubstantial wave functions. Material form springs forth from the primordial frequency within pure consciousness which progresses to generate different frequencies and their corresponding material forms. As Maharishi puts it,

> The picture is like this: Take a dish full of water. Create a gentle stir in the water by tilting it and leaving it. First you will see one holistic stir, one holistic wave generated throughout. If the process of stirring continues, specific waves develop in different structures within that one holistic wave—the initial holistic wave sequentially develops into waves of specific categories.[126]

From the initial vibrational frequency within pure consciousness— the eternal 'Hum' of creation—emerge the Vedas. The Vedas are not books written by the ancient seers; rather, they are acoustic records of the self-interacting dynamics of the field of pure intelligence as it takes on its expression as creative intelligence. The primordial sounds of the Vedas are the vibrations, the rhythms of self-referral consciousness cognized within the fully awakened consciousness of the Vedic seers. The impulses of the Vedic Literature are ever-present within the field of pure existence; they can be perceived by anyone whose awareness is open to the primordial rhythms. Veda is also known as *Shruti*, 'that which is heard.' The Vedic seers, attuning their own consciousness to this finest level of nature's functioning, cognized the primordial impulses of creativity that are lively within the field of unity. For each sound, Maharishi explains, there is a frequency, and that frequency also constitutes *the form* of the sound—the quantum wave function which turns into an expressed material value. The Vedic sounds are the vibrational states of the fundamental field of consciousness associated with the reverberation of existence into its manifest values.

The Levels of Mind and the Five Mahabhutas

The expressed values of consciousness emerge spontaneously and sequentially from the inherent dynamics of pure consciousness. Creation proceeds progressively from the fine, subtle, abstract levels of the subjective aspect of existence to the gross, concrete levels of material expression. From all the possible relationships between Rishi, Devata, and Chhandas emerge the qualities of the mind, the senses, and the objects of the senses.

Each new quality emerges spontaneously by virtue of its inherent presence within the structure of the 'previous' quality. The quality of self-referral consciousness is known as *Atma*, the Self; this is the self-sustaining, self-interacting level of unboundedness. From this emerges the ego, the sense of an 'I' that exists—it emerges as the 'I am' cognition of the subject, the knower. Inherent within Atma also exists the value of *buddhi*, the intellect aspect of the mind—the quality that discriminates the three-fold structure of knowing. This cognition belongs to the intellect, and the more elaborated fluctuations of it become the level of the mind. (Due to the limitations of the English language, the term 'mind' is often used to denote both a specific faculty of mental functioning and all the levels of subjectivity other than pure consciousness.)

The sequential unfoldment proceeds from the emergence of the subjective qualities of the mind to the first sprouting of objective existence. The finest level of matter is described in terms of five basic constituents, each of which has a subtle aspect and a gross, concrete aspect. The subtle aspects are known as the *tanmatras*—'the measure of That,' i.e. of totality. The five tanmatras constitute the essences of the objects of the five senses. These are the finest material expression of the five principles of nature; they exist on the borderline between consciousness and matter and are associated with the five senses, the link between subjective and objective existence.

The gross, more expressed aspect of the tanmatras constitute the five fundamental elements, the five *mahabhutas* that make up the objects of the senses and form the material basis of the objective universe, including the human body. The five mahabhutas are known as *Akasha* (space), *Vayu* (air), *Agni* or *Tejas* (fire), *Apas* or *Jal* (water), and *Prithivi* (earth). In the same way as the qualities of mind emerge spontaneously from the self-interacting play of pure consciousness, the five mahabhutas unfold spontaneously and sequentially, independent of any outside force. Maharishi highlights this point in the following passage:

> In the simultaneous cognition of Samhita and Rishi, Devata, and Chhandas, there is emergence of specificity on the non-changing plane of generality. So there is a move [vibrational quality]. And wherever there is a move, there is sound, there is Shruti. When Samhita looks upon itself as the knower, known, and process of knowing, there is a shift. The [sound exists in] some quality of Vayu [air], some impulse, some frequency in the self-referral state. . . .
>
> The sound is not only an isolated sound, because it is not an isolated move, it is the move of the totality. . . . It's the move of the total infinite field, of the ocean of pure intelligence, the infinite field of unbounded wakefulness, pure wakefulness . . . reverberating within itself. In the singularity of Samhita, Rishi is popping up. In this popping up of Rishi, there is dynamism, and that is Devata. In the Devata-value there is an overshadowing of silence, of Samhita and of the popping up of Rishi, so there is . . . Chhandas [that which hides]. These three values are functioning within themselves by virtue of some quality of Akasha [space]. Unboundedness, pure wakefulness, the eternal state of fully awake consciousness, of Intelligence, is knowing itself as pure singularity of Samhita and as the diverse values of Rishi, Devata, and Chhandas. This diversification, however, is in the unmanifest state because Samhita is unmanifest. It is unmanifest, because it is ever the same. But nevertheless, it is space within itself, it is air within itself, fluctuating within itself. And then, wherever there is flow, there is friction. So along with sound, there is some quality of heat, some warmth, some Agni [fire]. Wherever there is Agni, the Agni melts something. . . . [T]hat flow is the value of Apas, the value of water, and once it begins to congeal, it is Prithivi [earth]. So all these, Akasha, Vayu, Agni, Apas, and Prithivi are all the specific values

in the nonspecific, eternally the same, pure wakefulness of self-referral consciousness. . . .[127]

The five fundamental elements and forces of creation in turn combine into the three *doshas,* the three basic principles that rule the functioning of the human body. These three doshas are *Vata, Pitta,* and *Kapha.* Akasha and Vayu combine to form Vata; Tejas and Apas become Pitta; and Apas and Prithivi become Kapha. Vata is the principle of biological movement, Pitta is linked to all converting, metabolic processes, and Kapha is associated with the quality of structure.

Maharishi Vedic Science describes a level of nature's functioning where all matter and energy correspond to specific 'sounds' or fundamental vibrational patterns. In terms of physics, the five mahabhutas—the fundamental categories of matter and energy—are parallel to the stable vibrational states of the unified field of quantum physics. Theoretical physicist John Hagelin has studied the parallels between the Vedic understanding of the mechanics of transformation of unity, and modern physics' description of fundamental particles and forces as the resonant modes of an underlying unified field. Hagelin points out that the emergence of the relationship between wholeness and point and between Rishi, Devata, and Chhandas represents a 'break' in the perfect symmetry of the silent, nonmaterial unity of pure unmanifest existence. This is similar to modern physics' understanding of how space-time and the universe itself emerge through a succession of spontaneous, sequential symmetry breaking of the initial unbroken supersymmetry of the unified field.

Although close comparisons are difficult due to the disparity in languages associated with the two systems of knowledge, Hagelin has found a number of parallels between Vedic Science[SM] and the process of symmetry breaking in modern physics. "One of the most obvious and basic structural similarities between pure consciousness and a supersymmetric unified field (i.e. a superfield or superstring field)," Hagelin explains, "is the 'three-in-one' structure of pure consciousness in which the observer, observed and process of observation are unified. A parallel structure is found in supersymmetric theory. . . ."[128]

111

Structure of the Unified Quantum Field

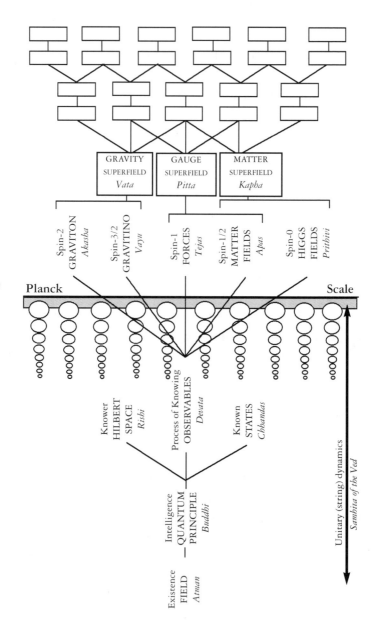

Planck   Scale

GRAVITY SUPERFIELD *Vata*

GAUGE SUPERFIELD *Pitta*

MATTER SUPERFIELD *Kapha*

Spin-2 GRAVITON *Akasha*
Spin-3/2 GRAVITINO *Vayu*
Spin-1 FORCES *Tejas*
Spin-1/2 MATTER FIELDS *Apas*
Spin-0 HIGGS FIELDS *Prithivi*

Knower HILBERT SPACE *Rishi*
Process of Knowing OBSERVABLES *Devata*
Known STATES *Chhandas*

Intelligence QUANTUM PRINCIPLE *Buddhi*

Existence FIELD *Atman*

Unitary (string) dynamics
Samhita of the Ved

FIGURE 1.

As this figure shows, there are striking parallels between modern physics' delineation of the unfoldment of matter from the unified field and Vedic Science's description of the manifestation of increasingly concrete expressions of the unitary state of pure existence. The observable phenomena of the universe are to the right of the Planck scale (in the middle of the figure). The empty boxes to the right denote the various fields of study in physics, which emerge as increasingly more concrete expressions of the five fundamental categories of matter and energy.

(From: Hagelin, J. S. (1989). Restructuring physics from its foundation in the light of Maharishi's Vedic Science. *Modern Science and Vedic Science*, 3: 3-74. p. 14.)

Hagelin likewise notes that there exists a close correspondence between the Vedic description of the vibrational states represented by the five tanmatras, and the five quantum mechanical 'spin types' of unified quantum field theory. These five spin types are specific vibrational states of the quantum field. They constitute the five fundamental categories of the quantum field, which give force fields and particles their *unique* characteristics. According to Hagelin, the Vedic description of the space tanmatra bears similarities to the spin-2 graviton, which is responsible for space-time curvature and the force of gravity. The spin-3/2 gravitino, which appears in the context of supersymmetric field theory, is similar to the air tanmatra, which constitutes a link between space and the other elements. The spin-1 force fields are parallel to the fire tanmatra, which is responsible for chemical transformations. And the spin-1/2 and spin-0 matter fields correspond respectively to the water and earth tanmatras.[129]

In the same way that the subtle elements combine to form Vata, Pitta, and Kapha, within the framework of supersymmetric theory there is a pairing of the five quantum-mechanical spin types into three types of $N=1$ superfields: the gravity superfield, the gauge superfields, and the matter superfields respectively. Hagelin also points out there is a correspondence between the more gross expression of the five tanmatras—the five mahabhutas: space, air, fire, water, and earth—and classical space-time and the four states of bulk matter: gaseous, plasma, liquid, and solid respectively.[130]

The Five Spin Types and the Five Tanmatras

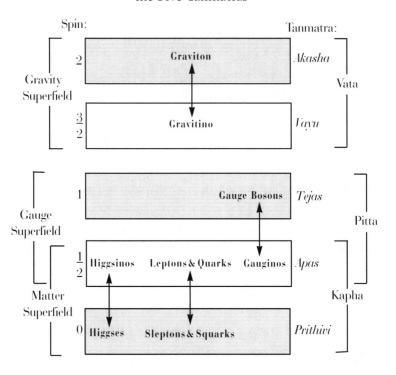

FIGURE 2.

In physics, the five quantum-mechanical spin types represent specific stable vibrational states of the field, which in supersymmetric unified field theories pair together to form gravity, gauge, and matter superfields. In Vedic Science, the tanmatras represent the five elementary categories of matter and energy, which pair up to form the three doshas—vata, pitta, and kapha. The three doshas represent the fundamental dynamics of intelligence inherent in structures of matter.

(From: Hagelin, J. S. (1989). Restructuring physics from its foundation in the light of Maharishi Vedic Science. *Modern Science and Vedic Science*, 3: 3-74. p. 32.)

The Structure of Natural Law

According to physics, the mathematical structure of the unified field provides a blueprint for the unfoldment of the entire creation. Emerging from this level are the individual laws of nature—the mathematical relationships that describe the non-changing relationships among changing entities in creation. The specific laws of nature that govern physical processes at various scales are derivatives of the basic mathematical structure of the unified field.

In the same way, according to Maharishi Vedic Science, the three-in-one structure within the fabrics of pure consciousness constitutes the *architectural theme* of the universe, the basic cosmic law, which is reflected in the functioning of the numerous specific laws of nature that guide the evolution and emergence of specific forms and phenomena. The dynamism and structure of nature's intelligence have their origin in the dynamics and structure of self-referral consciousness. The self-referral, three-in-one structure of primordial existence constitutes the non-changing relationship that generates change at all the expressed levels of creation. This is the universal dynamism that serves as the unmanifest blueprint for the entire creation.

The word 'Veda' means 'knowledge.' The Vedas are complete expressions of the structure of pure knowledge. They are acoustic records of the dynamism inherent within the nature of pure self-referral consciousness. Maharishi explains that total knowledge is found in the eternal three-in-one structure of pure consciousness as it becomes aware of its own existence. The order we observe in creation, he points out, comes about because creation, in essence, is nothing other than the precipitated expression of the structure of pure knowledge within the field of pure existence. This structure of pure knowledge is at the basis of all life. The orderly, sequential unfoldment we observe in creation is a reflection of the orderly, sequential unfoldment of the self-referral dynamics of pure consciousness, the structure of pure knowledge. The impulses of self-interacting pure consciousness are the primordial impulses of intelligence which generate the more precipitated and progressively more quantified values of expression that we observe as the manifest phenomena of creation. The impulses of self-referral consciousness detailed in the Vedas therefore form the *laws of nature*—the impulses of intelligence that guide and give direction to all processes in the universe. The primordial sounds of the Vedas, Maharishi says, are "the laws of nature murmuring to themselves. They are Natural Law describing itself and its own structure and function—eternally the same, total potential of Natural Law on the self-referral level of intelligence."

The Vedic sounds are the laws of nature in their primordial state, seated in the transcendental field of pure existence and orchestrating the expression of manifest creation from there. The Vedas, Maharishi asserts, are the cosmic blueprint that unfolds into manifest creation. They are the Constitution of the Universe, the fundamental set of laws that generates the expressions of the entire universe. The Vedas are the in-volved order that e-volves into the orderly sequential unfoldment of the universe. They are the fine structure of intelligence whose precipitated expressions are the forms and phenomena, the entire range of subject and object relationships of physical creation. The orderliness and regularity we observe in the universe is the surface appearance of this enfolded, hidden blueprint of intelligence.

Whole and Parts

The organizing intelligence of the universe effortlessly orchestrates the perfect alignment of wholes and parts at every level of creation. This holistic expression of natural law has its origin in, and is sustained in, the infinite dynamism between infinity and point, in the perfect flow of information—the infinite correlation—between wholeness and parts. The property of *infinite correlation*—the union of parts and whole—is inherent in the ongoing dynamic movement from unboundedness to the point-value of specificity, which happens at infinite speed. As Maharishi explains,

116

The evolution of consciousness into its object-referral expressions, ever maintaining the memory of its self-referral source—ever-evolving structure of consciousness, maintaining the memory of its source—progresses in self-referral loops—every step of progress is in terms of a self-referral loop.

As every point of consciousness is infinitely correlated with every other point, the entire field of consciousness is structured in self-referral loops of infinite frequency.

The basic process is the same—flow and stop . . . flow and stop . . . flow and stop. This basic process of change, this basic process of transformation, continuously maintains the momentum of evolution of different levels of expression, creating different levels of manifestation upholding the process of evolution.[131]

In the transformation of unity into diversity, unity and unboundedness are maintained as the foundation of change and boundaries. Wholeness is ongoing, eternal, ever-present, as are the infinite, self-referral mechanics of transformation—"an eternal, continuous phenomenon [going on at] every moment, at every minute particle of creation."[132]

Inherent within the dynamism between wholeness and part, is the holistic balancing function of nature's intelligence, the architectural theme of emergent wholeness reflected in every phenomenon of creation. The intelligence of the universe is expressed in the perfect attunement of wholes and parts. Although innumerable specific laws of nature guide the functioning of individual objects and systems, the functioning of each law is holistic in its structure—within its specific range of functioning it is in perfect alignment with the functioning of the total value of natural law. Every expression of intelligence has within it the totality of natural law.

The delicate interdependence of parts and whole that we observe at all levels of the organization of the universe, is difficult to fathom only if we think of the components of the universe as separate entities. When the universe is viewed as a dynamically self-interacting wholeness, this delicate attunement becomes a natural outgrowth of the nature of life. The masterly coordination of everything in manifest creation is an expression of the inherent holistic structure of natural law. The self-referral dynamism and the relationship between wholeness and point form the inherent dynamics of every value of creation. Wholeness remains continuously and infinitely correlated with every point in the universe. Every point contains the whole and every point is contained within the whole. From within, everything is connected with everything else. The capacity of doing everything at once, the infinite dynamism, is sustained within the perfect order, the unbounded knowingness that, knowing everything, maintains connectedness among everything.

The self-referral structure at the basis of creation is mirrored in the creative unfoldment of the universe toward ever more sophisticated structures with ever-increasing capacity for self-knowledge. Maharishi often quotes the following verse from the *Bhagavad Gita*, to illustrate the inherent creativity and self-organizing power within the self-referral structure of the absolute field of life:

Prakritim swam avashtabhya
visrijami punah punah
bhutagramamimam kritsnam
avasham prakritervashat

Taking recourse to My own self-referral Nature,
I create again and again—
creation and administration of creation,
both are a natural phenomenon on the basis
of My self-referral consciousness.[133]

The Three-in-One Structure

In the same way that the dynamic relationship between wholeness and point within self-referral consciousness is reflected in every phenomenon in creation, the three-in-one dynamism of Samhita and Rishi, Devata, and Chhandas forms an architectural theme common to all forms and phenomena. Every structure in creation reflects and expresses the same self-referral three-in-one pattern of consciousness.

> The repeating formula of Rishi, Devata, and Chhandas is not only the internal structure of pure consciousness, but is also *the formula* through which consciousness becomes manifest in a precise and lawful manner as the diversity of material forms found in nature. This diversity includes the whole range of organization of the physiology.[134] [emphasis added]

To fully appreciate this point, we must understand the implicit characteristics and mutual relation of Rishi, Devata, and Chhandas, which get reflected in the organization of manifest structures and systems. Rishi is the witness, the wakeful quality of Samhita, the silent observer, the structure of intelligence, the experiencer who 'knows' Devata and Chhandas. Devata, the value of 'knowing,' represents the mediating link, the dynamism or activity that connects Rishi and Chhandas. Chhandas is the 'object' of observation that 'hides' Rishi and Devata. Devata and Chhandas, the process of knowing and the known, emerge from within Rishi, the knower; in the same way, organizing functions (Devata) and their end products (Chhandas) emerge from the structure of knowledge (Rishi).

In biological systems, the knower aspect of Rishi is reflected in *biological information,* the mediating quality of Devata corresponds to biological activity—*relations, transformations, and processes*—and the hiding quality of Chhandas, which obscures the relations and information, is reflected in biological *products and structures*. In the human physiology, for example, the DNA can be taken to represent the Rishi value, the inner knower, the silent *immovable structure of knowledge* from which emerge the organizing activities of RNA, the Devata value. RNA is the *mediating link* that gives expression to the organizing power inherent within the knowledge of the DNA. From the activities of the RNA emerges protein, the *expressed* aspect of the three-fold dynamism—the Chhandas value. Although the silent knowledge inherent within the structure of the DNA and the mediating activity of the RNA are as much—or even more—a part of the reality of the protein as its actual manifest expression, the manifest form of the protein tends to 'hide' or obscure the mediating activity of the RNA and the unmanifest structure of knowledge within the DNA.

While they may appear separate, Rishi, Devata, and Chhandas are in reality simply aspects of the same underlying unity. Remember that the three-in-one distinction is a *conceptual* distinction only, each mode simply representing a specific viewpoint from which the unitary nature of reality can be experienced. In our description or perception of a phenomenon, however, it is easy to highlight only the form, the Chhandas aspect—at the cost of overlooking the internal dynamism of the form's existence. In physics, for example, the description of the electron in its particle aspect, which dominated physics until the advent of quantum theory, can be said to represent the Chhandas aspect of the particle. Viewed from the more fundamental perspective of quantum theory, however, we now know that we cannot pin down a particle as being an independently existing entity; the particle is essentially a set of relationships—interconnections that reach out to other interconnections. Viewing the particle from this perspective, we would be contemplating the Devata aspect of its existence.

Modern science tends to focus on the Chhandas level of reality to the exclusion of the less obvious levels of Devata and Rishi. In focusing on the more superficial levels of reality expressed in material objects, we overlook the subtler values of creation that are an equally, or even more important part of the reality of those objects. This is obvious within the field of medicine, where the focus on specific diseased parts of the body has led to a disregard of the subtle biological intelligence that gives rise to both physiological processes and expressions.

Some physicists and biologists have attempted to draw attention to the importance of shifting our understanding from the level of isolated units and material objects (Chhandas) to the relational links that underlie the objects (Devata). The British physicist David Bohm, for example, maintained that focusing only on the structural value of objects deceives us about the true nature of reality. Reality is a dynamic process, said Bohm, and all objects in actuality are processes, not the static forms that we perceive them to be. The very nature of our language misleads us about the characteristics of reality. Instead of talking about 'a window' or 'a tree,' argued Bohm, we ought to talk about 'window-ing' or 'tree-ing,' to denote the fact that the true nature of objects is more that of interactive processes than of stationary, isolated units.

Twenty years ago, the Swiss biologist Paul Weiss tried to draw attention to the fact that the essential nature of biological objects lies in their relational processes and constant interactions. The entire notion of isolated biological entities is an abstraction, he pointed out. Biological units are conceptual representations of what are, in actuality, nodal points in a network of relations—an undivided continuum in which both units and environment form an integral entity. And these units are not static objects or forms, but rather a flux of continuously changing processes. "What we recognize as the form of a system must be regarded as the derivative manifestation of *formative,* or more precisely, 'transformative' *dynamics*," wrote Weiss.[135] He continued, "[T]he isolation and delineation of a 'unit' [is an expedient artifact]. . . . [A] living cell is not the neatly and stably delineated unit suggested by the visual impression of the microscopic . . . picture of the dead or fixed object. . . . [T]he dynamics of the whole cell unit extend way beyond that visible boundary, attracting and repelling molecules and ions from their surroundings according to electrical charges and chemical affinities, sharp definitions dissolving into fuzzy halos."

As we saw in Chapter Five, biologists working within the framework of the emerging sciences of complexity are making a similar point, arguing that organisms should be understood not so much in terms of their parts as their relational properties. T. Ingold puts it succinctly, "Organisms and persons are not the effects of molecular and neuronal causes, of genes and traits, but instances of the unfolding of the total relational field. They are formed from relationships which in their activities they create anew."[136]

Reductionist analytical methods are optimally suited for studying the Chhandas level of structure and form. However, in the process of isolating units for analysis, we tend to overlook that these units are meshed in a network of dynamic interactions within the continuum of the universe. The reductionist method neglects the dynamic processes that give rise to biological entities, and the latent biological knowledge of which these dynamic processes are an expression. As Paul Weiss commented, "Each downward step [of reductionist analysis] involves a further degree of dismemberment of the primary unitary image of the Universe; it involves cumulative abstractions due to either the disregard or the deliberate mental severance of those relational ties that link the abstracted 'units' into the cohesive total fabric of the Universe."[137] In reality, a unit is 'a composite fragment of the universe' which we give a name because it preserves its identity over time; it retains its unique and measurable properties against continuously fluctuating background phenomena.

The criteria of a unit, maintained Weiss, are "unity and conservation of pattern."[138] From the point of view of Maharishi Vedic Science, when we start focusing on the underlying *pattern* that unites and conserves the activity of a system, we shift our conceptual focus from the Devata level to the Rishi level. Devata is the converting activity that brings latent order to overt expression. This latent order, the pattern of intelligence inherent in the converting activity, resides in the Rishi value.

Remember that Chhandas and Devata, form and mediating processes, emerge from within Rishi—the silent structure of knowledge. The organizing power that gives rise to biological processes and form is inherent within the 'pattern' of information. Again, drawing a parallel to the DNA will make this clearer. The DNA constitutes the pattern of information, the code, that unfolds into the formation of the entire physiology. The DNA nucleotides are arranged in a specific sequence which is a nonmaterial pattern of intelligence. The specific nucleotide atoms may change, but the basic pattern, the fundamental structure of knowledge, remains, in spite of the changing material values.

As noted previously, everything in the universe is continuously being recreated. The elementary particles and atoms of our eyes, our hands, our neurons, and our entire body are constantly being interchanged with the elementary particles and atoms in the air we breathe and the food we eat. In the same way, the elementary particles and atoms in the surrounding objects are constantly being interchanged. Everything is in continual flux. The only thing that remains constant is the pattern, the basic blueprint, the structure of intelligence inherent in the value of Rishi. From this unfolds the mediating and converting activities of Devata, and their end product, the form or structure of Chhandas. It is the pattern that is primary; this is the inner continuum that constitutes the basic reality of the 'object.' The pattern is the implicit value of intelligence from which emerge the activities of Devata—the medium of its expression—and the resulting form.

The uncanny plasticity and regenerative ability of biological systems derive from the inherent pattern of intelligence within the Rishi value, which enables an organism to retain its wholeness and regain its unique characteristics. Because the pattern of information, the specific mode of knowledge, remains constant within a given value of Rishi, the expressions of Devata and Chhandas will remain constant despite infinite variation of detail caused by environmental fluctuations. The self-organizing properties of living systems thus emerge from the inherent dynamism within the three-fold structure—mediating processes and form unfold from the pattern of intelligence within the Rishi value. Due to this unchanging pattern of intelligence inherent in the Rishi value, the functioning of parts maintains a continuous configuration—even in the face of environmental changes and nondestructive disturbances. The patterned, self-organizing processes of biological systems exhibit their invariance not because they unfold mechanistically in a prearranged, single-track sequence of activities, but because the activities of parts unfold from within the inner continuum of the specific pattern of intelligence contained within the Rishi value.

At each level of evolution, we find the progressive development of wholes of greater magnitude and complexity. Each layer represents another permutation of the three-in-one structure inherent within the nature of self-referral consciousness. Each layer expresses the same primordial configuration, the self-referral dynamism that constitutes the diversifying mechanics within the unified field of pure existence. The emergence of a wholeness greater than the sum of the interactive processes and parts is an expression of the Samhita value, the inherent wholeness that will always be more than the sum of Rishi, Devata, and Chhandas.

The self-referral process constitutes the structuring dynamism by which unity transforms into diversity and governs the infinite range of phenomena in the universe. Through the property of infinite correlation structured within this self-referral dynamism, the universe unfolds, at every step maintaining the perfect coordination and attunement of even the minutest particle in relation to the whole. This is the source of the finely tuned intelligence we see functioning in the human physiology and in the universe as a whole. Only when parts are disconnected from their source in wholeness do limitations in the complete expression of this creative intelligence arise. Only when the basic value of intelligence is obscured do parts fall out of alignment with the wholeness of which they are a part.

Chapter Nine

THE SEED OF DIS-EASE

The Ayurvedic model of the disease process is generally identified with the theory of the three doshas, Vata, Pitta, and Kapha. These are the three psychophysiological principles that govern the functioning of the physiology. Vata dosha is the subtle quality of intelligence associated with the space and air elements, and is responsible for all bodily movement; with its five subdoshas, it is involved in such functions as breathing, heart activity, speech, peristalsis, assimilation, elimination, menstruation, labor and delivery, circulation, muscle movement, nervous system activity, and mental clarity. Pitta dosha is associated with the elements of fire and water, and governs processes of transformation, such as metabolism, digestion, absorption, body temperature, and intelligence. Kapha dosha is responsible for structure (the earth element) and lubrication (the water element). Physiological strength is associated with Kapha, as is the building of bones, moisturizing of skin, joint lubrication, and stability of mind. When the three doshas are in balance, the individual enjoys excellent health. Conversely, if any of the doshas or subdoshas go out of balance, it generates an irregularity in the functioning of those parts of the mind-body system governed by that particular dosha or subdosha. Consequently, most Ayurvedic treatments focus on restoring the balance of the doshas, and eliminating the consequences of their imbalanced activity.

The state of equilibrium or disequilibrium of the three doshas plays a crucial role in the disease process which cannot be ignored. The tri-dosha theory, however, and other physiological descriptions of the development of disease, form only part of the total Ayurvedic knowledge. As Maharishi

125

has highlighted, the most powerful healing connection of all is found not in the physiology, but in consciousness itself.

As we have seen, there is continuity between pure consciousness, mind, and physiology; both mind and body are different vibrational states of the fundamental field of pure existence. The most fundamental cause of breakdown in the equilibrium of the body takes place at the level where the impulses of consciousness are transformed into the physiology. Vata, Pitta, and Kapha are closely linked to the three-fold dynamism of Rishi, Devata, and Chhandas—the three doshas are the finest material expressions in the body of the three-fold structure of pure consciousness. If the Chhandas value starts to dominate the individual's awareness, the dynamic balance between Rishi, Devata, and Chhandas is lost. This in turn is reflected in the more precipitated expressions of the primordial three-in-one relationship as a disequilibrium among the three doshas. The Chhandas value will start to dominate if pure consciousness starts to identify with the 'small self' and becomes absorbed in the objects of experience. The *buddhi* aspect—the intellect or *discriminating* value of consciousness—then gets lost in the complex, ever-changing vision of the world. Individual consciousness, we can say, becomes *object-referral* instead of *self-referral*, in the process losing sight of the fundamental wholeness of which both object and subject are a part.

This process of individual consciousness 'forgetting' its essential nature is called *pragya aparadh*—the mistake of the intellect. Pragya aparadh is the essential mechanism involved in the emergence of disease. Due to a 'mistake' in the discriminating power of *buddhi*, wholeness is lost. The value of pure consciousness is obscured when the mind is absorbed in the objects of perception and the memory of its own essential nature is overshadowed. Because the physiology is a precipitated expression of pure consciousness, this creates a 'shadow' in the mind-body wholeness. The parts are as if cut off from their connection to wholeness, and this results in limitations in the expression of the creative intelligence of the physiology. Returning to the analogy of the sun reflecting off the water in a glass, we can say that the water in the glass has become murky, and therefore does not reflect the full value of the sun's rays. When the self-referral value of consciousness is lost, then within the physiological expression of pure consciousness, some value of wholeness is lost. The wholeness of the silent, nonmaterial field of existence is no longer fully expressed in all aspects of the material body. Nature's creative intelligence is no longer completely lively in the physiology, and this gives rise to imbalance, a lack of the perfect attunement to the whole. The more 'dense' the shadow that obscures the value of pure consciousness, the greater the imbalance.

Self-referral functioning, being the essential dynamism inherent within the structure of the physiology, is also the basis of health. The human physiology is structured in layers of self-referral wholeness; the property of self-interaction forms the basis of the holistic integration and functioning of the physiology. At all levels of emerging wholeness, it is a self-referral dynamism that coordinates and harmonizes the activity of parts in relation to wholes. The hierarchy of physiological organization exhibits increasingly more sophisticated and more complex self-referral systems. At the macro-level of organization—the human nervous system—all the body's hierarchical layers of organization are joined into one all-inclusive, self-referral feedback system that synthesizes all the elements of the human physiology into a unified conscious whole.

One obvious example of the self-referral organization of the physiology is found in the homeostatic feedback mechanisms, which retain balance between the parts and the overall system. By calibrating the functioning of the parts of the physiology in relation to the needs of the physiology as a whole, self-regulating homeostatic systems retain the internal order and stability of the body in the face of a constantly changing environment. Homeostatic systems are found on each level of physiological organization, be it the level of atoms, macro-molecules, cells, tissues, organs, organ systems, or the organism as a whole. They regulate vital parameters such as temperature, blood pressure, acid-base balance, blood glucose levels, oxygen and carbon dioxide levels, and water and electrolyte balance.

The functioning of the homeostatic system is essentially self-referral. As the Australian physician Timothy Carr points out, "Every homeostatic self-regulatory system has its own 'self' reference point. . . . In this multi-layered organisation of cybernetic feedback systems there is a hierarchy of 'selves.' The self [is] a higher order of organisation entraining the activities of the lower order within its sphere of influence. The 'self' transcends the level of the genetic programme because even the genetic programme is constantly undergoing self-repair and restructuring and hence must have a more fundamental 'self' to refer to. The 'self' represents *the basic blue print* of the system which must necessarily contain 'memory' of the system's origin, its developmental staging and its ultimate end point. . . . If this basic memory or blueprint is altered, or if it is not so accessible, then the whole system is jeopardised."[139] [emphasis added]

As you will remember, the root meaning of the word *health* is 'whole.' With loss of wholeness, we become disconnected from the source of order in the physiology, and the blueprint or pattern that gives rise to physiological expression becomes less accessible. The result is impaired self-regulation, which in turn leads to reduced order and coordination in the functioning of the system. Individual cells or other elements of the physiology begin to lose their connection to the whole of the physiology. Once this happens, the seed of dis-ease has been sown.

Disease, in other words, is basically a loss of intelligence, an invasion of disorder in an otherwise highly sophisticated and orderly system. In the case of a disease such as cancer, for example, it is clear that dysfunctioning cells or cell networks are involved in the development of malignancies. When a cell loses sight of the fact that it is part of a larger organism, and ceases to regulate its duplication processes accordingly, the result is the wildly proliferating cell growth of malignant tumors.

Even aging is nothing but a progressive loss of biological intelligence. As aging advances, more and more cells lose their highly specialized functions and revert to a nonspecific status—as the scientist Richard Cutler puts it, they become "dysdifferentiated."[140] This dysdifferentiation of cells basically happens because of a disconnection with the biological blueprint inherent in the DNA. Genes turn off or on incorrectly, causing each cell to lose its differentiation. Even a slight deviation from its perfectly attuned status might cause a cell to lose its ability to perform specific tasks or respond appropriately to the instructions of hormones or neurotransmitters. Over time, the cumulative effects of the loss of intelligence on a micro-level will give rise to global disturbances in physiological functioning.

The fragmented perception of pragya aparadh not only creates problems on the level of the physiology; it is the source of imperfections and limitations on the level of the mind as well. When the mind loses touch with the limitless source of intelligence, organizing power, and creativity at the basis of its own existence, this results in shortcomings, inability to fulfill desires, feelings of loneliness and isolation, impediments to achievements, reduced expression of love, or suffering. Maharishi explains,

> All problems of life arise from some weakness of mind. All weakness of mind is due to the mind's ignorance of its own essential nature, which is universal and the source of infinite energy and intelligence. This ignorance of one's own Self is the basis of all problems, sufferings and shortcomings in life. In order to root out any problem of life it is only necessary to be brought out of ignorance, to be brought to knowledge.[141]

Pragya aparadh is a shift in our mode of knowing, which consists of an apparent separation from the most intimate part of our own Being. We forget or lose sight of the unbounded potential of our innermost self—the field of pure existence that lies beyond the subject-object division within the structure of knowing. In Maharishi's words, "the mind's essential nature is obscured."[142] We start to identify with the limited 'self' of self-awareness, the 'I' of the subject-object experience within the structure of pure consciousness—the ego. The ego is only an object of experience with the reflected light of consciousness, yet because it is the seat of the synthesis of individual experience, we identify with it, and thus lose sight of the grandeur of our true nature.

When the experiencer changes, so does the experience; the quality of experience is a function of the experiencer. As the saying goes, "The world is as we are." Our perception is colored by who we are. When we lose touch with the underlying essence of wholeness beneath the ever-changing phenomenal world, our way of experiencing is restructured. Pragya aparadh in this way changes the way we perceive reality. Rather than being established in the unbounded self-sufficiency of our own Being, our sense of happiness becomes linked to the ever-changing phenomenal world. Once pragya aparadh seeps in and the strong core of our inner Being is overshadowed, we are like a leaf being whirled around at the mercy of external forces.

Perception is one avenue through which the influence of pragya aparadh on the physiology is mediated. The body responds instantaneously to experience—our interpretation of and reaction to the environment is the key element in a domino chain of interrelated processes that shape our physiological status at any given moment. Modern research has made it clear that the functioning of both the autonomic nervous system and the immune system is linked to the manner in which we sort out and integrate experience.[143] As long as our experience of the world is predominantly object-referral, we will identify with the limitations of the phenomenal world and lose sight of the larger perspective. The resulting worry, anxiety, stress, or feelings of limitations are mirrored in the functioning of our physiology as it produces the biochemicals corresponding to these emotions.

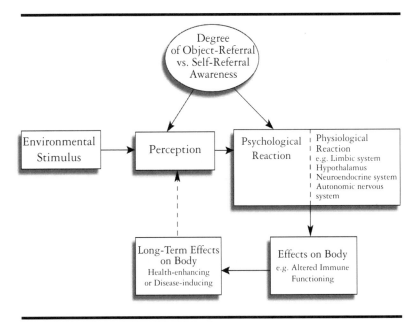

FIGURE 1. THE MECHANICS OF PRAGYA APARADH.
Our psychological and physiological reaction to environmental stimuli is determined by whether we perceive a stimulus as threatening or non-threatening. Our perception, in turn, is determined by the degree to which we are in touch with the deeper levels of our own inner nature. If our awareness is predominantly object-referral, outside events will easily be perceived as threatening and overshadow our mind. On the other hand, in a more self-referral state of awareness, the memory of the fundamental wholeness of our inner Being is not lost, and the transient fluctuations of experience will not cause us to lose sight of our essential, invincible nature.

Our reaction to outside events sets off a global neuroendocrine and hormonal response which influences the body via its effects on, for example, the immune system. Depending on the nature of the response, this chain reaction in the long run may either enhance or decrease the body's health status. It furthermore may contribute to specific patterns of behavior, as the individual for example tries to deal with the internal biochemical pandemonium through compensative behaviors such as smoking, overeating, alcohol use, or drug use.

The environmental stimuli that trigger this chain reaction need not be earth-shattering events. The little nagging worries or frustrations over daily affairs are sometimes the most destructive, because these are the ones we unconsciously turn on for long periods of time. Even irrespective of external stimuli, a continued sense of isolation, loneliness, or powerlessness will generate the same physiological effects.

The key element in triggering this psychophysiological chain reaction, as we saw above, is perception. However, our perception is determined by yet deeper factors. Our ideas and expectations play a role, but even more fundamental than these is our degree of object-referral versus self-referral. As Maharishi puts it, "What we see, we become." Experience gets translated into physiological reality. The placebo effect provides an excellent illustration of this. The patient who experiences that he or she is receiving a powerful pain reliever, will obtain relief from physiological pain even though the drug is actually a powerless sugar pill. When everything in the environment signals to a participant in a cancer treatment study that he or she is receiving a powerful chemotherapy drug that causes hair loss, the subject will lose his or her hair, even though the substance is innocuous. The heart patient who receives what he or she has come to perceive as an effective new surgical procedure, will experience highly satisfactory improvements although the surgical procedure is later found to be ineffective. As M.D. Sullivan comments, "[P]hysicians can manipulate the physiology by manipulating meaning."

Our body, being a more precipitated aspect of mind and consciousness, literally *embodies* events in the mind. The status of our physiology consequently is closely linked to our fundamental way of relating to the world. And this, in turn, is intimately connected with the degree to which we maintain the perspective of wholeness in our lives. If we perceive ourselves as isolated fragments in a hostile world, this will be mirrored in the biochemistry of our physiology. On the other hand, if we are established in a deep state of inner peace and well-being, the limitations of the phenomenal world will leave little trace in the functioning of our physiology.

"Atman [pure consciousness] is essentially devoid of all pathogenicity," writes Charaka in *Charaka Samhita*, his monumental work on Ayurveda. "[Atman] is the cause of consciousness through the mind and the specific qualities of the basic elements. He is eternal. He is an observer—he observes all activities."[144] At the very core of our existence lies the most intimate part of our Being, which never falls prey to sickness or suffering, and is beyond the ups and downs of relative existence. The more we are able to stay in touch with this profound level of our own existence, the greater will be our health and well-being.

In Search of the Missing Link

As we saw in Chapter Four, over the past decade researchers have accumulated a vast amount of evidence that mind and body are partners—for better or worse, in sickness and in health. The negative emotional states associated with certain personality types influence the functioning of the body, and have been linked to the emergence of diseases such as heart disease, cancer, gastrointestinal disturbances, and certain types of headaches. In the case of heart disease, research has centered on the role of strong emotions such as anger, hostility, and cynicism and the sense of urgency and time pressure associated with Type A personalities. In the case of cancer, bereavement, divorce, and loneliness are all factors that have been shown to predispose the physiology to this disease.

These emotions are simply the outward manifestation of a more fundamental cause. They are reactions to perceived limitations in one's life, which in turn derive from loss of inner wholeness and fullness. The greater the pragya aparadh—the more we identify with the limitations of the phenomenal world and lose the vision of wholeness—the greater will be the biochemical imprint on our body. Social support—feeling part of a larger whole, such as family or a network of caring and supportive friends—to some degree counteracts the influence of pragya aparadh. An individual's degree of social support is one of the most important predictors not only of resistance to many chronic diseases, but also of the chances for recovery and survival if one is treated for a chronic disease.

As well as being an arbitrator of the deleterious physiological events that result in imbalance and disease, the mind can also be a powerful force for health. Doctors and researchers have explored a variety of ways to harness the healing magic of the mind in the treatment of disease. Biofeedback, imagery and visualization exercises, relaxation techniques, and support groups are just a few examples of the many healing modalities that broad-minded medical practitioners are exploring. These approaches, however, all suffer from the same limitation—they lack a full understanding of the nature of the mind-body relationship. The discovery of the neuropeptide communications network has provided a framework for understanding some of the ways in which mental processes and the body are interrelated. However, there is still insufficient understanding of the source of the coordinating, integrating intelligence that in a nanosecond translates a mental impulse into physiological reality. Without this, medical researchers are forced to resort to a trial and error approach when seeking to identify ways of harnessing the mind-body relationship to enhance health.

From the point of view of a doctor trained in the Maharishi Vedic Approach to Health, this trial and error approach is only necessary because most mind-body modalities affect the superficial levels of the functioning of the mind, and therefore will be very limited in their results. For lasting healing to take place, such modalities must be able to effect changes at the most fundamental levels of the mind. Remember, in the Vedic model the different levels of the mind—ego, emotions, intellect, thinking mind, and senses—emerge sequentially in the process of unfoldment of pure consciousness. The ego is the seat of our sense of 'I,' the 'experiencer' that integrates and synthesizes the ceaseless input of experience. The level of emotions denotes the mental processes associated with feelings, motivation, intuition, creativity, and basic values. The level of the intellect represents the properties of discrimination and decision making. Memory and association are linked with the next level, the conscious mind, i.e. the mind in its limited connotation as a specific faculty of mental functioning. And lastly, the senses process environmental information, serving as a link between the individual and the world.

The more subtle, abstract levels of mental functioning are 'deeper' in the sense that they are more fundamental. Our emotional timbre, for example, takes precedence over intellectual and sensory processes. Feelings can 'color' other levels of awareness; specific moods will influence the quality of our perception, our thinking process, memory recall, and so on. Similarly, the functioning of the ego—the level of the experiencer—is fundamental to the functioning of other parts of the mind. From modern psychology we know, for example, that if the ego during the course of development is not allowed to unfold in a fully nurturing environment, the individual will not develop his or her full emotional and experiential capacity.

Treatment approaches that do not address the deeper levels of the mind will have very few long-term effects. Mind-body practitioners have been known to recommend clients to adopt a 'positive attitude' or simply 'be happy' in order to shift the internal environment of their body from a harmful, 'stressed-out' biochemistry to the immune system-enhancing biochemistry associated with happy emotional states. However, as we have seen, our moods and thoughts are intimately connected with the way we synthesize and integrate experience—in other words, how we interpret reality. Most of us can do a fair job of making ourselves 'feel happy' for a couple of minutes or even hours—until the next worry about a job deadline, regret about a missed promotion, or recall of last night's disagreement with our spouse flashes through our minds. Constantly having to remind ourselves to maintain a positive attitude only creates further stress in the mind, because our mood and attitude are a function of how we experience reality, and not something under our conscious control. Moreover, if a patient with a terminal disease erroneously believes that he or she should be able to control or cure the disease through positive thinking, the individual might start to feel guilty about having the disease. This is a deplorable and not uncommon effect of adopting a superficial perspective on the mind-body connection.

Similarly, visualization and imagery exercises may harness the mind-body link to produce short-term measurable changes in, for example, immune functioning. However, the fact that visualization exercises—such as imagining a pleasant scene in a beautiful environment—create some effect on the level of the body is one thing; to claim that they have general healing effects is quite another. Certainly, the pleasant emotions that accompany positive imagery will produce some positive effect in the physiology. However, if the person's experience of reality outside the visualization session generates frequent negative emotions, or feelings of inadequacy and an inability to cope, little has been achieved to enhance health.

Common to many mind-body approaches in use today is that they fail to address the core of the mind-body relationship—the experiencer, the Rishi value. If we want to change the mental and emotional concomitants of experience, we must first change the experiencer. Unless we address the level of the experiencer—the Rishi—no lasting changes on the Chhandas level of the physiology will occur. Permanent changes in conscious mental functioning can only be brought about by changes at deeper levels in the sequential unfoldment of the mind. In the same way as the structural weakness of a building cannot successfully be addressed by changing the roof, the imbalances at the more expressed levels of the mind—for example, at the level of emotions or perception—can only be addressed by correcting the lapse in the sequential unfoldment of mind and body from which the imbalances derive.

If we want to effectively harness the mind-body relationship, we need to go to the deepest level of reality of the experiencer—the innermost core of our Being. This is not something that can be done on the basis of thinking or volition. The essence of our Being lies beyond phenomenal reality, and cannot be experienced in the same way we commonly experience the outside world of phenomena. The innermost core of our Being can only be reached by introducing an entirely different way of knowing.

Chapter Ten

ANOTHER MODE OF KNOWING

I n 1958, not long after Maharishi arrived in the U.S., a San Francisco newspaper ran an article about the Transcendental Meditation (TM) technique, with the headline "Yogi Teaches New Sleeping Method." When Maharishi read that headline, he almost returned to India. "Here I bring them a technique to wake up to the full value of life," he said to himself, "and they use it to fall asleep!" Fortunately for the four million people in the West who have since received instruction in the technique, he decided to stay, concluding that regardless of the reasons for which a person starts the TM® program, he or she will still derive the full benefits.

This is a theme that has been repeated with many variations in the West ever since. Because meditation is a concept largely foreign to Western culture, researchers and the media alike tried to understand the phenomenon by fitting it into a more familiar framework—describing it as a sleeping aid or a 'non-medicinal tranquilizer.' And later, in the early 1970s, when the first research on the Transcendental Meditation technique showed that the practice is associated with a deep state of rest, it was concluded that the technique could be understood as evoking an innate 'relaxation response.'

There can be no denying that practice of the TM technique is associated with deep physiological rest. This profound rest is experienced immediately from the first session, and countless research studies attest to this measurable physiological effect. However, to infer from this that the TM technique is simply another form of relaxation is to confuse a descriptive attribute for a full explanation. Such a simplified portrayal fails to recognize the essential properties and purpose of Transcendental Meditation.

Even today, after the TM technique has been practiced in the West for almost four decades, there is little understanding of its true import. Granted, parts of the medical community have started to embrace it, and meditation in general is close to becoming a household word in the West. Yet, many people still attempt to fit the phenomenon into the framework of the materialist, mechanistic paradigm, discounting features that are less compatible with mainstream Western thinking in an effort to make it more palliative. Such efforts may be well-intentioned, but to the extent that they disregard the essential intent of meditation practices, they deprive us of the tremendous potential these ancient consciousness techniques have for improving our lives and our health.

Beyond Relaxation

Techniques of meditation have been generally available in the West for more than 30 years. Introduced in the late 1950s by Maharishi, the Transcendental Meditation technique is by far the most widely practiced and most thoroughly researched among these. Approximately 500 original research papers and reviews on the effects of the TM technique have been completed at 200 universities and institutions in 30 countries; these studies have been published in more than 100 refereed professional journals. This large body of research paints an excellent picture of what happens during and after the TM practice. Surveying the research, it is obvious that characterizing the TM technique as a form of relaxation is an oversimplification. Relaxation and reduction of stress are certainly important benefits of the practice, but other reasons for which people continue to practice the technique are long-term benefits, such as improved health, personality development, increased intelligence, enhanced creativity, improved social skills, increased happiness, and on and on.

From a simple start with doctoral dissertations and pilot studies, the research on the TM program has matured into a full-grown body of well-controlled, grant-funded studies. It would take a separate book to present this research in full, so I will limit myself to a brief review of the technique's effects on health and psychological growth.

In 1987, psychologists Michael Dillbeck and David Orme-Johnson published a meta-analysis in *American Psychologist* which made it clear that the profound relaxation gained during the TM practice is much deeper than the relaxation of simple rest.[145] The findings of the meta-analysis corroborated the results of some of the early 1970s studies on the TM program,[146] from which the notion of the TM technique as a form of relaxation originated. A meta-analysis is a statistical technique that integrates the results of several studies that measure the same variable. It detects the effects that are large and consistent enough to be clinically meaningful, and thus provides a more reliable assessment of the *overall* results of the studies in question. Based on the results of 31 studies, the Dillbeck and Orme-Johnson meta-analysis showed that TM practice is associated with a slower breathing pattern, increased basal skin resistance (skin resistance decreases under stress), and reduced levels of plasma lactate, a biochemical stress indicator.

The deep relaxation achieved during the TM practice reduces the individual's level of stress outside the practice as well. A meta-analysis done in 1989 by Stanford researcher K.R. Eppley compared the effects of the Transcendental Meditation program to those of a number of other 'stress reduction' techniques. Eppley found that on a measure of trait anxiety, TM practice reduced chronic stress substantially more than any of the other techniques in the study, including Progressive Muscle Relaxation, the Relaxation Response, and EMG Biofeedback.[147,148] In Japan, a longitudinal study of nearly 800 industrial workers who practiced the TM technique found significant improvements in such physical and mental health parameters as anxiety, depression, insomnia, digestive disturbances, neurotic tendencies, physical complaints, and psychosomatic problems.[149] And in Sweden, a nationwide epidemiological study conducted by the government's national health board found that the country's 35,000 TM practitioners were 150-200 times less likely to be admitted to the hospital for psychiatric care.[150]

In the U.S., TM practice has been found to significantly reduce substance abuse of illegal drugs, as well as alcohol, tobacco, and prescribed drugs. Drug use, including smoking and alcohol abuse, has become one of the most serious medical problems in the U.S. today, and one of the most difficult to cure. An average of 50 percent of patients in traditional substance abuse treatment programs drop out within the first month. Even among those who complete treatment, almost 65 percent relapse within 90 days.[151] Drug use is often linked to feelings of inadequacy and an inability to cope with external pressures or internally generated stress; therefore, to be effective a treatment must address the concomitant emotional or personality problems. A landmark meta-analysis has provided strong evidence that the TM technique constitutes one of the best tools for accomplishing this. Based on 198 studies which compared the effects of TM practice to those of other substance abuse treatment programs, the meta-analysis made it clear that TM practice produces far greater and longer lasting effects than any other treatment intervention.[152]

Another disorder closely linked to stress is hypertension. It is also one of the medical conditions most immediately responsive to regular TM practice. A large body of research, including several large, federally-funded, random-assignment studies, has found consistent and substantial improvements in hypertension in populations as diverse as working professionals,[153] elder African Americans,[154] and residents of retirement homes,[155] when the TM program is practiced. Other studies indicate that high cholesterol levels may also normalize in those who practice the TM technique regularly.[156] Both hypertension and high cholesterol levels have been linked to the development of heart disease.

Nothing undermines our health so consistently as the daily wear and tear that comes from the pressures and tensions of modern life. If this stress is reduced, better overall health and increased longevity should result. The overall effects of the TM technique on health can be seen in the decreased incidence of disease among TM practitioners. Based on insurance data, one field study compared the medical utilization statistics of 2,000 TM participants with those of other members of the same health insurance carrier. The TM technique group averaged half the health care utilization of other members of this insurance carrier who were in the same categories of age, profession, gender, and type of health insurance policy. TM practitioners were about one tenth as likely as the population norm to be hospitalized for heart disease and nervous system disorders, and half as likely to be hospitalized for tumors. The overall illness rates for the TM technique group were lower in 17 separate categories of disease.[157]

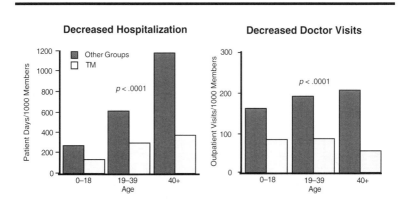

FIGURE 1A.

A five-year study on the health insurance statistics of over 2,000 people practicing the TM technique found that TM practitioners needed medical care much less frequently than other groups of comparable age, gender, profession and insurance terms. The difference became increasingly pronounced in older age brackets. TM practitioners in the 40+ age group visited their doctor about one fourth as frequently and had only about one third the number of hospital days as non-TM practitioners.

Reference: Orme-Johnson, D.W. (1987). Medical care utilization and the Transcendental Meditation program. *Psychosomatic Medicine*, 49: 493-507. p. 500.

Decreased Hospital Admission Rate in
All Categories of Disease

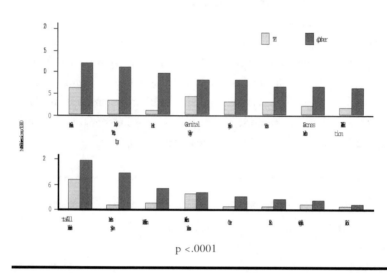

p <.0001

FIGURE 1B.
The same study showed that TM practitioners had fewer hospital admissions for illness in 17 medical treatment categories when compared to the norm. TM practitioners had 87% less hospitalization for heart disease, 55.4% less for benign and malignant tumors, 87.2% less for nervous system disorders, and 73% less for nose, throat and lung problems.
Reference: Orme-Johnson, D.W. (1987). Medical care utilization and the Transcendental Meditation program. *Psychosomatic Medicine*, 49: 493-507. p. 501.

A similar study conducted in Canada compared meditators' pre-TM medical expenditure patterns with those of the general population and with the meditators' expenditure patterns after they learned the TM program. It was found that medical expenses for the TM technique group declined for seven consecutive years after they started the TM practice. This decline was especially pronounced among high-end health care users.[158]

All of these effects add up—on the average, TM practitioners appear to remain healthier and age more slowly. On a standard test which measures biological age (i.e. age as determined by the degree of physical functionality retained) versus chronological age (i.e. a person's actual age), individuals who had practiced the TM technique for more than five years had an average biological age 12 years younger than their actual age. Study participants who had practiced the TM program for less than five years had an average biological age five years younger than their chronological age.[159]

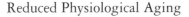

Reduced Physiological Aging

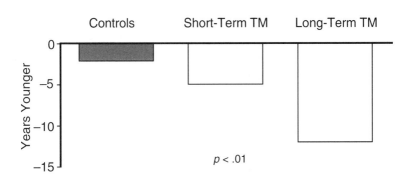

FIGURE 2.

The Adult Growth Examination is a standard test for measuring a person's biological age. In this study, the test was given to a group of individuals practicing the TM technique and to a group of non-meditating controls. Individuals who had practiced the TM technique for more than five years were 12 years younger, on the average, than their chronological age, while people who had practiced the technique less than five years were about five years younger than their chronological age. The study controlled statistically for the effects of diet and exercise.

Reference: Wallace, R.K., Dillbeck, M., Jacobe, E., and Harrington, B. (1982). The effects of the Transcendental Meditation and TM-Sidhi program on the aging process. *International Journal of Neuroscience,* 16: 53-58. p. 55. Copyright © 1982 by Gordon and Breach Publishers.

Aging is linked to a reduction in the secretion of certain hormones. One of these hormones, known as dehydroepiandrosterone sulfate (DHEA-S), is a marker of aging; levels of DHEA-S consistently decline as people advance in age. In men, relatively high levels of DHEA-S are associated with less atherosclerosis and heart disease, and lower mortality rates from all causes.[160] In women, low levels of DHEA-S have been linked to breast cancer,[161] and high levels to greater bone density in late menopause.[162] In a study published in the *Journal of Behavioral Medicine*, Dr. Jay Glaser and colleagues found higher values of DHEA-S in the blood of 423 TM practitioners, as compared to 1,253 controls. The ages of study participants ranged from 20 to 81 years, and results were gathered in five-year age ranges. The effects of diet, obesity, and exercise were statistically ruled out. Depending on their age range, people who practiced the TM technique exhibited DHEA-S levels that were equivalent to those of study participants in the control group who were five to ten years younger.[163]

Psychological Growth

One could explain the effects of the TM program on health and aging by saying that regular practice of the technique induces deep relaxation and enables the individual to more effectively manage and recover from stress. But this explanation falls short when we consider the effects of the TM technique on psychological growth and personality development. Yet, it is in the enhancement of human potential that the true significance of the Transcendental Meditation technique lies. People continue to practice the TM technique year after year, not just because it is a pleasant means of relaxing, but because the immediate and long-term reward of the practice is a profound personal transformation and growth. The TM technique helps an individual to blossom and unfold from the inside out, enlivening the latent possibilities that each of us carries within.

A wide range of studies provide an account of some of the changes involved in this pervasive personal transformation. A meta-analysis published in 1991 compared the effects of the TM program with those of other forms of meditation and relaxation on a measure of psychological health known as self-actualization. The construct was developed in the early 1960s by the well-known psychologist Abraham Maslow, who described self-actualized individuals as people who have an integrated perspective on themselves and the world, have high self-esteem and a great capacity for intimacy with others, are lively and creative, and have a clear sense of purpose. Researchers in the field maintain that only a small part of the adult population is self-actualized, and it is a quality that has proven exceedingly difficult to create or enhance.

The meta-analysis included a total of 42 independent study outcomes, 17 of which focused on the effects of the TM program. It was found that meditation techniques involving concentration led to no increases in self-actualization. Greater results were obtained from relaxation techniques and other forms of meditation, but the effect sizes of these techniques did not exceed the effect size of placebo treatments—in fact, they remained somewhat below the highest effect size for placebo treatments. The only intervention to show a substantial statistical effect size was the TM technique. The effect of TM practice was found to increase with longer treatment periods, which was not the case for the other techniques, indicating the results were unlikely to have derived from the expectations associated with being part of a study.[164,165]

Development of Personality
Increased Self-Actualization

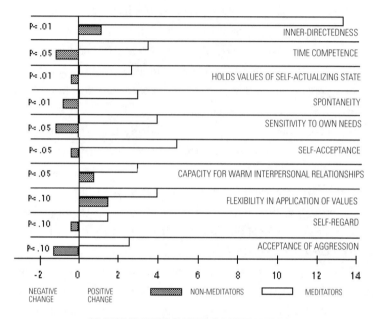

CHANGE IN SCORE OVER TWO-MONTH PERIOD

FIGURE 3.

Self-actualization provides a general measure of a person's psychological health. It is defined in part as a high level of maturity, health, and fulfillment, and increased integration, wholeness, and unity of person. A 1973 study (see chart) found significant growth of self-actualization in TM practitioners compared to controls.

Summarizing the results of 42 studies that focused on the development of self-actualization, a 1991 meta-analysis found that the overall effect of the TM technique was significantly greater than other forms of meditation and relaxation.

References: Nidich, S., Seeman, W., and Dreskin, T. (1973). Influence of Transcendental Meditation: A replication. *Journal of Counseling Psychology,* 20: 565-566. p. 566. Copyright © 1973 by the American Psychological Association. Adapted with permission.

Alexander, C. N., Rainforth, M. V., and Gelderloos, P. (1991). Transcendental Meditation, self-actualization and psychological health: A conceptual overview and statistical meta-analysis. *Journal of Social Behavior and Personality,* 6: 189-247.

The personality growth that results from regular TM practice is evident not only with this one variable, however; it can be seen in a broad range of measures. A ten-year longitudinal study, for example, compared the ego development of TM practitioners with that of a group of controls. In spite of the fact that ego development, as measured by Loevinger's ego development scale, is not thought to change beyond a certain age, TM practitioners had a marked increase in scores from pretest to posttest. In fact, at the ten-year posttest almost 40 percent of the TM technique group placed within the two final stages of ego development—a larger segment than found in more than 40 other studies of adults.[166] The same picture of overall personal development is painted by many other studies, which have found such longitudinal changes as increased intelligence,[167] enhanced creativity,[168] improved field independence,[169] heightened self-identity,[170] greater ego-strength,[171] better marital relations,[172] and so on.

One may wonder how a single technique could give rise to such a broad range of effects. After all, if a pill was invented that could produce one or two of the above benefits—e.g. enhanced self-esteem and greater ego development—it would be widely heralded as the greatest medical breakthrough ever. We are accustomed to thinking in terms of mechanistic, linear, cause-and-effect relationships in which *one* particular intervention gives rise to *one* specific effect. Blood pressure medication treats hypertension, stress management techniques help the individual relax or improve specific coping abilities, drug treatments target addictive behavior and the specific problems that underlie this behavior, and psychotherapy attempts to locate and address the unique causes of clients' specific problems, be it low self-esteem, neuroticism, general lack of fulfillment, or something else.

The individual is an organic whole, however. Hypertension is not a problem that occurs in isolation from the overall functioning of the physiology, and in turn, the feeling of stress and pressure that is often the psychological counterpart of hypertension does not exist independently of the overall psychological makeup of the individual. Personality, personal history, degree of social support, ego development, intellectual capacity, and educational background are all related to the overall health status of the individual.

Regular TM practice generates such a wide range of effects because it changes the individual from the inside out. Maharishi explains that the technique employs the same principle applied to the care of a plant. If the leaves lack luster and the sprigs droop, you don't start polishing the leaves or binding up the sprigs. You simply supply nourishment to the root of the plant, and the inherent intelligence of the plant takes care of the rest. Life unfolds from the inside out. If we bring nourishment to the root of our individual existence, all other aspects of our life will blossom. The TM technique changes the Rishi value, the knower, the experiencer. It is in this aspect that the true significance of Maharishi's Transcendental Meditation technique lies.

Turiya Chetana—The Fourth State of Consciousness

From the research studies, we have a delineation of some of the physiological changes associated with the practice of the TM program. But description does not equal understanding; it does not give us much of an idea of what actually happens during TM practice. Maharishi gives the following explanation of what occurs during the practice of the Transcendental Meditation technique:

> The TM technique is an effortless procedure for allowing the excitations of the mind gradually to settle down until the least excited state of mind is reached. This is a state of inner wakefulness with no object of thought or perception, just pure consciousness aware of its own unbounded nature. It is wholeness, aware of itself, devoid of difference, beyond the division of subject and object—transcendental consciousness. It is a field of all possibilities where all creative potentialities exist together, infinitely correlated but as yet unexpressed. It is a state of perfect order, the matrix from which all the laws of nature emerge, the source of creative intelligence.[173]

The phrase 'Transcendental Meditation' derives from the fact that during the practice of the TM technique, the mind *transcends*, i.e. goes beyond the finest impulse of thought and reaches the state of pure awareness, or pure wakefulness. This state is known as 'transcendental consciousness.' It is consciousness knowing itself, dwelling in its pure, unbounded form, simply awake to its own existence. It is a state of restful alertness in which consciousness is completely settled, without a trace of activity, yet at the same time completely alert. In this state, consciousness is without the specific representations of phenomenal experience; it is like the white screen in a movie theater without the projections of thought.

Maharishi explains that the experience of transcendental consciousness is the experience of a *fourth state of consciousness—Turiya Chetana—* which is distinctly different from the waking, dreaming, and sleeping states of consciousness. In the *Mandukya Upanishad*, this experience is described in the following way:

> Not conscious of the internal, nor conscious of the external, nor conscious of both . . . unseen, beyond the texture of all relativity, incomprehensible, without any distinguishing mark, unthinkable, indescribable, of the essence of the consciousness of the Unity of the Self, the very cessation of the world of relativity, peaceful, full of bliss and non-dual—this is what is known as the *Turiya* or the Fourth.[174]

If human beings have the capacity to experience a fourth state of consciousness, why don't we experience it without the aid of a technique? In fact, although it is not part of our common repertoire of experience, human beings can and do have spontaneous experiences of the fourth state of consciousness. People of all cultures and ages have left us countless reports of experiences that do not fit into the framework of the three normally experienced states of consciousness. However, for reasons which we shall address later in this chapter, the fourth state of consciousness is much more rarely experienced than the three other states of consciousness.

William James, who studied such rare experiences, heavily suspected that our waking state was only one type of consciousness. "[A]ll about it parted from it by the filmiest of screens, there lie potential forms of consciousness entirely different. We may go through life without suspecting their existence; but apply the requisite stimulus, and at a touch they are there in all their completeness, definite types of mentality." James referred to such unusual experiences as 'states of assurance,' noting that we pass into these states "from out of ordinary consciousness as from a less into a more, as from a smallness into a vastness, and at the same time as from an unrest to a rest. We feel them as reconciling, unifying states. . . . In them the unlimited absorbs the limits and peacefully closes the account."[175]

Let us take a few moments to explore some examples of these spontaneous experiences of the fourth state of consciousness. The 19th century British writer J.A. Symonds has left us the following passage:

> Suddenly at church, or in company, or when I was reading, and always, I think, when my muscles were at rest, I felt the approach of the mood. It consisted in a gradual but swiftly progressing obliteration of space, time, sensation and the multifarious factors of experience which seem to qualify what we are pleased to call our Self. In proportion as these conditions of ordinary consciousness were subtracted, *the sense of an underlying or essential consciousness acquired intensity.* At last nothing remained but *a pure, absolute, abstract Self.* The universe became *without form and void of content.* But the Self persisted, formidable in its vivid keenness.[176] [emphasis added]

Symonds' description of "an underlying or essential consciousness" clearly evokes characteristics of the fourth state of consciousness. It is an experience of the essence of awareness—other modes of awareness are simply more excited states of this "essential consciousness." Similarly, William Wordsworth in his poem "Tintern Abbey" speaks of

> . . . that serene and blessed mood,
> In which the affections gently lead us on,—
> Until, the breath of this corporeal frame
> And even the motion of our human blood
> Almost suspended, we are laid asleep
> In body, and become a living soul:
> While with an eye made quiet by the power
> Of harmony and the deep power of joy,
> We see into the life of things.

In the fourth state of consciousness, we 'see' with "an eye made quiet by the power/ Of harmony and the deep power of joy." The fourth state can also be described as a state of supreme harmony and bliss, a reunion with the most intimate core of our own existence. This is expressed in the following quote from the French playwright Eugene Ionesco:

> Once, long ago, I was sometimes overcome by a sort of grace, a euphoria. It was as if, first of all, every notion, every reality was emptied of its content. After this emptiness . . ., it was as if I found myself suddenly *at the center of pure ineffable existence. . . . I became one with the one essential reality*, when, along with an immense, serene joy, I was overcome by what I might call the stupefaction of being, *the certainty of being. . . .*
>
> I say that with words that can only disfigure, that cannot describe the light of this profound, total organic intuition which, surging up as it did from *my deepest self*, might well have inundated everything both my other self and others.[177] [emphasis added]

And finally, the philosopher Jacob Needleman tells of the following experience:

> [T]ime passed much more slowly and I saw my thoughts in front of me as if they were written on a screen. So I was quite aware that there's a difference between awareness and thought. At the same moment I was aware of the thousand things going on inside me

with a global awareness, with *a center of attention that was in touch with all parts at the same time.* . . . If one could have more access to those states, science would be quite different. One's vision of the universe would be quite different.[178] [emphasis added]

Needleman's report is actually of a more advanced experience of pure consciousness, or a higher state of consciousness, because he is clearly able to experience both the pure awareness of the Self *along with* thoughts. We will explore this type of experience in greater detail in a later chapter. At the risk of getting ahead of myself, I have included Needleman's report here, because it provides a clear delineation of the contrast between more excited mental states and the silent field of pure awareness.

States of consciousness have two attributes: first, they are characterized by different qualities of experience, and second, they are associated with qualitatively different modes of physiological functioning. Modern research has shown that transitions from waking to dreaming or to sleeping are associated with global physiological changes in heart rate, blood pressure, blood chemistry, and organ and gland activity. The fourth state of consciousness likewise has its own unique physiological signature. In the above examples, both Symonds and Wordsworth make reference to the more settled physiological state associated with the experience. Symonds recalls that this experience arrives when his muscles are at rest; Wordsworth in his poetic parlance speaks of the suspension of "the breath of this corporeal frame/ And even the motion of our human blood."

It is the shift in our level of mental activity that gives rise to the pervasive physiological changes that take place during the practice of the TM technique. As the mind settles down into more and more refined states of mental activity and eventually transcends even the finest impulse of thought, the physiology shifts into a more restful, settled mode of functioning corresponding to the decreased mental activity. Researchers charting these changes note that the pattern of physiological functioning during the TM practice is characteristic of a state of physiological rest accompanied by heightened alertness. The increased alertness is indicated by a unique EEG pattern of brain activity during the TM practice, together with such features as increased blood flow to the brain and increased arginine vasopressin production.[179]

Normally, only advanced practitioners experience the fourth state of consciousness for the entire duration of the TM practice. For other practitioners, any given sitting consists of both 'inward' strokes, in which the mind settles down and experiences the state of pure awareness, and 'outward' strokes, in which the mind becomes involved in thought processes. Therefore, in some studies subjects are asked to press a button immediately after an experience of the fourth state of consciousness. From such studies we have a clear picture of the unique physiological parameters that are specifically associated with the experience of transcendental consciousness. These are mainly characterized by global increases in EEG coherence, which can be taken as an indication of long-range spatial ordering of brain activity, and extended periods of virtual respiratory suspension. This deeply restful and integrated state of physiological functioning sustains that completely settled and integrated state of awareness which is devoid of even the finest impulse of thought.

Another Way of Knowing

How can we understand the nature of the fourth state of consciousness? According to the Vedic tradition, *Turiya Chetana* is a direct appreciation of the unbounded field of Being, the most intimate core of our own existence. As Carl Gustav Jung, one of the most well-respected of the early European psychologists observed, "I simply believe that some part of the human Self or Soul is not subject to the laws of space and time." What Jung intuited, the ancient Vedic seers had developed the capacity to directly explore. Millennia before the birth of Western psychology, the Vedic seers had acquired a remarkable degree of knowledge regarding the nature of higher states of consciousness and how to attain them. The following passage from the *Mandukya Upanishad*, for example, is almost a textbook presentation of the characteristics of the four different states of consciousness:

Atman, the Self, has four conditions.

The first condition is the waking life of outward-moving consciousness, enjoying the . . . outer gross elements.

The second condition is the dreaming life of inner-moving consciousness, enjoying the . . . subtle inner elements in its own light and solitude.

The third condition is the sleeping life of silent consciousness when a person has no desires and beholds no dreams. That condition of deep sleep is one of oneness, a mass of silent consciousness made of peace and enjoying peace. . . .

The fourth condition is Atman in his own pure state: the awakened life of supreme consciousness. It is neither outer nor inner consciousness, neither semi-consciousness, nor sleeping consciousness, neither consciousness nor unconsciousness. He is Atman, the Spirit himself, that cannot be touched, that is above all distinction, beyond thought and ineffable. In the union with him is the supreme proof of his reality. He is the end of evolution and non-duality. He is peace and love.[180]

The source of objective and subjective existence is one—the objects of the phenomenal world, our bodies, and our minds are the precipitated expressions of the same primal substance. When the basic source of objective and subjective existence is conceptualized as the same underlying field of wholeness, or consciousness in its pure form, it follows that individual consciousness cannot exist as a phenomenon outside the underlying field of pure consciousness. It is simply a more precipitated expression of that very consciousness. To experience it, all one has to do is settle down and Be it.

All the major traditions of knowledge maintain that there is a dimension of reality that lies beyond the common experience of the waking state of consciousness. The Jewish Kabbalah talks about the transcendent and the immanent orders of reality, representing respectively, unmanifest wholeness and the 'world of separation.' The Sioux Indians talk about

Waken, the inner source of life. The Vedic tradition, however, is unparalleled in the manner in which it details the relationship between 'normal' objective experience and the experience of the finest level of reality. And the Vedic tradition contains a treasure trove of techniques for developing this state of awareness.

The Vedic seers knew that if the human mind becomes still and settled enough, it will merge with the field of pure existence, its own essential nature. As the mind's activity is transcended, it beholds the finest fluctuations of its own intelligence in its pure unexpressed form. With the experience of the fourth state of consciousness, a completely different mode of knowing—and a different level of reality—opens up. In the waking state of consciousness, we know only the precipitated expressions of the underlying field of existence as they are revealed to us through the senses. In contrast, in the fourth state of consciousness we suddenly gain access to the unmanifest underlying reality that forms the basis of phenomenal existence. Both Wordsworth and Needleman make reference to such different modes of knowing. Needleman talks of "a center of attention that was in touch with all parts at the same time" and Wordsworth speaks of seeing "into the life of things." And, as Needleman remarks, "If one could have more access to those states, science would be quite different. One's vision of the universe would be quite different." The British poet Robert Browning expresses this recognition beautifully in the following passage:

> Truth is within ourselves; it takes no rise
> From outward things, whate'er you may believe:
> There is an inmost centre in us all,
> Where truth abides in fulness; and around
> Wall upon wall, the gross flesh hems it in,
> This perfect, clear perception—which is truth;
> A baffling and perverting carnal mesh
> Blinds it, and makes all error; and, 'to know'
> Rather consists in opening out a way
> Whence the imprisoned splendor may escape,
> Than in effecting entry for a light

> Supposed to be without. Watch narrowly
> The demonstration of a truth, its birth,
> And you trace back the effluence to its spring
> And source within us, where broods radiance vast
> To be elicited ray by ray, as chance
> Shall favour. . . .[181]

"And you trace back the effluence to its spring/ And source within us, where broods radiance vast/ To be elicited ray by ray, as chance/ Shall favour. . . ." As Browning so eloquently puts it, in the West glimpses of the fourth state of consciousness have been elicited only "as chance/ Shall favour." This profound experience has remained a rare and precious visitor, seeking one out in moments of quiet and calm. But if such occurrences are possible, why are they not part of one's common repertoire of experience?

The Importance of a Technique

In the same way as we cannot shift from the waking to the sleeping state of consciousness at will, we cannot make the transition to transcendental consciousness simply by intending to do so. We slide automatically from waking into sleeping; likewise, the shift from the excited mental activity of the waking state to the state of least excitation of consciousness, i.e. transcendental consciousness, happens spontaneously.

In Western society, one is habituated since birth to projecting the awareness outward, into the field of phenomenal existence. However, when the mind is projecting awareness outside, it fails to realize the abstract transcendental aspect of its existence. As Maharishi explains,

> Pure Being is of transcendental nature because of Its status as the essential constituent of the universe. It is finer than the finest in creation; because of Its nature, It is not exposed to the senses which primarily are formed to give only the experience of the manifest reality of life. It is not obviously exposed to the perception of the mind, because the mind is connected for the most part with the senses.

156

Experience shows that Being is the essential, basic nature of the mind; but since it commonly remains in tune with the senses, projecting outwards toward the manifest realms of creation, the mind misses or fails to appreciate its own essential nature, just as the eyes are unable to see themselves.[182]

Even if we consciously attempt to turn our attention inward and experience our own essential nature, however, we will meet with little success. The field of Being lies beyond relative existence; as a consequence, it cannot be reached simply by thinking about it. As philosopher David Hume mused, "When I enter most intimately into what I call *myself* I always stumble on some particular perception or other, of heat or cold, light or shade, love or hatred, pain or pleasure. I can never catch *myself* at any time without a perception, and never can observe anything but the perception."[183]

The field of pure Being can only be experienced by Being it. Transcendental consciousness can only be experienced by *transcending* the finest impulse of thought. Any effort to unite with the absolute sphere of existence belongs to the relative sphere of life. Any attempt to comprehend or conceive of it with the mind is just another mode of mental functioning, another object of thought projected onto the screen of awareness. Any conscious attempt to experience pure consciousness automatically precludes the experience. The *Khanda Upanishad* summarizes this paradox as follows:

He by whom it is not thought, by him it is thought; he by whom it is thought, knows it not. It is not understood by those who understand it, it is understood by those who do not understand it.[184]

Because it lies beyond our habitual, representational states of awareness, the fourth state of consciousness cannot be reached by imagining it, thinking about it, or striving for it, no matter how hard we try. It is a tribute to the magnificence of the Vedic tradition that the TM technique resolves this dilemma in a very simple and elegant way. The technique makes use of the fact that, although it is impossible to experience the fourth state of consciousness at will, it can happen spontaneously when no effort is involved. The Self, or pure transcendental consciousness, is the most intimate feature of the mind's existence. The mind may therefore settle into this state at times when it is not distracted by outside factors and when the nervous system is in a sufficiently settled and integrated state to sustain this level of experience. The TM technique is so natural and effortless, because it simply sets up the right condition for this to happen. It provides a means for turning the attention *inward* so that the mind, instead of being caught up in the outside world of sensory experience, spontaneously opens to its own transcendental nature. All that is needed is to set up the initial condition, and the rest will proceed by itself. In the TM technique, the Vedic tradition has left us a delicately tuned methodology that enables the mind to naturally settle into the supreme bliss of self-referral transcendental consciousness. As the practice advances, the physiology becomes cultured to sustain clearer values of this experience for longer periods of time.

Maharishi's contribution in making the Transcendental Meditation program widely available to our global society cannot be underscored enough. For centuries, meditation has been considered an excessively difficult discipline, mastered only after years of practice. What happened, Maharishi explains, is that over the years the teachings of the Vedic sages became misunderstood. The Vedic seers described meditation in terms of a state of pure awareness in which the mind is completely silent, and completely 'empty of thought.' As the purity of the original teachings got lost, the 'end state' of meditation came to be mistaken for the process, and people started to think of meditation as a process of subduing the activity of the mind or 'emptying' it of its mental content. This is one of the great tragedies of knowledge—it can only be understood at the recipient's level of awareness. Although the Vedic sages had developed a full vision of the nature of reality and how to experience it, the people who come after them could only understand the ancient seers' vision at their own level of consciousness.

The ultimate aim of meditation certainly is the state of pure consciousness in which the mind is devoid of mental activity. However, the 'emptying of the mind' is *a characteristic* of the meditative state and *not a prescription* for how to reach it. The effort involved in such attempts, Maharishi points out, in itself keeps the mind from settling down. If you have the intention to have no thoughts, that intention is itself a thought. If you attempt to still the mind, that attempt is itself activity. Greater awareness or 'an empty mind' is a finer state of mental functioning which can only be brought about by the spontaneous settling down of mind and body to subtler states of functioning.

Even today, such misunderstandings are pervasive. Noting the many potential health benefits of meditation, a number of Western health practitioners have sought to revamp ancient consciousness techniques to fit a modern mold. The prevalent notions of meditation among such practitioners, however, often fail to appreciate the true depth of the phenomenon. Without having full insight into the mechanics and nature of techniques to develop consciousness *and* the subtle levels of reality they explore, such derivations do not produce results that are comparable in range and potency. Precious few are the individuals who have been or are in touch with the fine levels of reality that meditative techniques seek to explore. Their legacy is something to be treasured, not manipulated and altered according to superficial criteria. From the point of view of the Vedic tradition of knowledge, blindly changing meditation techniques to make them more palliative is like handing out pebbles where people could have gotten gold.

It is to preserve the integrity of the teaching that Maharishi has always insisted the Transcendental Meditation technique be taught by a certified teacher and according to the ancient Vedic procedures for passing on consciousness techniques. Teaching and learning the TM technique is an experiential and interactive process—it is not a transfer of intellectual knowledge that can be done through a book. Certain procedures need to be elicited to produce the proper experience, and questions need to be dealt with in the sequence in which they arise. Although the TM technique is easy to learn and practice, it is also a delicate procedure; to retain maximum efficiency, the instruction follows the time-tested format and sequence for imparting consciousness techniques. Apart from preserving the purity of the teaching, this standardized, systematized method of imparting the knowledge has also had the advantage of making the TM technique more amenable to scientific study.

The Transcendental Meditation program provides us with a means of systematically exploring the full range of human consciousness. It opens our awareness to a different dimension of reality which has until now been shrouded in mystery and misunderstanding. It provides a technique for refining the human nervous system to sustain that level of experience in which individual existence unites with the pure field of existence, the essential wholeness of the universe. This opens up new dimensions of knowing, as the mind develops the ability to dwell at the finest levels of existence. It opens up new dimensions of being and of living, as we develop the full potential and range of consciousness and start to express in our daily lives the unlimited creative intelligence residing at this supreme level of existence. And it opens up new dimensions of healing as we become blessed with the sublime experience of our own essential wholeness. As the memory and perfect symmetry of the silent, nonmaterial, unified field is infused into the activity of our apparently material body, health and healing take on a whole new dimension of meaning.

Chapter Eleven

DISSOLVING PRAGYA APARADH

The essence of healing is "the restoration of memory." Pure consciousness is always there, but without a technique that enables us to 'know' this level of reality, it remains as if hidden beneath the flurry of habitual mental activity. "Complete transcending is the best among the sources of health and happiness," wrote Charaka in the ancient Ayurvedic text *Charaka Samhita*.[185] The benefits of transcending are not limited to the actual meditation sitting, but extend far into the daily activity of the individual. As the mind repeatedly experiences the field of wholeness or pure Being, it becomes as if infused with the primordial wholeness of existence. Over time, as the individual alternates regularly between the experience of the silent state of pure consciousness and normal everyday activity, the changes at the level of the knower get permanently integrated into the functioning of the physiology. As the knower blossoms, so does every aspect of his or her life. The physiological and psychological changes charted by the vast body of scientific research done on the TM technique, are just some of the changes that come about as the manifest states of creation are brought in tune with the unmanifest field of self-referral wholeness.

These changes can be described as a shift from an object-referral toward a more self-referral mode of functioning. It is a gradual dispersal of pragya aparadh—the mistake of the intellect. As the mind gets imbibed with the unboundedness at the source of its own existence, it spontaneously develops a more universal perspective and gradually becomes less overshadowed by the limitations of relative existence. The positive emotional states associated with this heightened sense of Being harness the mind-body relationship for greater health. As pragya aparadh dissolves, we less frequently elicit the vicious cycle of the emotional stress response; in fact, the cycle gets reversed for the creation of better health. This is the reason the first step toward healing in the Maharishi Vedic Approach to Health is to restore the memory of wholeness.

The transformation and healing that is initiated when an individual starts to experience pure consciousness is a profound psychophysiological shift—the increased connection to the integrating source of existence happens on the level of the mind-body system as a whole. The activity of each part of the physiology becomes better regulated with respect to the needs of the organism as a whole. We can also describe this process as a progressive release of stress, i.e. removal of blockages that impede the normal functioning of the physiology. The development of greater self-referral functioning also makes one more attuned to the needs of the body; it increases one's awareness of the body and of the effects created by harmful health habits. This leads to a spontaneous shift toward more positive health habits, such as reduced alcohol consumption, smoking cessation, preference toward healthier foods, etc. These are commonly observed changes in people who begin practice of the TM program. The source of gratification shifts from predominant reliance on outside sensory experience to the self-effulgent joy that comes from being in touch with one's deep inner fullness.

As the mind becomes habituated to the experience of pure consciousness, it gets infused with the value of wholeness. Identifying itself with this level of nature's functioning, it also gains the ability to function at this level and to perform in the same style with which nature performs its activity at its most fundamental level. With this, a whole new realm of possibilities for harnessing nature's intelligence opens up.

The TM-Sidhi Program

The TM-Sidhi® program is a more advanced technique for exploring the full range of human consciousness; together with the TM technique, it forms the principal technology of Maharishi Vedic Science. Whereas the TM technique allows the mind to experience the unbounded, unchanging source of all mental impulses, the TM-Sidhi program enables one to function from the level of this least excited state of awareness.

The TM-Sidhi program is based on the *Yoga Sutras* of Patanjali, who was one of the great sages of the Vedic tradition. The Sanskrit word *sidhi* means perfection. The purpose of the TM-Sidhi program is to create perfection in the coordination between mind and body, which in this context means to infuse the full value of pure consciousness on the level of the physiology. The program does this by developing optimal functioning in the various channels of mind-body coordination. In this way, the finest level of awareness becomes increasingly coordinated with the most expressed value of the individual's existence—the physiology.

The TM-Sidhi program can be learned after a few months of TM practice, when the individual has become habituated to the experience of pure consciousness. The key to the technique is learning to project a fine impulse of thought from the junction point between the active mind and the silent field of pure consciousness. As Maharishi explains,

> In this program, human awareness identifies itself with that most wide and most powerful level of nature's functioning and starts to function from there. The purpose of the TM-Sidhi program is to consciously create activity from that level where nature performs.

> Because the state of least excitation is basic to all excited states, the mind in this state gains the upper hand. The mind becomes more basic to its own excited states, which is the body. On that level where the awareness becomes more basic to the body, the mind-body relationship has reached its climax. *The ultimate relationship between mind and body is that the mind is the master of its own projections. The body is a projection of the mind, and therefore the mind can be master of the body.*[186] [emphasis added]

The thinking process at this level takes on a new dimension—it becomes one with the self-referral dynamics of the field of pure consciousness. At this level, one's transcendental consciousness, functioning within itself, is the field of wholeness, the field of pure existence functioning within itself. The TM-Sidhi program is performed at that self-referral, self-interacting level where specific manifestations emerge from the field of pure potentiality. At this level resides the total organizing intelligence of nature. When the mind is stationed at this level it gains, as Maharishi puts it, "the upper hand." In this state, the mind can be master of the body, and command it at will.

Different aspects of the TM-Sidhi program enliven different aspects of the mind-body system. Some techniques focus on developing the senses, which form the junction between the mental and the material spheres of existence. Some aim at developing the fine emotional qualities of the heart, while others stimulate the individual's ability to cognize the finest fluctuations of intelligence as they gain expression from the field of pure consciousness. Yogic flying, considered by many to be the most supreme of the sidhis, provides the individual with a technique to master the mind-body connection in such a way that he or she transcends the usual limitations for bodily motion, and lifts off the ground by the exercise of merely a mental impulse.

Gaining full mastery over the sidhis involves a pervasive psychophysiological transformation. For the sidhis to be performed successfully, the mind must be so established in pure consciousness that the impulse of thought does not overshadow the unbounded, pure awareness. This requires a high degree of neurophysiological refinement, which is developed over time with continued practice. It is important to understand that the mastery of specific sidhis is not an end in and of itself, but a means to stimulate this comprehensive psychophysiological refinement and transformation.

As part of the psychophysiological development that is stimulated by the TM-Sidhi program, the mind-body system starts to normalize imbalances and release the shadows of old stresses still lodged in the system. This healing process takes place over time and is largely noticed as an increasing sense of well-being, vitality, and increasing physiological balance.

However, it can also manifest in more dramatic ways. New dimensions of healing open up when one gains access to the junction point where self-referral consciousness assumes material form. The following report by Mary (name has been changed), who has practiced the TM and TM-Sidhi programs for a number of years, provides a vivid illustration of the healing that is associated with directly experiencing the mechanics of pragya aparadh.

For years I had a stabbing, almost crippling pain in one of my shoulder blades, which at times would leave me practically paralyzed. Frequent visits to chiropractors provided some relief, but the pain always returned.

While on a residential meditation course, I was going through a period when I would sink very deep during the practice of the TM-Sidhi program and become one with this unified, infinite wholeness. I felt completely nonlocalized and everything around me was completely nonlocalized, just space—well, not even that, because everything was just nothingness, a wonderful, beautiful nothingness. At the same time, there was this immense feeling of fullness and bliss.

At one point, as I was deep in this wonderful unboundedness, I began to hear a faint sound. Hearing is not the right word, because it was not like hearing a sound through your ears. It was just a reality that this sound was there.

It didn't influence me at all, because it seemed to be somewhere in infinity. It was so far away, I couldn't even judge where it was coming from. The sound kept getting louder and louder, and then at the point where it was becoming very loud, I began to be aware of a localization of myself. I became aware that if I could be located in space, it was like I was all these fluctuations of consciousness. There was a particular flow to these fluctuations and that flow was really my localization—my body. There was nothing concrete, just this flow of energy.

As the sound reached its loudest point, I became aware of a localization in this energy flow that was my body. The sound was right at the point in my back where I had always had a pain. It as if created some solid block and the fluctuations of energy were blocking up there and couldn't flow.

Somehow I knew that this block in the flow of consciousness was actually what created the experience of pain. The pain that I had experienced all these years came from some impression deep in consciousness rather than from some physical factor. On one level of consciousness—the level that was deeper than my physiology—it was not a physical block.

I was right on the junction point where my attention could be with both the relative and the transcendent aspects of my being. When my attention flowed in one direction, I was a relative, concrete being, and that sound and pain were right there in my shoulder blade. When my attention flowed another direction, I was in the transcendent field of consciousness witnessing this pain that had been created by this 'sound,' which was somewhere deep in my consciousness.

Being in the transcendent, I still experienced the body as having no concreteness to it at all. Then a silent knowing came —I realized that when this body is really just a flow of energy, these fluctuations aren't blocked by anything solid.

Very subtly I initiated an impulse to the fluctuations of energy, saying, this can't even happen, there is nothing there to stop you, so just keep moving. And immediately, there was no block and the fluctuations were just flowing like before. I went on with my program, and the pain, the sound was gone. I was again immersed in a feeling of unboundedness.

When I finished my program, I remembered what had happened, and I began to think about it intellectually. At the same time, I noticed a lot of bliss in that area. Over the next couple of days, I would sometimes feel a faint sensation in that area. But never the pain that had been there before—that has never since come back.

Mary describes a direct experience of the body as a field of intelligence in motion, as the fluctuations of wholeness within itself. Her account provides an excellent illustration of how pragya aparadh can be spontaneously dissolved when the true nature of Self and body is experienced.

When the memory of the basic wholeness of the physiology is restored, any limitations that have arisen in this wholeness automatically dissipate. As long as wholeness is fully awake to its own nature, there is a frictionless flow between wholeness and parts, between the finest impulses of the unmanifest as it sprouts into the manifestations of relative existence, and between its more precipitated expressions in the physical body. When some value of wholeness is lost, however, some value of infinite correlation, of perfect alignment of wholes and parts is lost. It is this loss of perfection that we experience as disease, pain, and suffering.

Creating World Health

The TM-Sidhi program is the most far-reaching of all the programs in the Maharishi Vedic Approach to Health. There is a well-known phrase from the Vedic Literature which reads, *Tat sannidhau vairatyagah*—"In the vicinity of the settled mind, hostile tendencies fall away." When a person contacts pure consciousness, a harmonious influence is not only created in his or her own mind; this influence extends to the environment as well, because pure consciousness is the primordial field of wholeness, the essence of everything that exists. When the source of thought is enlivened, all the impulses in the individual's mind and in the environment start to become aligned with the unbounded field of cosmic intelligence that is the source of all evolutionary impulses in nature. When a sufficiently large number of people contact the field of pure consciousness, it creates a powerful influence of harmony and coherence in the environment. As Maharishi explains,

> [T]he Unified Field of Natural Law . . . has the character of infinite correlation. The impulse of coherence from this level instantly reconstructs and transforms unnatural, stressful, negative, undesirable tendencies in the brain physiology, and brain functioning becomes coherent.
>
> Considering this phenomenon in the light of the Unified Field Theories of modern Physics and Quantum Cosmology, we under-

167

stand that the scale of Super Unification at the level of the Unified Field is associated with a fundamental phase transition in the
structure of Natural Law from a diversified state to a completely
unified state. The defining characteristic of such a phase transition is that the 'correlation length,' which is a measure of the connectedness or correlation of different components of a system,
expands to finally become infinite. . . . A delicate impulse at any
point in space and time can create a precipitous change throughout
the entire universe. This long-range correlation explains how
action on the level of the Unified Field, at the scale of Super Unification (transcendental field of intelligence), can have a profound
influence that can spread anywhere and everywhere throughout the
universe.[187]

This phenomenon is known as the Maharishi Effect. The Maharishi
Effect is not just an abstract notion; it can actually be measured. The first
studies on this phenomenon were conducted in 1974 in U.S. cities. When
one percent of a city's population practiced the TM program, the trend of
rising crime was reversed.[188] With the more advanced TM-Sidhi program,
this effect becomes even more pronounced; when the square root of one
percent of a population practices the TM-Sidhi program, a number of
effects can be observed: decreased crime rate and reduction of violent
deaths, fewer traffic accidents, decreased incidence of infectious disease,
fewer suicides, and improvement on a number of economic indicators such
as inflation and unemployment.[189] A study performed in the Middle East
and published in the *Journal of Conflict Resolution* found that the effect of
a large group of people practicing the TM-Sidhi program was even reflected in a reduction of war hostilities in the surrounding area.[190]

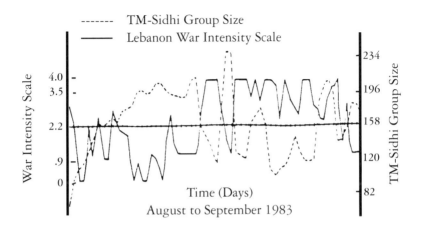

FIGURE 1.

This figure illustrates the inverse relationship between the number of TM-Sidhi participants (dashes) and intensity of war in Lebanon during an extended TM-Sidhi course in Israel during August and September 1983. The number of TM-Sidhi participants accounted for a 45% decrease in war intensity and a 75.9% drop in war deaths. War intensity was measured by content analysis of the nature of the hostilities in Lebanon each day as reported in newspapers. The content of the news report was rated blindly on a five-point scale with '0' indicating "no reported fighting" and '4' indicating "full-scale land battles." As the graph indicates, a high number of participants in the TM-Sidhi course coincided with decreased intensity of conflict in neighboring Lebanon, and vice versa.

A second study found the same results using ten leading international and Lebanese news sources and independent raters, who rated article content unaware of the date of the article.

References: Orme-Johnson, D. W., Alexander, C. N., Davies, J. L., Chandler, H. M., and Larimore, W. E. (1988). International peace project in the Middle East: The effect of the Maharishi Technology of the Unified Field. *Journal of Conflict Resolution*, 32: 776–812. Copyright © 1988 by Sage Publications. Reprinted by permission of Sage Publications.

Davies, J. L. and Alexander, C. N. (1989). Alleviating political violence through enhancing coherence in collective consciousness: Impact assessment analyses of the Lebanon war. Summary of a paper presented at the 85th Annual Meeting of the American Political Science Association, September 1989. (Refer also to: *Dissertation Abstracts International*, 49(8): 2381A, 1988.)

From the point of view of our habitual Newtonian-Cartesian paradigm, such effects are hard to understand. However, if we adopt the quantum mechanical perspective that reality is fundamentally one wholeness, it makes sense that an influence generated at the deepest level of creation will be nonlocal in its effects. The studies that have demonstrated some of the observable manifestations of increasing coherence in an area, have actually done so on the terms of our traditional scientific paradigm. Raymond Russ, Professor of Psychology at the University of Maine and Editor of the *Journal of Mind and Behavior,* made the following comments about two of these studies, which were published in this journal: "The hypothesis definitely raised some eyebrows among our reviewers. But the statistical work was sound. The numbers were there. . . . When you can statistically control for as many variables as these studies do, it makes the results more convincing."[191]

As much as we would like to, we cannot isolate ourselves from the social ills that are around us. Fear of crime, uncertainty about the nation's economic future, tension and hostility in the workplace—all these impact our mind and our body as well. For each of us to enjoy a supreme state of health, the state of health of our society cannot be ignored. The TM-Sidhi program opens up a completely new realm of possibilities for addressing age-old social ills and creating a healthy society.

Chapter Twelve

ACCESSING THE INNER INTELLIGENCE OF THE PHYSIOLOGY

T he regular practice of the TM and TM-Sidhi programs over time restores greater values of wholeness on the level of individual consciousness, mind, and body. These principal healing technologies of the Maharishi Vedic Approach to Health work by restoring the memory of wholeness on the level of individual awareness. These techniques, however, are just two of many therapeutic modalities in the Maharishi Vedic Approach to Health, which all aim at restoring the full value of wholeness and its structuring dynamics of intelligence. As Maharishi says, "Our message to the individual to live a well coordinated, integrated life is 'the intelligence is there inside, within you, which is absolutely, marvellously healthy because it is immortal, it is eternal.' . . . [We only] need to co-ordinate its relationship with its own expression—the physiology."[192] In the following, we will explore another consciousness-based healing modality, which provides a further means of enlivening the totality of the physiology, while also targeting and balancing the specific areas in which wholeness has been lost.

To explore this healing modality, we need to first develop a deeper understanding of the Vedas and the Vedic Literature. In the West, the Vedas have been generally understood as books written by ancient seers, which contain a body of knowledge to be intellectually comprehended. In fact, the Vedas have only recently been recorded in book form; for millennia before that, they had been preserved in the oral tradition of Vedic families. This is an important distinction, because it is in the *sound* value of the Vedas that their real significance is to be found. The Vedas are structured in con-sciousness—the Vedic sounds detail the primordial fluctuations within the unmanifest, eternal field of pure existence. The true meaning of the Vedas therefore is not probed by translating words and interpreting their meaning—it lies in the sounds and the sequence of their expression. The Vedas are the acoustic records of the eternal dynamics of the unmanifest, unified wholeness as it takes on its expression as creative intelligence. One of the early commentators on the Vedas apologized in the introduction to his commentary for 'killing' the Vedas by trying to commit them to intel-lectual understanding. The Vedas can only be fully fathomed when the mind settles into the state of least excitation and merges with the field of pure awareness. The Vedas are not limited to a specific culture or people— as Maharishi points out, they are universal and *Apaurusheya*, 'uncreated.'

Drawing on his own unique insights into the Vedic knowledge, Maharishi has brought out a detailed and complete description of the internal dynamics of the Vedic sounds. As significantly, he has intro-duced techniques that enable the individual to directly experience the Vedic level of reality on the level of their own consciousness. Maharishi explains that the Vedas are the 'fundamental seeds of intelligence,' the dynamic impulses which make up the implicit structure of the unbound-ed field of consciousness. He has further highlighted how every *specific aspect* of the Vedic Literature expresses a specific value of unfoldment of the primordial field of consciousness. In the Maharishi Vedic Approach to Health, this principle is applied by using the Vedic sounds that structure specific areas of the physiology to create balance in these areas. To under-stand how this is possible, we need to understand the structure of the Vedas and the mechanics of their unfoldment.

The unfoldment of the Vedas mirrors the unfoldment of creation, from the initial structuring dynamics of knower (Rishi), known (Chhandas), and process of knowing (Devata), through the increasingly elaborated trans-formation of all possible relationships between subject, object, and the con-nection that links subject and object. The infinite dynamism and eternal silence within the nature of pure self-referral consciousness is embodied in the very structure of the Vedic expressions. Maharishi has brought to light how the initial expression of the Rik Veda, the first of the Vedas, contains in seed form the totality of knowledge of the eternal flow of infinite silence and its collapse into a point. In the same way as the totality of a tree unfolds from the initial structure of knowledge within the seed, the Vedic Literature unfolds in a precise and symmetrical sequence as it details the progression of the self-referral transformation within the nature of pure consciousness. Each progressive expression elaborates and comments on the preceding expressions of the Vedic Literature. This is Shruti, 'that which is heard,' the eternal reverberations generated within the nature of self-referral consciousness, which were cognized by the ancient seers in their own self-referral consciousness. From these primordial frequencies within the nature of pure consciousness arise the forms and phenomena of manifest creation, which in their essence are nothing other than vibrational frequencies, fluctuations of the underlying field of intelligence. As Maharishi explains,

> Different aspects of the Vedic Literature categorize different qualities of consciousness in terms of vibrations or frequencies that are inherent in the holistic value of consciousness. These frequencies of consciousness are the expression of the intelligence that firstly gives rise to the Vedic structure, the structure of Rik Veda, and continues to evolve into particles of matter and different forms of material creation.[193]

Throughout this book, we have contemplated the many expressions of nature's intelligence apparent in living systems. Precisely proportioned and integrated structures of order are equally present in material phenomena as well. At every level of the universe, in every physical structure we find such finely tuned balances that, if the value of even one element was slightly different, the existence of the universe and the life forms within it would be entirely impossible. "[W]e find ourselves in a universe that breeds life and possesses the very particular properties that make that possible," notes Nobel Prize winner George Wald. "The more deeply one penetrates, the more remarkable and subtle the fitness of this universe for life appears. Endless barriers lie in the way, yet each is surmounted somehow."[194]

The entire universe, according to Western science, itself is known to exist in a delicate balance between two forces: a force of continuous expansion, which is brought about by the Big Bang, and a force of contraction or aggregation brought about by gravity. If the force of expansion had been slightly dominant, all matter would have dispersed and there would have been no large planetary bodies where life could emerge. Conversely, if the force of gravity had dominated, the universe would have gradually contracted and eventually collapsed. The fact that these two forces are in *exact* balance, has fulfilled the prerequisite condition for the emergence of life. Note how the delicate balance between the contracting force and expanding force at the level of the cosmos mirrors the precisely tuned balance between expansion and contraction, the simultaneous coexistence of infinity and point, within the nature of pure consciousness. The structure of the Vedas is reflected in the structure of creation. Everything is a reflection and more elaborated value of the three-in-one structure of pure consciousness and the infinite dynamism and eternal silence contained in the coexistence of infinity and point. The Vedas and Vedic Literature are the invisible matrix of the laws of nature that generates what we know as reality. As such, this matrix is lively in every grain of creation, including the human physiology. As Maharishi explains, "the holistic and specific values of the total intelligence of Nature are displayed in the impulses of sound (available in the Veda and Vedic Literature) and are further expressed in the physical aspects of the physiology."[195]

Healing Through Vedic Sounds

One of Maharishi's many contributions in restoring the Vedic knowledge is showing how it is possible, through the Vedic sounds, to access the inner intelligence that upholds the structure of the physiology, and harness it for healing and growth. The structure and function of the physiology itself reflects the sequential unfoldment of the structuring dynamics of intelligence displayed within the Vedas. The Vedas are the expressions of the unseen, 'enfolded' order which 'unfolds' into the dynamics of matter and cells, and brings them into manifestation on the level of reality we perceive with our senses. In the healing process, this order is the implicit principle, the impulses of intelligence that initiate and direct all of the isolated activities that act to restore the whole. Enlivening the impulses of the Vedas in the physiology therefore provides a powerful means of reactivating the healing intelligence in all parts of the body.

The restorative value of the primordial sounds of the Vedic Literature is two-fold—general and specific. Maharishi explains that reading, listening to, or reciting the primordial sounds of the Vedas provides a means of accessing the inner intelligence that structures everything in creation, including the human physiology. When listening to or reciting various aspects of the Vedic Literature and taking the awareness to the transcendent, the physiology over time gets cultured to reflect the total organizing power of pure knowledge within itself. Maharishi describes it in this way:

> [T]hrough daily recitation of the Vedic Literature, the brain physiology of every individual will become habituated to function in the same precise, orderly sequence in which the Samhita is eternally flowing at the unmanifest basis of all creation, spontaneously promoting evolution of all life.
>
> This habituation of the brain physiology to adopt the functioning of Natural Law spontaneously regulates the rise of every feeling, emotion, and thought in the evolutionary direction.[196]

On a specific level, it is also possible to use the primordial sounds of the Vedas to target and restore the functioning of specific areas of the physiology that have become imbalanced. Recall that different values of the universe are the expressions of the specific qualities of consciousness displayed in different aspects of the Vedic Literature. In the same way, different values of the physiology are the expressions of specific qualities of consciousness displayed in different aspects of the Vedic Literature. Therefore, it is possible to use the frequencies of specific parts of the Vedic Literature to enliven the corresponding aspects of the physiology. Dr. Tony Nader, a physician and neuroscientist trained at MIT, has under Maharishi's guidance produced ground-breaking work in discovering the parallels between the structures of the human physiology and the 40 branches which form the structure of the Veda and Vedic Literature.[197] Dr. Nader explains,

> [T]he structure of the various branches of Veda and the Vedic Literature correspond to specific structures in the physiology. These anatomical structures therefore have the same intelligence at their basis as that Intelligence which structures the Vedic sounds to which they correspond.
>
> It is thus reasonable to conclude, as Maharishi explains, that the recitations of the sounds of the Vedic Literature in their proper sequence will resonate with the same anatomic structures to which they correspond. Their specific sequence will also enliven a specific sequence of neuronal, physiological activity. This will induce the physiology to function according to its original and perfect design. Any imperfections in the form of blocks, stress, lack or excess of activity, or abnormal connections between the various components of the physiology, will be disfavoured by reading the specific aspect of Veda and the Vedic Literature that corresponds to that area of the physiology which is disfunctional.
>
> This clearing up and balancing applies to any kind of abnormality, structural or functional. Only the processes that are according to the original perfect design will be enhanced; all aberrations will be cleared out. It is like the rush of a powerful, pure stream which clears any mud or deposit blocking the free flow of a river.
>
> The value of reading the Vedic Literature is thus seen to be the most subtle, profound, and holistic therapeutic approach, and the most complete system of rehabilitation.[198]

To fully appreciate the merit of this approach to healing, it is necessary to shift our perspective on the physiology and recall that our body is not the solid, unchanging structure that we experience it as. In our daily lives, we experience the gross, Chhandas level of the physiology. But as we have seen, this level only serves to obscure the presence of the more fundamental dynamics that give rise to the level of reality we perceive as the physical structure. All of matter is basically vibrational states that take on the appearance of solidity. These vibrational states can be influenced by the fluctuations of the primordial Vedic sounds. The body in essence is a certain vibrational pattern—and this pattern can be affected by the vibrational pattern of the Vedic sounds. In our laboratory at The Ohio State University, the primordial sounds of Sama Veda, one of the four principal Vedas, were found to have an inhibitory effect on the cultured growth of human tumor cells. Playing a recording of Sama Veda in the laboratory incubator decreased the average growth of human tumor cell lines of lung, colon, brain, breast, and skin cancer. Hard rock music, on the other hand, increased the growth rate of these tumor cell lines.[199]

Reading or listening to the primordial Vedic sounds enlivens weak areas of the physiology to the full value of intelligence. It restores the full value of wholeness to areas in which it is not fully expressed due to the overshadowing influence of pragya aparadh. The central aim of each of these healing modalities in this way is to remove the veil that has fallen on pure consciousness.

Chapter Thirteen

THE MANY ROADS TO HEALTH

So far I have emphasized the consciousness-based healing modalities that are introduced in the Maharishi Vedic Approach to Health. The role of mind and consciousness in maintaining and creating health has not been well-understood in the West, yet this dimension of life is essential to healing. No healing process will be complete without addressing imbalances on the most fundamental level of the mind-body system, where consciousness is transformed into the material structure of the physiology.

The emphasis I have put on consciousness-based healing modalities, however, does not imply that therapeutic interventions which focus on the body are not important. The mind-body system forms an indivisible wholeness. The condition of the body impacts the functioning of the mind in the same way as the state of our consciousness and mind are reflected in the functioning of the physiology. The section of the Vedic Literature dedicated to optimizing the functioning of the physiology is Ayurveda. Ayurveda is one of the Upavedas, the four subsidiary Vedas. Whereas the Vedas deal with the inner value of life—the structuring dynamics of natural law in the unbounded field of pure consciousness—the Upavedas deal with matter, the most expressed value of the unfoldment of natural law.

The Maharishi Vedic Approach to Health draws upon the knowledge and techniques contained in the Upavedas for addressing various aspects of matter to enhance human health and happiness. In the following, we will explore the tools and techniques provided by the two Upavedas that deal with structures of matter: Ayurveda, which provides rich insights into the human physiology and the optimization of its functioning, and Sthapatya Veda, whose subject matter is the structures created by man, i.e. our living environment. We will also consider modalities that draw on parts of the Vedic knowledge other than the Upavedas.

In the Introduction, I emphasized the importance of multidimensionality in healing. The single-aimed magic bullet approach of allopathic medicine tends to carry over even into the practice of alternative and complementary medicine. Herbs, nutritional supplements, and single alternative therapies are often used to alleviate symptoms or treat disorders without any attempt to locate and address the deeper reality of the problem. For the process of healing to be complete, the physician must be able to activate and harness all aspects of intelligence involved in the transformation of consciousness into matter. As Maharishi has highlighted in the Maharishi Vedic Approach to Health, the ancient Vedas provide a rich source of therapeutic modalities, each of which provides a different channel for maintaining physiological balance and emotional and mental well-being. In this chapter, therefore, we will walk down a number of these roads to health and explore what they have to offer.

Enhancing the Expressions of Matter in the Human Physiology: The Healing Modalities of Maharishi Ayur-Veda

Each day we expose our body to a wide range of influences, each of which has an impact, for better or worse, on our health. If we are not aware of this, we may—as Larry, in the beginning of the book—adopt habits that, over time, slowly erode our health. And I am not just talking about 'bad habits,' such as smoking or consuming excessive amounts of alcohol. Every single activity we do throughout the day has an impact on our body and hence, over time, on our health. Our daily habits contribute not only to our long-term health status, but even more importantly, to our overall well-being throughout life.

The good news is that this fact can be turned to our advantage— positive lifestyle habits are therapeutic practices in the sense that they strengthen and facilitate the flow of biological intelligence in the body. If we learn to attune ourselves to the body's rhythms and day-to-day needs, we can create a powerful, preventive influence which will ensure that we retain not only health, but vitality and zest for life to a very advanced age.

As I discussed in the Introduction, much of the Vedic knowledge, including Ayurveda, was fragmented, overshadowed, and misinterpreted during years of foreign rule in India. Since the early 1980s, Maharishi has undertaken an extensive revitalization of Ayurveda, drawing on his own profound insights and the knowledge of numerous experts in the diverse aspects of Ayurveda; this comprehensive restoration is known as Maharishi Ayur-Veda. Maharishi Ayur-Veda consists of various therapeutic approaches relating to the human physiology, and reaches its full health-promoting potential as an integral part of the Maharishi Vedic Approach to Health.

In the following, we will review some of the modalities of Maharishi Ayur-Veda, which range from simple lifestyle recommendations to directly focused treatment interventions. To be most effective, each of these approaches should be individually tailored to address the unique makeup of imbalances in a person's psychophysiology, but the underlying principles of each approach are of interest in and of themselves.

The Three Doshas

The common focus of the treatment modalities that work on the level of the body is to purify the body and restore the balance of the three doshas. As we saw in Chapter Nine, the *doshas* are the three basic modes of intelligence involved in all bodily processes. The doshas govern both bodily and psychological functions, and disturbance in a dosha can manifest both on a mental and physiological level. *Vata* dosha is the subtle quality of intelligence that governs all bodily *movement.* With its five subdoshas, it is responsible for such functions as breathing, heart activity, speech, peristalsis, assimilation, elimination, menstruation, labor and delivery, circulation, muscle movement, nervous system activity, and mental clarity. Pitta dosha is responsible for *processes of transformation,* such as metabolism, digestion, absorption, body temperature, and intelligence. Kapha dosha is associated with *structure and lubrication* and is involved in the building of bones, moisturizing of skin, joint lubrication, and stability of mind. Each dosha has several subdoshas that govern specific aspects of physiological functioning.

The physiology of any individual exhibits the three doshas in varying proportions. The constitution of some people is dominated by Vata dosha, whereas others may be predominantly Pitta, and so on. Optimal health derives from the balanced functioning of the three doshas. A disruption in the functioning of one aspect of these modes of intelligence will generate an irregularity in the functioning of the parts of the mind-body system for which it is responsible. An imbalance of Vata dosha, for example, might manifest as a wide range of ailments, such as joint pain, constipation, or nervous aggravation. An imbalance in Pitta dosha could show up as an ulcer, poor absorption, or irritability, among others. An imbalance in Kapha dosha might give rise to obesity, dullness, or a strong tendency toward attachment. Only when the doshas are in the perfect balance that corresponds to our unique dosha proportions will the intelligence of nature be fully expressed in the functioning of both mind and body.

Knowledge of the doshas and their relative state of balance presents a unique means of monitoring the state of the body, and detecting imbalances long before they show up as symptoms of disease. Additionally, if symptoms are already present, assessing the dosha imbalances in a person's body enables the practitioner to pinpoint the underlying cause of the symptoms. Therapies can then be applied that address the physiological imbalance, rather than merely the symptoms themselves.

The principal means of assessing an individual's unique dosha proportions and current state of dosha imbalances is *nadi vigyan*, or pulse diagnosis. To the trained physician, the pulse provides a channel through which he or she can 'listen' to the symphony of the entire body. Through the pulse, the physician learns not only about the state of the bodily organs, but also about the interaction and balance of energies in the mind-body complex. The pulse gives the practitioner a direct feeling for the workings of the doshas at the junction point between consciousness and matter. There is nothing mystical about pulse diagnosis; with sufficient training, it can be learned by anyone. Many individuals find it useful to participate in one of the *self-pulse reading* courses that are offered at Maharishi Ayur-Veda Universities around the country (see Resources section). Self-pulse reading enables one to follow the state of one's physiology on a day-to-day basis. One can then make the necessary lifestyle changes if any dosha or subdosha starts to get out of balance.

TABLE 1. SIGNS OF DOSHA IMBALANCE.

This quick quiz can help you determine which of the three doshas you most need to balance. Put a check mark by each statement that characterizes you and then tally your score for each dosha. The highest of the three scores indicates which dosha you need to pay attention to.

I NEED CALMING	I NEED COOLING	I NEED STIMULATING
These are the signs of Vata imbalance:	*These are the signs of Pitta imbalance:*	*These are the signs of Kapha imbalance:*
❏ I often feel restless, unsettled	❏ I tend to be demanding or critical	❏ I often feel complacent or dull
❏ My sleep comes slowly or is easily interrupted	❏ I'm a perfectionist	❏ My skin is oily to normal
❏ I tend to overexert	❏ I get frustrated or angry easily	❏ I tend to have slow digestion
❏ I'm easily fatigued	❏ I have sensitive skin	❏ I feel lethargic
❏ I tend to be constipated	❏ I get irritable and impatient easily	❏ I can be possessive, over-attached
❏ I feel anxious, and worry too much	❏ My hair is prematurely gray, or thinning	❏ I tend to oversleep
❏ I'm underweight	❏ I don't tolerate hot weather well	❏ I'm overweight

Total Vata   Total Pitta   Total Kapha

Please note that a questionnaire like this of course only gives a very rough indication of the state of your dosha balance. It should not serve as a substitute for a consultation with a physician trained in the Maharishi Vedic Approach to Health.

TABLE 2. PREVENTING DOSHA IMBALANCE.

Imbalances develop as a result of many factors. Check this list to see how you can prevent a dosha imbalance from developing or help correct an existing imbalance.

VATA	PITTA	KAPHA
Keep a calming, regular routine. Here are some tips:	*Moderation is the key. It's best for you to:*	*Stimulation is the key for you to feel better:*
• go to bed early	• avoid excessive heat or exposure to the sun	• avoid excessive rest and over-sleeping
• eat meals at the same time every day	• abstain from alcohol and smoking	• favor spicy, bitter and astringent foods
• have regular elimination	• favor sweet, astringent and bitter foods	• get plenty of exercise
• keep warm in cold weather	• avoid excessive activity	• seek out variety in life
• drink plenty of warm liquids	• finish work on time to avoid stressful deadlines	• don't eat too much heavy, oily food
• avoid stimu-lants	• avoid skipping meals	• keep warm in cold, wet weather
• favor sweet, sour and salty foods	• avoid spicy, sour or salty foods	

Lifestyle Choices As Health Choices

Everything we do in life influences the functioning of the three doshas. According to *Charaka Samhita*, however, there are three activities or lifestyle habits that influence our health more than anything else, because they support physiological functioning on a day-to-day basis. These are known as the three pillars of life: diet, proper rest, and balanced behavior. The main focus of prevention should be on establishing daily health routines that are suitable to the individual's unique dosha proportions and current state of dosha imbalances, and strengthen these three sources of physiological nourishment.

Before we survey the influence of these lifestyle factors on health, a note of caution is in order. It is not easy to change one's lifestyle. Anyone who has tried to lose weight or quit smoking knows that old habits die hard. In most cases, much more is involved than simply deciding to change one's eating habits or stop smoking. For most people, bad habits are compensatory behaviors, the tip of the iceberg beneath which lie all our insecurities, dissatisfactions, frustrations, neuroses, or lack of fulfillment. Any physician knows that for most people to adopt healthier lifestyle habits, more is needed than simply good intentions.

For this reason, the first recommendation often made by a physician trained in the Maharishi Vedic Approach to Health is that the client should start practicing the TM technique. Research studies have demonstrated that regular TM practice leads to *a number of spontaneous* lifestyle changes: people stop smoking, normalize weight, start eating healthier foods, and so on. The TM technique is a key to developing a healthier lifestyle because it changes a person from the inside out, which as we have seen, is the only way that true change can take place. It is the knower that must be the focus of change, not the habits or behaviors that are only the expression of the inner state of the knower. When the knower changes, so does his experience of the world around him, and the need to indulge in compensatory behaviors subsides. Through the regular experience of pure consciousness, one gets in touch with the silent inner core of self-sufficiency and happiness at the source of one's being. As pure consciousness becomes stabilized in one's awareness, a new sense of confidence, self-sufficiency, vitality, and happiness takes center stage. With this, self-destructive or harmful behaviors spontaneously fall away, because the frustration or unhappiness that caused them in the first place no longer remains.

Keep these points in mind as we explore the principles that allow us to strengthen the three pillars of life. If the effort to introduce new behaviors adds strain and tension to the mind and body, it defeats the very purpose of making the change.

The Importance of Diet

Our daily intake of food constitutes the first of the three pillars of life and is the most important. Eating is the fundamental physiological activity that upholds our health on a day-to-day basis; the influence of diet is second only to the influence of consciousness. Food contributes the basic energy and material from which is formed not only our body, but the quality of our mind and intellect as well. All aspects of our daily diet—what we eat, how we eat, and when we eat—are important.

Not only are foods an important source of the nutrients that enable us to stay in good health, they also provide a plethora of healing remedies. Vegetables and fruits are loaded with a drugstore's worth of pharmaceutical activity—tranquilizers, antidepressants, analgesics, laxatives, anti-inflammatory agents, antibiotics, immune stimulators, cholesterol regulators, and cancer inhibitors, to mention just a few. Food can make our brain work faster or make us feel sleepy; it can influence our moods for better or worse; it can slow or speed the aging process. The therapeutic properties of foods are every bit as effective as those of the most sophisticated drugs. They require no expensive technology and do not have to be developed and tested—and they are without side effects.

As with all lifestyle factors, food is a double-edged sword. It can be an important force for disease as well as for health. "Wholesome food is one of the causes for the growth of living beings and unwholesome food for the growth of diseases," notes the ancient Ayurvedic text *Charaka Samhita*.[200] Modern researchers know that five of the ten major causes of death—including heart disease, diabetes, and cancer—are diet-related.[201] In one doctor's estimate, 90 percent of the patients that seek a doctor's help do so for problems related to diet—obesity, clogged arteries, allergies, sore joints, and cancer.[202]

If food is so important, what should we eat? Over the years we have been bombarded with an enormous amount of conflicting dietary advice. Nutritional science is hampered by the complexity of its subject matter—every food is constituted by hundreds or even thousands of organic compounds of which the majority remain unidentified. Furthermore, many plant substances appear to work synergetically and therefore cannot be understood fully by isolating them for study. As if this isn't enough, insight into the nutritional value of foods must include knowledge of their effects in the context of the body's complex metabolic processes. Modern science knows that this effect varies among individuals of different cultures—according to Maharishi Ayur-Veda, it varies even from individual to individual. Our dietary requirements are dosha-specific—they depend on our unique dosha proportions and the specific dosha imbalances we may have. Wholesale dietary recommendations simply don't work for everyone. A person of Vata constitution, for example, needs a certain amount of oil in his or her diet, whereas a person with a Kapha constitution should avoid oily foods.

Eating the *right foods* in the *right quantity* is a potent technique both for preventing disease and for extending our life span. In addition, diet can be used as a therapeutic modality by supplying the specific foods that will pacify imbalanced doshas and subdoshas and neutralize their effects. To address specific health concerns, rapid improvements can result from getting dietary advice that targets specific dosha and subdosha imbalances from a physician trained in the Maharishi Vedic Approach to Health. In addition, there are a few simple rules of thumb that go a long way toward creating a noticeable difference in health and well-being: Rely predominantly on fresh, natural, easily digestible foods, and take measures to strengthen the digestive process.

Natural Foods. In its naturally occurring form, each food item is like a little packet of nature's intelligence, which our body can use to counterbalance disruptive influences from the environment. In modern times, however, most foodstuffs are tarnished by synthetic materials—artificial fertilizers and pesticides leave residues in fruits and vegetables that remain even after washing and peeling. Some 3,000 artificial ingredients are added in the production of the foods that typically fill the supermarket shelves—preservatives, bleaching agents, flavorings, dyes, foaming agents, and moisture protectors. About 12,000 chemicals are used in packaging foods, some of which are absorbed into the foods under certain conditions.

At best, such artificial ingredients are just extra waste materials that the body must devote energy to eliminate. At worst, they interfere with the normal operation of our physiology by generating free radicals, functioning as carcinogens, and/or interfering with our metabolism. Standard scientific trials that seek to evaluate the health hazards of chemicals in our food look at the morbidity associated with a chemical, but fail to consider its influence on our well-being, energy level, and general quality of life. Furthermore, there is no way of knowing to what extent a chemical might interact with and magnify the effects of other chemical additives in our diet. Food additives already have been linked to hyperactivity in children; the most pervasive influences, however, are most likely too subtle to be detected by the standard methodologies available to science.

Another grave health concern is the rapidly expanding use of genetic engineering in the field of agriculture and the biotech industry. This process involves, for example, the transfer of genes from animals, fish, insects, and bacteria into agricultural crops to enhance yield or transfer a 'desirable' quality. The U.S. Department of Agriculture and Food and Drug Administration have decided these genetically modified foods do not require labeling, therefore consumers have no way of knowing if they are eating these altered foods. Many scientists assert that genetically modified foods have not been adequately researched and could cause serious damage to our health and our environment.[203]

The most alarming example, to date, of hazards involved in this area is that of the food supplement tryptophan. A company in Japan genetically manipulated the bacteria used to produce the food supplement tryptophan in order to make them produce larger amounts of this substance. Unknown to them, the genetic alterations also caused the bacteria to produce a powerful toxin. Before the mishap was discovered, 37 people had died and 1500 had become permanently disabled.[204] Genetic engineers have also created more insect-resistant crops by including the introduction of a bacterial gene into potatoes and corn, which creates a toxin that kills insects. This toxin is now produced inside these potatoes and corn. Supposedly, it is deactivated by the acids in our stomach, and research on animals supports this claim. But these studies determined that there were no *immediate* poisonous effects—the *long-term* effects are still unknown. Also, there is concern that these modified vegetables may cause allergies in susceptible people, or poisonous effects in people who take antacids or ulcer medications that reduce stomach acidity. Herbicide-resistant crops have also been created; this allows farmers to spray higher levels of herbicides without damaging the crops. As a result, there is a higher level of contamination of our food, soil, and water with these harmful chemicals. Since labeling is not required on any genetically-modified foods, there will be no way to trace allergic reactions, other toxic effects, or the emergence of new diseases that could result from eating these foods.

For these reasons, it is best to favor fresh, organically grown, unmodified, unprocessed foods in one's diet—ideally prepared in a way that best preserves nutrients, such as steaming or baking. Life begets life. Fresh foods contain more nutrients, both of the kinds already charted by science, and a host of other more unstable, but equally valuable nutrients. As they become less fresh, fruits and vegetables change both in color and taste— one indication that something is lost. Among these unstable constituents are the important compounds known as phytochemicals that, among other things, contribute color and taste to vegetables and fruits. The fresher the food, the more valuable it is in the diet.

It is also good to gradually eliminate stimulants such as sugar and caffeine from one's diet; the physiological and psychological price we pay for their short-lived reward is too high. Caffeine is suspected of contributing to osteoporosis, decreased fertility, and increased risk of miscarriage. The blood sugar rush that sugar creates can give rise to mood swings and anxiety. As one physician puts it, discontinuing the intake of sugar and caffeine can at times accomplish what years of psychotherapy cannot.[205]

In addition, many people find that adhering to a healthy vegetarian dietary regimen carries tremendous rewards. Vegetarian diets are easier to digest and therefore less taxing on the system. Among vegetarians, researchers have found a decreased incidence or severity of cardiovascular disease, cancer, osteoporosis, and diverticular disease. People on a vegetarian diet also run a much smaller risk of having high serum cholesterol levels, high blood pressure, kidney and gallstones, atonic constipation, obesity, and diabetes mellitus.[206] Vegetarians have a lower age-specific mortality rate than non-vegetarians. In a study involving a group of Seventh-day Adventists from California, for example, non-vegetarian men had a 50 percent greater risk of dying from heart disease.[207]

Decreased incidence of chronic diseases and reduced age-specific mortality are only the *measurable* manifestations of the health advantages of adhering to a vegetarian diet. Any vegetarian can relate a host of more immediately gratifying benefits—such as increased vitality, energy, clarity of mind, well-being, and overall better quality of life.

If you like meat, don't *force* yourself to become a vegetarian—just give yourself the chance to experience the psychological and physiological benefits of a healthier lifestyle, and you will find that you spontaneously start favoring more wholesome foods. Don't try to eliminate old habits, just build an alternative habit and allow it to grow. You can start by avoiding eating meat at night, when the digestive fire is very weak. A wholesome eating regimen also stimulates the body's own intelligence. Most people find that as their diet becomes more pure, i.e. free of synthetic and hard-to-digest elements, they develop a keener sense of which foods are good for them and which are not. Healthy eating is a prime tool for growth—growth of happiness, love, optimism, bliss, and the many other positive correlates of optimum health.

The Importance of Digestion. How we eat is as important as what we eat. As one colleague of mine put it, if you had to choose between a healthy diet and a perfect digestion, choose the impeccable digestion. It doesn't matter how wholesome our diet is if foods aren't digested properly; we will not derive the full health-promoting value from them, and in addition, the toxins or excess metabolic wastes that result from imbalanced digestion will gradually undermine our health. Underutilized carbohydrates, for example, can be an etiological factor in diabetes; high mineral concentrations may cause kidney stones or some forms of arthritis; and surplus protein by-products have been implicated in such diseases as osteoporosis and Alzheimer's.

The Ayurvedic term for these by-products of improper digestion and metabolism is *ama*. Ama consists of noxious, toxic substances which result mainly from poorly digested food, environmental chemicals, and negative emotions. According to *Charaka Samhita*, ama is the universal ingredient in the progression of any disease, because it blocks the innumerable minute channels of the body through which nutrients, hormones, neuropeptides, immune system cells, and wastes move. The accumulation of ama also aggravates the doshas, a process which leads to accelerated aging and disease if not arrested.

Bad breath, fatigue, a coated tongue, body odor, and joint pain are all signs of accumulated ama. Signs of poor digestion include feelings of sluggishness—especially after meals—mood swings, constipation, headaches, loss of appetite, loose stools, and gas.

Poor dietary and lifestyle habits, chemical additives, and stress are endemic to the Western culture. They are also a prescription for creating ama. If you feel that your digestion needs to be improved, the best place to start is to consult a physician trained in the Maharishi Vedic Approach to Health. People with different dosha proportions have different digestive abilities, and a properly trained physician can help you develop a greater awareness of the foods that people with your dosha proportions and specific dosha and subdosha imbalances should favor or steer clear of.

In addition, there are a few simple recommendations that go a long way in aiding the digestive process. It is best, for example, to eat the heaviest meal around noon, when the digestive fire is strongest. Similarly, it is advisable to eat as light as possible in the evening, when the digestive fluids and gut activity are decreased in preparation for the night's rest. Nothing facilitates digestion and assimilation as much as simply chewing one's food thoroughly. Ice-cold drinks should be avoided at mealtimes; they tax the system by quenching the digestive fire.

It is important to only eat when one is hungry. Hunger is a signal that the previous meal has been fully digested. The digestive process is a highly precise sequence which takes three to four hours, depending on how heavy the meal was. If the stomach has to deal with new material halfway through the sequence, the body has to start over again with some foods while still processing others. This is a sure way to create imbalance in a very delicately tuned physiological process. It is also best to eat at the same time each day, and to fill one's stomach only to three-quarters of its capacity—*Charaka Samhita* emphasizes that intake of food in excessive quantity causes serious types of indigestion.

The emotional backdrop of the meal is important as well. The atmosphere should be pleasant and settled; discussing business or indulging in any other activity that might create tension is simply not a good idea. Eating should be a special occasion approached with reverence, not something done while watching TV, negotiating business deals, or rushing out the door.

Alignment to Nature's Cycles

Everything in nature functions in cycles. There is the diurnal cycle of day turning into night and night into day, the annual cycle of seasons changing from one to another, cycles of activity and growth, and cycles of rest and integration. As a part of nature, the functioning of our body is linked to the daily cycle of night and day, and to the seasonal changes around us. Countless natural cycles in our body synchronize with our environment, fluctuating in distinctive patterns dictated by circadian or other environmental rhythms. Hormone production has its own rhythm, as does DNA synthesis; the concentrations of biochemicals change continuously in a complex, but highly regular pattern; immune system activity, metabolism and digestion, body temperature, and kidney and liver function vary dramatically in any given 24-hour period.

Our dosha proportions, diet, and lifestyle all interact with these daily rhythms and with seasonal changes. Each period of the day is dominated by a specific dosha. Vata dosha dominates the time from 2 am to 6 am and again from 2 pm to 6 pm. Kapha takes over from 6 am to 10 am and from 6 pm to 10 pm, whereas Pitta dosha is lively in the interval from 10 am to 2 pm and from 10 pm to 2 am. Each season, likewise, is dominated by a different dosha. In a temperate climate, the cold, dry, windy weather of late autumn and winter (mid-October to mid-March) is Vata season—its qualities will tend to accumulate Vata in the physiology. This must be counterbalanced by appropriate Vata-pacifying measures to avoid aggravated Vata. In the spring, from mid-March to mid-June, Kapha dosha dominates, and the period from summer to early autumn (mid-June to mid-October) is considered Pitta season.

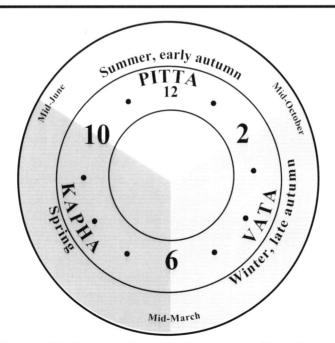

FIGURE 1. THE DAILY AND SEASONAL CYCLES OF THE THREE DOSHAS.

At the change of seasons, greater adaptive demands are placed on the body, and this time can be associated with increased susceptibility to disease if one is not careful to take precautions. To establish harmony between our individual rhythms and those of nature, Maharishi Ayur-Veda recommends specific daily and seasonal routines suited to the cycles of the day, the season, and the individual's unique dosha proportions and imbalances. Nothing is so taxing on the body as an erratic, constantly changing schedule. To maintain health and to slow the aging process, both regularity of schedule and living in accord with the natural cycles that support our physical existence are very important.

The main focus of the Ayurvedic daily routine, or *dinacharya,* is to help restore and maintain physical and mental purity. Rising early, even before dawn, is considered ideal. The day's first activity should consist of a number of purificatory procedures—massage and exercise to mobilize and expel metabolic waste products; removal of internal wastes by urinating and moving the bowels (without forcing); removal of external wastes by showering, brushing the teeth, and scraping the tongue if it is coated.

The most important part of the daily routine is to maintain a proper balance in the rest and activity cycle. Of all the rhythmical cycles that constitute the progression of time, none is more important than the sleep/wake system. Researchers consider it equal in importance to the major systems of the body, i.e. the circulatory, digestive, and reproductive systems. Unfortunately, the sleep/wake system is also the most neglected. Ninety percent of people in modern industrialized societies may suffer from chronic sleep debt,[208] a condition that is known to cause increased susceptibility to infectious disease and increased incidence of gastrointestinal disorders and cardiovascular disease.[209,210] Sleep deprivation lies behind one of every five highway accidents, and costs U.S. industry an estimated 70 billion dollars a year in reduced alertness in the workplace.[211]

The most immediate detrimental effect of chronic sleep debt is on our mood. Women who sleep seven hours or less have been found to experience

12 times as much nervous apprehension, seven times as much fatigue, and five times as much tension as women who get at least eight hours of sleep.[212] We all know how the psychological impairment and negativity associated with fatigue affect our social and family life—tiredness seems to bring out the worst in us. Many divorces could be avoided if the partners were able to maintain a restful, balanced, and health-enhancing daily routine.

"Happiness, misery, nourishment, emaciation, strength, weakness, virility, sterility, knowledge, ignorance, life and death—all these occur depending on the proper or improper sleep," notes the *Charaka Samhita*.[213] Sleep serves an important restorative function; its purpose is like that of the diet—to provide nourishment. Sleep gives the mind a chance to rest. In the same way as the body needs time to recuperate and rest, the mind cannot process sensory information nonstop. "When the mind including sensory and motor organs is exhausted and they dissociate themselves from their object, then the individual sleeps," explains Charaka.[214]

Too little sleep or irregular sleep patterns will cause aggravation of Vata and Pitta doshas. Vata dosha is also known as the king dosha. It has the dubious distinction of being responsible for four times as many diseases as, for example, Kapha dosha. As if this wasn't enough, aggravated Vata also causes the other doshas to go out of balance. When Vata dosha is strongly vitiated, it often causes restlessness and disturbed sleep patterns. Our fast-moving modern society is a Vata-aggravating environment. Irregular routines, long commutes and frequent travels, erratic and rushed eating habits, deadlines, and sleep deprivation are all too familiar characteristics of modern living. These are also precisely the things that will aggravate Vata dosha. So it should come as no surprise that sleep disorders are now epidemic. In the U.S., about one of every three adults has a sleep disorder, which could be: trouble falling or staying asleep; poor quality, non-restorative sleep associated with excessive daytime fatigue; disorganized and aberrant sleeping patterns; or other sleep disorders, such as sleep walking and sleep apnea.

As are all other bodily functions, the 'health' of the sleep-wake cycle is linked to how we treat our body. In the same way as the functioning of the cardiovascular system and immune system is influenced by health habits, the functioning of the sleep-wake system is tied to lifestyle habits and to a person's mental, physical, and emotional condition. Illicit drugs, many medications, alcohol, and smoking are all known to be associated with sleep disorders. So is an erratic and irregular lifestyle and poor eating habits, especially eating heavily in the evening. In addition, mental or emotional tension is one of the most common causes of sleep problems.

Sleep problems may be transient, emerging in response to specific stressful life events such as exams, a family crisis, or work pressure. Long-term sleep disorders indicate deeper imbalances in Vata and Pitta doshas, and are best remedied by consulting a physician trained in the Maharishi Vedic Approach to Health, who can give general advice and recommend Maharishi Ayur-Veda herbal mixtures that help calm the mind and pacify the doshas involved in creating the sleep disturbance.

Aids for inducing good sleep include an Ayurvedic oil massage, maintaining a tranquil, pleasant atmosphere in the bedroom (not watching TV while in bed, for example), engaging in relaxing activities in the evening, such as listening to music or reading something uplifting, and eating a light evening meal. Stay away from caffeine—even caffeine-containing beverages taken in the afternoon can keep one awake at night. If sleep doesn't come, it is best to simply lie and rest in the bed, trying to think of things that bring happiness. The body gets valuable rest just lying in bed, and knowing this, one can be patient and enjoy. Getting up to do one's taxes or reading a novel might be tempting, but inevitably it results in fatigue the next day. It is also far better not to succumb to the temptation of taking a drug to fall asleep. Sleeping pills inhibit REM sleep, a certain phase of sleep which might be the most important part of the sleep period. Drugs may result in habituation, and short-duration drugs can even increase insomnia during the later parts of the night as their effects wear off. The effects of long-duration drugs carry over into the day and diminish mental clarity.

Our need for sleep changes as we age. Whereas a child of ten might need nine or ten hours of sleep, it is perfectly normal for a person over 60 to sleep only six to seven hours a day. The reason is that different periods of our life are dominated by different doshas—from birth to 16, a person will sleep more because Kapha dosha is predominant. From 16 to about 60, sleep will be more moderate, often seven to eight hours a night, because Pitta exerts greater influence on the system. After 60, we enter the period which is dominated by Vata, and our need for sleep is reduced to typically around six hours a night. Likewise, our need for sleep may vary according to the dosha that dominates our psychophysiology. A person with a dominance of Kapha dosha may need nine hours of sleep at night, whereas a Vata-predominant person might need only seven.

For people with sleep disorders, practice of the TM program is a lifesaver. The deep emotional and mental calm that develops with the practice turns out to also be a formula for good sleep. Studies have shown that insomniacs overcome their sleep problems within a few weeks or months of starting the TM practice, and these changes are lasting.[215]

Balanced Behavior

The health effects of diet and sleep are intuitively quite obvious—we have all experienced them ourselves. Far more elusive are the effects of behavior and our general interaction with the environment. Although this area of life doesn't usually fall into the category of influences on our health, it matters a great deal. Everything in life affects our health. We get material for the reconstruction of the body through the food we eat, but also on a more subtle level, through the energy we take in mentally and emotionally. The 'drama of life' as it is played out on the screen of our mind is 'metabolized' and transformed into physiological reality. Every thought, every emotion, every experience is associated with a unique pattern of neuronal and biochemical activity. Even the most fleeting of thoughts transforms the psychophysiology in one direction or another, moving literally millions of molecules in fractions of a second. The biochemical signature of negative emotions is imbalanced neurotransmitters, excess adrenaline, and a host of other apparently innocuous changes which over time undermine health and well-being. On the other hand, positive emotions evoke physiological processes which support our well-being and health.

The key term when we consider behavior is *moderation*. Too much of any one thing will overload and unbalance the physiology. Too much sensual pleasure is best avoided; according to Ayurveda, it causes a depletion of *shukra dhatu*. Shukra dhatu is the subtle end product of the metabolic process; it is sometimes roughly translated as semen, but the term really refers to the subtlest physical essence of our bodies. This essence is closely linked to our sense of vitality and zest for life, so depleting it will take some of the charm out of life and, over time, weaken the system.

According to *Charaka Samhita*, overuse or misuse of any one of the five senses can also have serious effects on our health. Wrong utilization of sight, states Charaka, is to "see things that are awful or terrifying, frightful, deformed or alarming." Wrong utilization of hearing is the "hearing of harsh words, news about the death of friends, assaulting, insulting and terrifying sounds." Charaka's words might sound slightly archaic to modern ears, but think about it. We have all had the experience of someone talking harshly to us, and we know that it affects us not only emotionally but physiologically as well, making our heart race or tying our stomach into a knot. Likewise, seeing an act of violence, even if only on TV, creates an unwholesome effect as the biochemical pattern of the brain starts to reflect the quality of the experience. We may not notice this if we have become habituated to such experiences over many years. However, such habituation leads to a gradual coarsening of the mind. If the mind is repeatedly exposed to unhealthy states of experience, it becomes dominated by this mode of functioning and is thereby unable to reflect the more delicate states of mental experience associated with peace, joy, happiness, and calmness.

There are many activities which promote happiness and a healthy psychophysiology—these are known as behavioral rasayanas. The term *rasayana* means 'putting in the essence of life' and it usually refers to Ayurvedic herbal mixtures used for balancing the doshas and subdoshas. Behavioral rasayanas strengthen life by creating positive emotions and experiences, which promote the production of *ojas*, a vital substance that creates balance and health in our physiology. The behavioral rasayanas are actions and attitudes to be aspired to in various areas of life; by favoring them when one has a choice, they will promote the purity and clarity of the mind and aid in the development of consciousness. Refined emotions and a positive, loving approach to life are qualities that develop over time, from the inside out, through a deep integration of mind and body. The most important trigger of this process is the regular experience of pure consciousness.

There are many behavioral rasayanas; here are a few examples:

Interpersonal Relations. 'Do not entertain negativity.' It is good to avoid getting caught up in any negative emotion, be it anger, hostility, cynicism, or indignation, no matter how justified it may seem. This does not mean that one should suppress emotions as they come up—it is not good to curtail the natural response to a situation. We do have the option, however, to refrain from subtly encouraging a negative emotion over time. If a negative feeling comes up, *allow* it to go—it is in the letting go that our choice lies. It is best to invest one's energy in thoughts and actions that help the growth of positivity, and whenever possible, to make a choice for happiness. Bliss is the best recipe for eliminating ama.

'Keep the company of the wise.' We are influenced by the environment and people around us in many more ways than we realize. Our perception, judgement, choice of activities, and lifestyle habits are all affected in both subtle and obvious ways by the people with whom we spend time. Choosing to be with those who uplift and inspire us leads us to strive for greater knowledge, consideration of others, charity, and wisdom.

Speech. 'Speak the truth, but speak it sweetly'—i.e. in such a way that no pain is caused to anyone. Speaking the truth discourages deviousness, deceit, and other mental modes that complicate and muddle the mind.

Maintaining personal integrity enhances self-esteem and self-confidence. In addition, speaking well of others allows us to highlight their best qualities in our own mind. Everyone is a mixture of qualities, and for one's own sake, it is important not to freeze a person into a narrow mode based on one's own limited perception. By emphasizing other people's positive qualities, we create a positive psychophysiological state for ourselves; by highlighting their faults, we allow their shortcomings to be reflected in our psychophysiological functioning.

Cleanliness. 'Observe cleanliness in all things'—mentally, physically, environmentally. Adhering to daily and seasonal purifying routines will help maintain the internal purity of the body and curb the accumulation of ama. Practicing the TM technique twice a day will help purify the mind of negative impressions and stress. Maintaining a clean, dignified, and beautiful environment will uplift and inspire the mind, and create the positive emotions and sense of comfort and well-being that are health-inducing.

Charity. 'Be charitable in all areas of life.' Adopt an attitude of giving, whether it be sharing one's knowledge, giving advice, donating money to charities, or something as simple as a smile of encouragement. Such actions ultimately benefit oneself. No matter how small or great the gift, it directs one's attention and channels energy in a positive way. That energy is as valuable for our own healing as it is for that of others.

Spirituality. 'Follow the precepts of your spiritual beliefs.' Devoting time for spiritual practices that one finds appealing provides a beautiful channel for the heart to flow and our devotional nature to unfold. The higher emotions associated with heartfelt and balanced spiritual practice are the most noble and refined that humans can experience. To support and inspire these emotions, the psychophysiology must maintain a high level of integrated functioning.

Therapeutic Vehicles: Purification Techniques and Herbal Remedies

Lifestyle modifications should form the backbone of any program for creating better health. If our daily habits are such that they consistently undermine our health, therapeutic interventions will only slow the slide toward the disease-end of the health-disease continuum; they will not truly create health. Each of us is to a great extent the master of our own destiny—we can take responsibility for adopting daily habits that support and enhance health rather than undermine it. When done gradually, the process of adopting healthier lifestyle habits is a joyful one—a discovery of renewed energy and zest for life, new possibilities and potential as the mind-body system gets rid of imbalances and impurities that have hampered its functioning for a long time.

Therapeutic modalities also have an important role to play, however. Carefully targeted interventions are crucial in eliminating dosha and sub-dosha imbalances, especially when symptoms of disease are present. Even for the person of average health, therapeutic modalities provide a vehicle for moving further toward the health-end of the health-disease continuum. This can be an important part of the process of adopting a healthier lifestyle, because the more healthy we become, the more obvious will be the effects of negative health habits.

In the following, I will describe two therapeutic vehicles used in Maharishi Ayur-Veda—techniques that purify the body and eliminate the result of imbalanced dosha activity, and herbal remedies that strengthen the body and target specific imbalances.

Purification Techniques

The technique for purifying and balancing the physiology is known as *panchakarma*. Translated as 'the five actions,' panchakarma is a medley of treatments that all aim to clear impurities from the body and balance the doshas. The panchakarma treatments first dislodge ama from the cells and channels of the body, then flush it out through the organs of elimination—

the sweat glands, intestines, and urinary tract. The main focus of pan-chakarma is to clear the bodily channels, or *shrotas*. There are innumer-able shrotas in the body; some are large and well-known, such as the respiratory channel, the food channel (from stomach to large intestine), and the channels responsible for elimination of wastes. Most shrotas, how-ever, are tiny channels through which the entire activity of the body flows—immune defense units, biochemical messengers, waste materials, oxygen, nutrients, and the subtle form of biological intelligence known as *prana*. The shrotas provide the infrastructure for the flow of the dynam-ic processes that make up the body. If these channels are blocked by ama, the flow of bodily intelligence becomes restricted, leading to 'dark' areas where disease can develop and grow.

The structure of the panchakarma treatment varies from client to client, but in general a person starts out with a preparatory oleation treat-ment, or *snehana*, i.e. intake of large quantities of ghee (clarified butter) over several days in order to loosen impurities at the cellular level. This is followed by a purgative to flush out the toxins. The actual panchakarma treatment starts with *abhyanga*, an herbalized oil massage in which the client is rubbed with oil from head to toe. The mechanical pressure of the massage increases circulation and helps move excess doshas toward the central area of the body where they can then be eliminated through the intestinal tract. Because of its soothing, calming influence, abhyanga also helps balance Vata dosha. After abhyanga, the patient undergoes one or more of the following treatments, which are prescribed according to his or her constitution and specific imbalances. *Swedana*, an herbalized steam bath, further increases the circulation through the periphery of the body and helps loosen more impurities. People with aggravated Vata dosha gen-erally receive *shirodhara*, during which warm sesame oil is poured in a slow stream on the forehead; this treatment is surprisingly relaxing and sooth-ing. The *nasya* treatment is helpful in removing excess Kapha and is said to nourish the senses, brain, and eyes; it consists of an herbalized oil massage of head, neck, and shoulders, combined with steam inhalation and herbalized oil drops taken into the nostrils.

FIGURE 2. THE SHIRODHARA TREATMENT
This treatment is often used in panchakarma to create a deeply calming influence on mind and body, and helps release deep-rooted mental tension.
Photo courtesy of The Raj Health Center, Fairfield, Iowa.

Most treatment routines are capped with *basti*, an herbalized enema which eliminates the impurities that have been disposed to the intestinal tract during the other treatments. Basti strikes at the root of imbalanced Vata, whose main seat is in the colon. When aggravated Vata is balanced in the colon, vitiated Vata in other parts of the body is automatically alleviated.

Additional therapies employed along with panchakarma at Maharishi Ayur-Veda clinics include dosha-specific aromatherapy and Maharishi Gandharva Veda℠ music therapy. Gandharva Veda is another of the Upavedas; it is the ancient science of the use of sound to create harmonious effects in the environment, or to smooth the transitions in the progression of nature's daily and seasonal cycles. In the field of health, researchers have long known that music has numerous positive effects on the body, and in the West music therapy is used, for example in the treatment of pain. The benefits of Maharishi Gandharva Veda music go far beyond this, however. When precisely targeted, these subtle vibrations of sound can balance aggravated doshas, soothe the mind-body, and promote psychophysiological integration. Maharishi Gandharva Veda recordings can be integrated into one's daily routine to create a harmonious influence at various times of the day. This profound music is also an important part of the panchakarma treatment, as it smooths and facilitates the subtle inner restructuring of the physiology that is taking place.

A typical panchakarma treatment takes about two hours per day. The length of the treatment can vary from three to 14 days, depending on the individual's constitution. For maximum effect, a person should receive panchakarma several times a year, preferably at the change of seasons. However, many people find that even three days once a year makes a difference. Pilot studies have shown that panchakarma retards the aging process and improves both mental and physical health, including improvement in cardiovascular risk factors.[216] Participants report greater well-being and emotional stability, increased energy, vitality, and youthfulness, better appetite and digestion, and improvement in physical symptoms present prior to the treatment.

Rasayanas—The Bearers of Life

The Ayurvedic *materia medica* is enormous, containing knowledge of literally thousands of medicinal plants and herbal mixtures. Some of these are mild in their action, while others have more potent and specific effects. Among the mild medicinal herbs are several well-known spices and plants, which can easily be adopted as part of one's home pharmacy. Turmeric, for example, is an excellent blood purifier and is also useful for eliminating excess mucus from a sore throat. Ginger is an excellent digestive; nothing fans the digestive fire as much as a bite of fresh ginger with a bit of lemon juice before a meal. The cooling effect of aloe vera juice is helpful for Pitta disorders and is especially soothing and beneficial during hot spells in the summer. Licorice tea is good for balancing Vata, and peppermint is good for Pitta and Kapha. Black pepper, cinnamon, cayenne, ginger, and clove are all useful for removing ama. Integrated into one's daily diet, these spices and herbs provide a sort of 'apple a day' that helps ward off disease-causing influences.

For deeper dosha imbalances and specific disorders, however, the Ayurvedic physician turns to herbal rasayanas, the 'holy healers' of Ayurveda. Rasayanas are potent herbal mixtures that strengthen the physiology and target imbalances. They can best be described as 'tuning forks,' packets of vibrations that resonate with certain parts or systems of the body and help 'reset' the vibrations of the biological intelligence in that area. As Maharishi explains,

> As the basis of physiology and behaviour is the field of consciousness, or intelligence, within the body of everyone, it is clear that the quality of inner intelligence promotes the corresponding level of physiology. This means that *every state of physiology has a corresponding quality of inner intelligence.* This is true in the case of the human physiology and it is also true in the case of the physiology of plants.

Considering the physiology of a plant, there is the physiology of the root, stem, leaf, flower, and fruit; at each level the inner intelligence has a specific quality.

The knowledge of Natural Law available in the Veda and Vedic Literature identifies the quality of intelligence of the root, leaf, or flower of any specific plant in terms of its favourable reaction with the intelligence of a particular area of the physiology in order to revitalize intelligence in favour of balance.

. . . [W]hen the knowledge of Natural Law is properly applied, the matching quality of intelligence within the physiology and within the plant will create a balancing effect, and the balanced functioning of the physiology will be restored.[217]

In the wake of the British occupation of India, only a few individuals were truly knowledgeable about the full range of Ayurvedic herbs. Maharishi spent many years working together with some of the remaining experts on herbal mixtures to create a series of Maharishi Ayur-Veda rasayanas. These are now available to help support and improve almost any bodily function, and they are an important part of the healing repertoire of vaidyas and physicians trained in the Maharishi Vedic Approach to Health. A single rasayana may contain up to 50 ingredients, each of which is handled in the traditionally prescribed way during harvest and preparation to retain maximum potency.

Of all the Maharishi Ayur-Veda rasayanas, the most well-known and well-researched is Maharishi Amrit Kalash™, which comprises two rasayanas known as Maharishi Amrit Kalash-4 and Maharishi Amrit Kalash-5. These rasayanas were developed in collaboration with three of the most prominent experts on Ayurvedic medicinal plants in modern India: the late Dr. V.M. Dwivedi, former Vice-Chairman of the Ayurveda Pharmacopoeia Committee, Government of India; Dr. Brihaspati Triguna, former president of the All-India Ayurveda Congress; and Dr. Balraj Maharshi, Chief Adviser for Ayurveda, Andhra Pradesh Government (India), and a preeminent Ayurvedic herbalist who, training for more than

40 years in the Himalayas, developed personal familiarity with more than 6000 medicinal plants. Dr. Balraj Maharshi was especially responsible for restoring the formula for Maharishi Amrit Kalash-5, which had been lost in its original form.

Amrit Kalash is a Sanskrit name which means *vessel of immortality*, and it is the most renowned of all the rasayanas described in the ancient Vedic texts. Maharishi Amrit Kalash-4 (MAK-4) is in paste form, and Maharishi Amrit Kalash-5 (MAK-5) is in tablet form. The two mixtures complement each other, and between them contain more than two dozen herbs and dried fruits. Some are commonly known, such as licorice, turmeric, cinnamon, and cardamom. Others are rather rare Ayurvedic herbs, such as Indian pennywort, heart-leaved moonseed, butterfly pea, Indian gallnut, trumpet flower, Uraria pitch, Bengal quince, Cashmere bark, and many others.

My initial interest in Maharishi Ayur-Veda was stimulated by a series of research studies I and my colleagues conducted on the general health-promoting and specific disease-preventing properties of Maharishi Amrit Kalash. In studies carried out at South Dakota State University using laboratory animals, we found that MAK is highly effective in preventing the formation of chemically-induced breast cancer. In addition, when the 'control' animals (animals used for comparison, which were not originally fed MAK) with tumors were fed MAK, the tumors shrank or disappeared completely in nearly two thirds of the cases.[218] A study on animals carried out at Indiana University showed that MAK-4 reduces the size and number of metastatic nodules of an aggressive form of lung cancer.[219] A study has also been conducted on cultured cell lines of neuroblastoma, a neurological cancer that strikes in childhood. The results revealed that MAK-5 is able to reverse the malignant process, so that the tumor cells revert back to cells with normal morphological and functional properties.[220]

These impressive results may in part be due to the immune system-enhancing properties of Maharishi Amrit Kalash. In studies carried out at the University of Kansas and Indiana University, we found that animals treated with MAK-5 had a 32 to 88 percent increase in the induced production of immune system cells known as lymphocytes, compared to control animals.[221] A study conducted in Japan confirmed these results for MAK-5, and showed that MAK-4 has the same immune-enhancing effect.[222] In addition, MAK-4 was shown to significantly increase stimulated spleen cell production of interleukin-2, a protein involved in regulation of the immune system.[223] Animals fed MAK-4 or MAK-5 have also shown enhanced production of nitric oxide in activated macrophages, another type of immune system cell. Nitric oxide is used by macrophages to destroy tumor cells and invading bacteria.[224,225] Many people who take MAK on a regular basis report reduced susceptibility to infections and decreased allergy symptoms—this may be due to the beneficial effects MAK has on the immune system.

In addition to the cancer prevention and treatment properties of MAK, several studies have shown that MAK reduces the toxic side effects of chemotherapy treatment. A clinical pilot study showed that use of MAK-4 and MAK-5 in patients undergoing intensive combination chemotherapy decreased blood toxicity and lipid peroxide (a marker of free radical damage; see below for more on free radicals) levels, as well as vomiting and diarrhea. These patients also experienced improvements in sleep, weight, and overall well-being.[226] Studies on lab animals have shown that MAK decreases toxic side effects of the chemotherapeutic drugs Adriamycin[227] and cisplatin.[228]

Undoubtedly, one of the mechanisms of MAK's beneficial effects is its remarkable ability to scavenge free radicals. These chemically unstable atoms or molecules arise in part as a byproduct of the normal metabolism of the body, and they are capable of causing severe damage if not held in check. The body has its own mechanisms for neutralizing free radicals; however, several factors may cause free radicals to be produced faster than the body can scavenge them. Some of these factors are: smoked and barbecued foods, peroxidized fats in meats and aged cheeses, processed foods, alcohol, cigarette smoke, certain drugs, pesticides, air pollution, overexposure to the sun, and chemotherapy.[229] When the balance is tipped in favor of free radicals, they wreak extensive havoc in the physiology, causing damage to key components such as DNA, proteins, and the lipids in cell membranes.

The excessive generation of free radicals has been linked to almost every chronic disease imaginable, including cancer, heart disease, stroke, emphysema, maturity-onset diabetes, rheumatoid arthritis, ulcer, cataract, and Crohn's disease, to mention just a few. The well-known Japanese biochemist and free radical researcher Dr. Yukie Niwa estimates that at least 85 percent of chronic and degenerative diseases are the result of oxidative (free radical-induced) damage.[230] Excessive free radicals are also known to accelerate the aging process and lead to the onset of senility.

When Dr. Niwa conducted chemical analyses of the herbs in Maharishi Amrit Kalash, he found that these mixtures are rich in low-molecular-weight substances that are well-known antioxidants (substances that help prevent free radical damage), such as vitamin C, vitamin E, beta-carotene, polyphenols, bioflavonoids, and riboflavin. Dr. Niwa also found that MAK scavenges free radicals more effectively than any of the 500 substances he has tested over the course of 30 years. In a laboratory study we conducted at The Ohio State University, MAK was shown to be 1000 times more potent than vitamin C, vitamin E, or the pharmaceutical antioxidant probucol, in preventing oxidation of human low-density lipoprotein (LDL).[231] Other laboratory studies have shown that MAK effectively scavenges many different types of free radicals.[232]

Free radicals are etiological factors in the development of atherosclerosis, the disease commonly known as 'hardening of the arteries.' The oxidation of LDL, the 'bad' cholesterol, plays a significant role in this form of heart disease. In a clinical study we conducted at The Ohio State University, patients with high levels of cholesterol were given MAK as a dietary supplement. These patients showed a substantial increase in the resistance of their LDL to oxidation.[233] An investigation conducted on 'Watanabe heritable hyperlipidemic' rabbits, which are genetically predisposed to extremely high cholesterol levels and severe atherosclerosis at a young age, showed that the rabbits fed MAK-4 had an increased resistance to LDL oxidation and an astonishing 53 percent reduction in atheroma (the plaque which lines atherosclerotic blood vessels).[234] An additional factor which contributes to atherosclerosis is blood platelet aggregation; MAK-5 has been shown to decrease platelet aggregation induced in the laboratory by several different substances.[235] A clinical study conducted in India also revealed that MAK decreases the occurrence of angina pectoris, a heart condition characterized by severe chest pain.[236]

The results of this extensive research conducted on Maharishi Amrit Kalash indicate it has valuable health-promoting and disease-preventing properties. It has the beneficial effects one would expect from the ancient Vedic formula for this 'ambrosia of immortality.'

Handling Matter on the Level of Structure: Creating a Health-Promoting Living Environment through Maharishi Sthapatya Veda

The domain of Maharishi Ayur-Veda treatments is matter in the form of the human physiology. Just as our health habits and daily activities create an influence on our body and mind, everything in our surroundings creates an effect as well. Matter, in the form of the structures that humans build—be they houses, sculptures, institutions, or whole cities—is the domain of another of the Upavedas, Sthapatya Veda.

As in the case of Ayurveda, the knowledge of Sthapatya Veda remained fragmented and scattered after the British occupation of India, and Maharishi has worked with leading experts in Sthapatya Veda to restore this important body of knowledge.

The purpose of the Maharishi Sthapatya Veda® program is to bring every aspect of the individual's 'built' environment into harmony with the laws of nature—the supreme intelligence that comprises all the mechanics of transformation in the universe. Everything in the universe is part of the same wholeness, and sharing a common source, simultaneously interacts with everything else. We are part of nature, not separate from it; yet modern man is increasingly oblivious to the subtle workings of the infinite order that breathes life into life. As Dr. Noel Brown, Director of the U.N.'s Environmental Programs comments, "We need to develop a better sense of connectedness with all of life, and when that reverence is developed I think we will find ourselves more at home and at peace in this world."[237]

The secret of this "connectedness with all of life" is the alignment of human life with the subtle mechanics of nature's intelligence. On the level of consciousness, this is achieved by purifying our mind through such practices as the TM and TM-Sidhi programs, which help expand our immediate awareness of the fundamental unity of creation. These programs structure the ability to act spontaneously in accord with the subtle laws of intelligence that govern the unfoldment of creation. On the level of the body, we can align ourselves with the laws of nature that guide physiological functioning by adopting habits and activities that enhance health rather than produce disease. On the level of structures and buildings, we can achieve harmony with nature through designs that respect and optimize nature's resources, and create a living environment attuned to the progression of nature's daily and seasonal cycles.

As we have seen throughout this book, progress unaligned with the subtle dynamics of nature's intelligence brings unfortunate and often dangerous side effects in its wake. In allopathic medicine, this is evidenced in the debilitating side effects of drugs and the sharp rise in iatrogenic, or physician-induced, disease and death. In our living environment, technological advances have brought us skyscrapers, air conditioning, and a host of other modern comforts. It has also brought us toxic building materials, polluted air, and crowded, stressful working and living spaces.

The most common ailment of today's living environment is known as the 'sick building syndrome.' Buildings are constructed using synthetic dyes, paints, glues (in wood products), and carpets, and are sealed tight to preserve heating and air conditioning. As a result, toxic fumes emitted from the synthetic materials are trapped inside. This is not a trivial concern, as indoor pollutants generated from synthetic or chemically treated materials in many cases far exceed the highest levels of outdoor pollutants in cities.[238] Whereas people sensitive to chemical pollutants will be the first to fall victim to this indoor pollution, long-term exposure to high levels of indoor pollution may eventually undermine the health of anyone living or working in the structure.[239]

Many researchers feel that the effect of low-level electromagnetic fields emitted from high voltage power lines, video display terminals, and electric blankets is another cause of concern. Countless processes at the cellular and subcellular levels function via delicately balanced electric signals, and it is easy to imagine the havoc that long-term exposure to outside electrical fields can wreak on these processes. Exposure to low-level electromagnetic fields has been linked to male breast cancer and childhood leukemia, lymphoma, and tumors of the nervous system.[240]

The knowledge of Maharishi Sthapatya Veda provides tools and techniques for creating living spaces that promote the health and welfare of the individual and the environment as a whole.[241] The fundamental focus is on the integration of man and nature by creating a living environment in which each element is designed in accord with the laws of nature that guide man's life and his interaction with the environment. Once we act in accord with natural law, rather than against it, we can use nature's bounty for maximum health and gain in life.

Emphasis is put on the use of natural materials, not only in buildings, but in carpets and furniture as well. Materials derived from nature are more beneficial for the people working or residing in the structure, and they are healthy for our global living environment as well, since less toxic waste material is created during their manufacture.

Another important consideration in Maharishi Sthapatya Veda is on creating an energy-efficient living environment with adequate circulation of fresh air. Buildings are designed to suit the climate and to work with nature in providing protection from temperature changes. Passive solar energy techniques, thick-walled construction, proper placement in surroundings, and landscaping with water, landforms, plants, and trees are some of the tools used for tempering the influence of changing climatic conditions. Special emphasis is put on creating a constant flow of fresh air through buildings, as well as through communities and cities. Air is a major source of bodily renewal. We breathe in a new supply of oxygen molecules about ten times per minute, 600 times per hour—almost 15,000 times every 24 hours. If the air we breathe is stagnant and full of pollutants, bacteria, or waste products from the exhalation of other people, it will not provide the energy and renewal we need, but rather will burden the system with unnecessary impurities.

In making the plans for a building using a Maharishi Sthapatya Veda design, the architect draws up a *Vastu Purusha Mandala*. This is essentially a site diagram that seeks to maximize the positive influence of nature by taking into consideration the unique natural conditions of the site, along with the specific requirements of the project. Homes are oriented with respect to all environmental factors, whether geographic, topographic, demographic, or climatic. Buildings and landscape are seen as different aspects of the same wholeness.

Great care is taken to find the ideal location for the building and the right orientation in relation to the sun. The sun is primary to all life on Earth. The functioning of our physiology is intimately linked to the circadian rhythms dictated by the sun, and the processes of nature are aligned to the daily movement of the sun as well. The architect places the rooms in the building in such a way that they utilize the changing qualities of energy produced by the sun throughout the day, bringing occupants' patterns of activity in harmony with the changing cycles of nature. Mr. Eike Hartman is a German-born artist and scholar who under Maharishi's guidance has studied at length with a team of expert Sthapatis (professional practitioners of Sthapatya Veda) in India. As he notes, "Maharishi Sthapatya Veda is the only science in the world capable of allocating the different rooms in a house according to our activity. When the kitchen, dining room, living room and bedroom are in the proper places, natural law becomes very supportive of the cycle of our daily activity, thereby eliminating the cause of fatigue and stress which otherwise might give rise to some discomfort and even disease."[242]

Planning for a Healthy Future: Maharishi Jyotish

Quantum physics has forced us to consider the possibility that the world in essence is an unbroken wholeness, not an aggregation of separate things. Reality is an unbounded web of vibrational states, each of which exists as relations between the parts of a unified whole, and each of which gains its observable properties through its interaction with other systems. In this unbounded interwoven web, everything is connected to everything else and everything influences everything else. As Maharishi eloquently puts it, the master weaver of the fabrics of creation, pure unbounded consciousness, creates everything from within itself and always sustains Unity.

One of the many implications of the discoveries of quantum physics is that time as we know it doesn't really exist. Certainly, we have the impression that time is moving or flowing from past through present to the future. However, although events are ordered in time as a sequential unfoldment of the processes of the universe, time is something that is never measured directly. We may measure it in terms of the movement of a clock, the rotation of the Earth on its axis, or the rotation of the Earth around the sun; none of these are time, however, but rather the sequential movement of certain points in the universe in relation to other points. There is no ultimate time, which our clock measures. The progression of events that we know as time is based on relations of entities with other entities. As physicist Paul Davies explains, "The ultimate clock is the Universe itself, which through its progressive expansion in size defines a 'cosmic time.'. . . But when we try to study the origins of this expansion of the Universe in terms of the best scientific description of mechanics, quantum mechanics . . . cosmic time drops out of the equations altogether! The gravitational equations that govern the motion of the cosmos impose a restriction which has the effect of eliminating the time coordinate. As a result all change must be gauged by correlations. Ultimately, everything must be correlated with the size of the Universe. Any vestige of a moving present has faded completely."[243]

In the same way as the body is the expression of the primordial wholeness, pure consciousness, everything in the universe derives from this unbounded field of all possibilities. In this way, there is an intercorrelation between the individual and the universe, because both derive from a common source. The state of the universe at the time an individual first enters this world constitutes a single point in the cosmic web, a sort of blueprint for the energies and forces present in his or her life.

Jyotish, the 'science of light,' is the ancient knowledge contained in the Vedic texts of how to gain knowledge about all aspects of a person's life by calculating the coordinates of the heavenly bodies, or 'cosmic counterparts,' at the time of birth. Because everything is one wholeness, what is present in the macrocosm is simultaneously present in the microcosm. The cosmic counterparts, i.e. sun, moon, planets, and solar and lunar constellations, are points in the universal existence which are mirrored in the individual's existence; they have corresponding areas in the human physiology and anatomy where they exert an influence.[244] If the cosmic counterparts are not in proper correspondence with these areas of the body, disorders and disease can result. For example, the hypothalamus corresponds to the moon, and is involved with emotions and the physiological response to emotions. The hypothalamus has daily, monthly, and seasonal cycles; some of its many functions are: control of feeding behavior, body temperature, reproductive behavior, and hormonal cycles of various frequencies (e.g. women's 28-day menstrual cycle). The functions and characteristics of the hypothalamus are like those described for the moon in Jyotish. Any afflictions in the correspondence between the hypothalamus and the moon can result in disorders and disease affecting hypothalamic functions.

A physicist, by knowing the coordinates of a photon's emergence from the unified field, can determine a particle's future spin, energy, direction,

215

and decay; likewise, a trained expert in the Maharishi Jyotish℠ program, by knowing the coordinates of an individual's birth, can determine the relations and forces present throughout the individual's life and predict how these will manifest, be it in the area of health, personality, profession, or relationships. This analysis is tremendously helpful in a number of ways. For instance, it gives insight into one's strengths and weaknesses, something which is useful in helping one build on strengths, while avoiding too much exposure to situations that hit on one's weaknesses. This goes a long way toward ensuring 'health' in all areas of life, such as relationships, work, family life, or wealth. For example, the knowledge that during a certain period of time one will have a propensity to lose money through investments, could prompt a person to adopt a more conservative investment strategy during that period and save untold amounts of grief and frustration. Likewise, knowing that one has great potential for success as an artist, but little as a teacher, might give a recent art graduate the confidence to make the difficult decision to work as a full-time artist, whereas the conventional choice would have been to opt for the financial security of a teaching position. This is a choice that will go a long way toward ensuring work satisfaction, something that is crucial to both mental and physical well-being.

When it comes to physiological health, a Maharishi Jyotish analysis is useful both for prediction and for illumination of the deeper mechanics involved in a specific problem. A well-trained expert in Maharishi Jyotish can determine which areas of the body are more likely to develop health problems and at which time. Based on this, a person can focus on dissolving the patterns of present behavior that might be associated with a future physiological weakness, long before these behaviors give rise to actual problems. For example, knowing that one has a propensity for weakness of the liver can motivate a person to avoid behaviors that might tax the liver, such as eating excessive amounts of fats or impure foods or drinking alcohol.

But not all situations and conditions on a person's life path can be solved simply by changing one's patterns of behavior. At times we are up against relentless obstacles and challenges that do not yield, no matter how hard we try. In such a situation, a Maharishi Yagya℠ procedure is recommended. A yagya is a traditional Vedic performance done by trained Vedic pandits in India; it can help counteract influences that might otherwise lead to disease, accidents, lack of success, or marital conflict. As Maharishi explains, "Yagya is regarded as the means to that complete success in life which consists of all possible achievements in the world together with freedom from bondage. Yagya, in fact, is a means to accomplish perfection in life. It brings the blessings of the powers which control and direct the evolution of the entire Creation, wins the favor of almighty nature and ultimately brings fulfillment."[245]

With their deep insights into the nature of the unbounded wholeness at the source of our nature and the mechanics of its unfoldment into matter, the Vedas and the Vedic Literature provide us with a number of useful tools to manage human existence. Essentially, the focus of all the therapies used in the Maharishi Vedic Approach to Health is to eliminate the sources of limitations in human life. These healing modalities are far more than mere remedies; they serve to restore to life its full possibilities. We have already seen how techniques such as the TM and TM-Sidhi programs, which work on the level of consciousness, not only enhance health but enable the individual to unfold in fuller values of life. The growth of self-actualization, the increase in ego development and intelligence, and the many other indications of psychological growth are the objective expressions of the comprehensive changes that unfold as the individual taps into the latent unbounded potential within themselves. All the facets of the Vedas and the Vedic Literature provide a means to cultivate the physiology to reflect the full value of nature's intelligence. As pure consciousness gets infused into the functioning of the body, the floodgates of nature's creative regulating intelligence open, eliminating imbalances and causing all aspects of the mind-body system to function more in accord with its original design.

217

The theme of increasing health is thus a theme of growth. Moving toward the supreme end of the health continuum, we get rid of various symptoms of physiological imbalance. And since the mind and body are sequential expressions of the same underlying field of pure existence, as the body starts reflecting fuller values of life, so does the mind. Human growth is the process of restoring the full value of nature's intelligence on the level of both mind and body. It is the process of restoring balance to the physiology and developing a more refined state of physiological functioning which will uphold more refined states of awareness. As such, it is an exploration of the furthest reaches of our own intimate nature, which opens up unparalleled possibilities for growth of fullness, creativity, accomplishment, and happiness.

Chapter Fourteen

HEALTH AND HAPPINESS

Throughout this book, we have explored the disease process from different angles, delving deeper and deeper into the levels of causality. Disease can be viewed as increasing imbalance on the level of the physiology, which over time gives rise to specific symptoms of disease. The disease process can also be understood in terms of the mounting impediments to the expression of the subtle physiological intelligence responsible for harmonizing and integrating the trillion processes that at any one moment constitute the dynamic reality of the human body. And, at its deepest level, disease can be viewed as the phenomenon of pragya aparadh—loss of the memory of the transcendent wholeness within which the dynamism of nature's self-organizing, structuring intelligence unfolds. The seed of disease at this deepest level of causality is sown where the impulses of consciousness are transformed into the physiology. When wholeness is lost on the level of individual consciousness, wholeness is lost on the level of the precipitated expression of consciousness—the physiology—as well.

We have also seen that the loss of wholeness is the seed not only of disease, but of pain and suffering in life. The limitations that arise in the individual's existence when individual consciousness 'forgets' the dignity of its unbounded nature, arise on the level of both the body and mind. Under the influence of pragya aparadh, the mind doesn't reflect the unbounded fullness and infinite creative potential at the core of its own existence. The result is limitations, inability to fulfil desires, frustration, unhappiness, suffering, and so on. The healing modalities of the Maharishi

Vedic Approach to Health aim to dissolve pragya aparadh by reenlivening the memory of wholeness on the level of individual consciousness. As the quality of self-referral becomes lively on the level of individual consciousness, infinite correlation becomes lively on the level of the physiology, and the immense healing power of the body's self-organizing intelligence is gradually restored to its full value. In aiming to eliminate the very source of limitations in human life, these healing modalities are far from being simply remedies; they give the individual access to the infinite creative potential of his or her deepest nature. In this chapter we shall therefore explore the positive end of the health continuum—the state of supreme health.

As one develops greater health, the true meaning of the notion that 'health is more than the absence of disease' becomes obvious. The 'side effects' of greater physiological health are greater happiness, more energy, vitality, zest for life, and enhanced overall well-being. The greater well-being associated with the development of a more balanced and fine-tuned physiology is more than simply feeling good. It is an unfoldment from the inside out, a realization of our latent, unexpressed possibilities. This is a profound point. The side effect of developing a finely tuned physiology is psychological growth—of mind, personality, and consciousness. Because mind and body are expressions of the same fundamental reality, the perfect functioning of the physiology is associated with the realization of perfection at the level of mind and consciousness.

Please note, however, that the link between health and the growth of consciousness is not a principle that can be used to compare individuals in different states of health. The changing quality of awareness applies only *within* the individual's own experience continuum. It obviously would be wrong to say that because one individual is in better health than another, he or she has greater mental clarity or emotional maturity. A host of other factors, including genetic differences, personality disposition, life experiences, and so forth come into play *between* individuals, making it impossible to draw any parallels. However, within the individual's continuum of experience, when every part of the physiology is perfectly attuned with wholeness, consciousness is fully expressed at the level of matter—the individual physiology.

Higher States of Consciousness

As we saw in Chapter Ten, our understanding of the nature of consciousness has been limited, because we have only had access to the waking, dreaming, and sleeping states of consciousness. Yet, as we saw, human beings have the capacity to experience a fourth state of consciousness—*Turiya Chetana*—the state of pure consciousness in which awareness is in its most settled state, simply awake to its own existence. *Turiya Chetana* is what we might call a nonsymbolic, nonrepresentational state of awareness—a state devoid of thoughts or any other form of mental activity. The transition into the fourth state of consciousness can happen spontaneously. However, to experience it repeatedly and regularly, one needs a technique that will entice the mind to turn inward instead of maintaining its usual outward-directed flow.

Individuals from all cultures and all times have left us reports of spontaneous glimpses of a deeper, glorified dimension of reality dramatically different from our common perception. Such sublime experiences often become the source of artistic inspiration, far-reaching achievements, or selfless service to society. However, these experiences have never received the prominent place in our conceptual universe that they deserve, because they could not be properly depicted and fit into a conceptual framework developed on the basis of the experience of our 'ordinary' waking state of consciousness. Furthermore, in the West there had been no means of systematically inducing these experiences so that they could be closely studied and understood.

From the standpoint of ordinary waking consciousness, experiences of the higher, more exalted states of consciousness are profound anomalies. They are 'irregularities' whose nature and significance simply cannot be accounted for within our usual conceptual framework. As such, they have suffered the fate to which most anomalies are subjugated—they have been classified as irrelevant—and they have been largely ignored by the disciplines under whose domain they naturally fall—philosophy and psychology. The vast majority of psychologists either ignore the existence of such states or contend that the field can more fruitfully focus on more easily accessible mental phenomena.

But what if these experiences in fact are instances of a higher order of psychological functioning? What if they give us invaluable insight into untapped human growth potential? Developmental psychologists already know that what is currently considered the end state of cognitive development—the so-called formal operations stage—is only reached by a fairly small percent of the adult population. And this stage of cognitive development is only a shadow of the full cognitive, emotional, and sensory range of our Being. What if these experiences provide examples of end states of human development that lie far beyond what most people realize in their lifetime? Surely, we then would not want to ignore the phenomenon just because it rarely occurs—that would be like saying diamonds are insignificant because they are found only rarely in nature.

After devoting considerable time to studying these experiences, the American psychologist William James concluded that, "Most people live, whether physically, intellectually or morally, in a very restricted circle of their potential being. They make use of a very small portion of their possible consciousness, and of their soul's resources in general, much like a man who, out of his whole bodily organism, should get into a habit of using and moving only his little finger."[246]

In the ancient Vedic tradition of knowledge, these experiences have always been considered of utmost importance. They are regarded as instances of higher states of consciousness, sublime states in which the full potential of mind, emotions, and consciousness are expressed in all aspects of the individual's life. The Vedic tradition delineates a taxonomy of *several* higher states of consciousness, in the framework of which our ordinary waking consciousness seems but a mediocre expression of the human repertoire of experience. The waking state of consciousness gives us access to the surface level of sensory experience, in the same way as Newtonian physics gave us access to the mode of reality that appears as the classical mechanistic mode of the universe. Classical mechanics obscured the existence of the vast 'hidden' realm of quantum mechanics; similarly, our normal waking mode of awareness obscures the value of finer levels of mental functioning and the least excited, transcendental state of consciousness that exists beyond the finest mode of mental activity.

With the introduction of his Vedic Science, Maharishi has provided a conceptual framework for understanding these experiences, and a practical methodology for extricating them from the obscurity in which they have been veiled. In the Transcendental Meditation program, he has provided a technique that makes the fourth state of consciousness a tangible reality to the steadfast practitioner. Furthermore, he has cast light on how the experience of higher states of consciousness begins to unfold naturally from the repeated experience of the fourth state of consciousness. The experience of pure consciousness in this way is only the first step in unfolding the otherwise latent potential for human growth.

The Fifth State of Consciousness

"The Self reveals its essence only to him who applies himself to the Self," says the *Katha Upanishad*. As the mind, through the practice of the TM technique, repeatedly experiences the state of pure consciousness—the Self—the sublime dimensions of experience that apprehend the finest, subtlest levels of reality start to unfold.

The mechanics of this development of consciousness must be understood in terms of the physiological changes associated with it. The growth of higher states of consciousness is, in essence, a growth of supreme health—a growth toward a state of complete psychophysiological integration. Because there is a reciprocal relationship between mind and body, only a perfectly fine-tuned physiology is able to uphold higher states of consciousness. The repeated experience of transcendental consciousness refines both mental and physiological functioning so that, over time, the physiology becomes capable of sustaining the experience of pure consciousness even when the mind is engaged in activity outside of meditation. During the practice of the TM technique, the nervous system adapts to a new style of functioning. Over time, as this style of physiological functioning alternates with the activity of waking, dreaming, and sleeping, the physiology starts to uphold a mode of experience in which pure consciousness coexists *along with* normal activity. This is the experience of a fifth state of consciousness, Maharishi explains. In the Vedic terminology, this state is referred to as *Turiyatit Chetana*, or 'cosmic consciousness,' to signify the all-inclusive, greatly expanded mode of knowing and being which is associated with this state of awareness.

In this state, the conscious mind has grown to realize the full range of its own existence, from the most active, expressed levels of mental functioning, to more silent values of mental activity, to the transcendent core of the Self. Even when engaged in activity, the individual never loses sight of the unbounded wholeness that is the essence of his or her nature. The state of cosmic consciousness involves a permanent shift in our level of identification. Whereas before, our sense of self might be linked to events on the level of the ego, emotions, intellect, or even sensory experience, in cosmic consciousness the individual remains established in his or her essential nature, the unbounded inner silence of pure consciousness, while engaged in normal activity.

The experiences below provide some examples of the pervading sense of wholeness associated with the experience of cosmic consciousness. The first excerpt you may recognize as the quote from philosopher Jacob Needleman in Chapter Ten. The last quote is from Hakuin, a Zen saint of the 18th century, who describes the state of those who have realized the Zen ideal.

> *Time changed; {it} passed much more slowly* and I saw my thoughts in front of me as if they were written on a screen. So I was quite aware that there's a difference between awareness and thought. At the same moment I was aware of the thousand things going on inside

me with a *global awareness*, with *a center of attention that was in touch with all parts at the same time.* [emphasis added]

—Jacob Needleman[247]

I was experiencing deep, wonderful silence, and having my first clear experiences of infinite correlation—that is, being in such an unbounded, infinitely orderly and harmonious state of awareness *that an impulse in my awareness seemed to be instantly connected with all of creation.* When I say 'instantly' connected with creation I mean that there was no time value separating me from any part of creation.

—practitioner of the TM and TM-Sidhi programs[248]

A continuum of awareness has become more predominant. The sense of events and time has given way to an interconnectedness within a whole.

—practitioner of the TM and TM-Sidhi programs[249]

Abiding with the non-particular which is in particulars,
Going or returning, they remain for ever unmoved.
Taking hold of the not-thought which lies in thoughts,
In their every act they hear the voice of Truth.
How boundless the sky of contemplation!
How transparent the moonlight of the four-told Wisdom!
As the Truth reveals itself in its eternal tranquillity,
This very earth is the Lotus-Land of Purity,
And this body is the body of the Buddha.

—Hakuin[250]

"Taking hold of the not-thought which lies in thoughts," and "abiding with the non-particular which is in particulars," clearly refers to the fifth state of consciousness in which the abstract, nonrepresentational Self is experienced together with the ordinary thinking process and the 'particulars' of everyday existence.

Cosmic consciousness is a state of perfect psychophysiological integration, and the growth toward cosmic consciousness consists of a profound psychophysiological transformation. Maharishi has highlighted how this transformation is brought about when the activity of the nervous system regularly alternates between physiological activity that upholds the experience of the ordinary waking state of consciousness and the physiological functioning associated with transcendental consciousness. He explains it this way:

> [The] gradual and systematic culture of the physical nervous system creates a physiological situation in which the two states of consciousness exist together simultaneously. It is well known that there exist in the nervous system many autonomous levels of function, between which a system of coordination also exists. In the state of cosmic consciousness, two different levels of organization in the nervous system function simultaneously while maintaining their separate identities. By virtue of this anatomical separation of function, it becomes possible for transcendental consciousness to co-exist with the waking state of consciousness and with the dreaming and sleeping states of consciousness.[251]

When the experience of cosmic consciousness becomes a permanent reality, the highest degree of human perfection, enlightenment, is attained. This is a state of spiritual, mental, and physiological perfection, a state in which the individual reflects the full value of unbounded pure consciousness. In this state, the fullness of unbounded Being illumines all aspects of the individual's existence.

As the memory of pure consciousness grows, an inner sense of stability, strength, wholeness, and peace becomes increasingly dominant in the individual's awareness. There is an increasing inner sense of evenness, bliss, and self-sufficiency that exists independent of outside circumstances. This increasing awareness of the more silent values of the Self unfolds spontaneously from the repeated experience of pure consciousness. It is not something that is contrived or imagined, and then again forgotten when a familiar or unfamiliar stressor pops up. As Maharishi explains, in the waking state of consciousness, stressful events are like lines scratched on the surface of stone—they leave behind a permanent trace. As the light of pure consciousness starts to be infused into waking state activity, stress becomes like a line drawn in water—it leaves its mark, but no permanent trace is left. Finally, in cosmic consciousness, any stressful event is like a line drawn in air—it happens, but it leaves behind no physiological trace, because everything is experienced on the backdrop of the inner fulfillment and wholeness of one's unbounded, essential Self.

The Sixth State of Consciousness

Cosmic consciousness forms the first of several higher states of consciousness. It represents the state in which the development of the *inner* value of life has reached its zenith, as our conscious mind has grown to realize the full range of its own existence. Subsequent development encompasses the *outer* dimension of existence, as the individual starts to fathom finer and finer values of the objective sphere of life. This is a progressive *refinement of perception* which mirrors the progressive refinement of mental functioning. In the same way as the mind, in the growth toward cosmic consciousness, developed the ability to experience more and more refined and silent modes of its own 'subjective' existence, it now starts to apperceive finer and finer qualities of 'objective' existence. The nervous system starts to filter reality in such a way that one begins to perceive a broader spectrum of the reality of the object. It is the awareness of the unbounded value of life inside that causes perception to spontaneously move from the surface of the object and start to appreciate deeper values of the object.

One way this development is initially experienced is that perception gains depth—whereas before, one might simply see a face, one would now sense the whole personality of the person as it is mirrored in the face. Whereas before, one might see a tree in a park, one would now *sense* the silent values of beauty lively in the very being of the tree, as it resonates with the silence inside. This development culminates in the sixth state of consciousness, in which, according to Maharishi, "perception is so refined that the finest relative is capable of being spontaneously perceived on the gross, surface level."[252] In the Vedic terminology, this state of consciousness is known as *Bhagavad Chetana*, or 'refined cosmic consciousness.' The British poet Kathleen Raines describes an experience of this state of consciousness in the succeeding passage, which is followed by additional accounts of this refined and glorious state of awareness:

> I dared scarcely to breathe, held in a kind of fine attention in which I could sense the very flow of life in the cells [of the hyacinth]. I was not perceiving the flow but living it. I was aware of the life of the plant as a slow flow or circulation of a vital current of liquid light of the utmost purity. I could apprehend as a simple essence formal structure and dynamic process. This dynamic form was, as it seemed, of a spiritual not a material order; or of a finer matter, or of matter itself perceived as spirit. There was nothing emotional about this experience, which was, on the contrary, an almost mathematical apprehension of a complex and organized whole, apprehended as whole, this whole was living; and as such inspired by a sense of immaculate holiness. . . . By 'living' I do not mean that which distinguishes animal from plant or plant from mineral, but rather a quality possessed by all these in their different degrees.
>
> —Kathleen Raines[253]

There were days when I felt my heart melting as if I could take everything in creation into myself and cherish it with the greatest love. Often I would have long periods of the day when everything I saw seemed to be glowing with divine radiance. Sometimes I would even be able to see the tremendous energy at the basis of every object, minute particles of energy . . . moving very rapidly at a different rate and pattern for every object, yet unified somehow in a 'unified field.'

> —practitioner of the TM and TM-Sidhi programs[254]

The corn was orient and immortal wheat, which never should be reaped, nor was ever sown. I thought it had stood from everlasting to everlasting. The dust and stones of the street were as precious as gold. The gates at first were the end of the world. The green trees, when I saw them first through one of the gates, transported and ravished me; their sweetness and unusual beauty made my heart to leap, and almost mad with ecstasy, they were such strange and wonderful things. The Men! O what venerable and reverend creatures did the aged seem! Immortal Cherubim! And young men glittering and sparkling angles, and maids strange seraphic pieces of life and beauty! Boys and girls tumbling in the street, and playing, were moving jewels. I knew not that they were born or should die. But all things abided eternally as they were in their proper places.

Eternity was manifested in the light of the day, and something infinite behind everything appeared; which talked with my expectation and moved my desire. The city seemed to stand in Eden, or to be built in Heaven. The streets were mine, the temple was mine, the people were mine, their clothes and gold and silver were mine, as much as their sparkling eyes, fair skins and ruddy faces. The skies were mine, and so were the sun and moon and stars, and all the world was mine; and I the only spectator and enjoyer of it. . . .
—Thomas Traherne[255]

The Seventh State of Consciousness

As we shall see, this last passage also illuminates the transition to the seventh state of consciousness, unity consciousness. The experience of higher states of consciousness is intimately familiar and natural, more natural than "dull common consciousness," in the words of the British poet Kathleen Raines. Her experience, Raines comments, was of something "infinitely familiar, as if I were experiencing at last things as they are, was where I belonged, where in some sense, I had always been and would always be."[256] Despite its sense of familiarity, the perception in the sixth state of consciousness is of an entirely different quality than perception in the waking state of consciousness. Raines distinguishes this quality of perception when she explains that she "was not perceiving the flow but *living* it" [emphasis added]. The refinement of perception that takes place in the development of *Bhagavad Chetana* is associated with a continuously growing intimacy with that which is experienced. The TM-Sidhi practitioner in the second account above, describes this growing intimacy in terms of growing love. As individual consciousness expands, the fine fluctuations of manifest existence start to resonate with the fine reverberations of one's own existence.

The development of consciousness culminates when perception reaches such a refined quality that the individual is able to appreciate the very finest aspect of the object's existence—and behold the object as fluctuations of the infinite, unbounded, unmanifest field of Being. In the Vedic taxonomy of higher states of consciousness, this state is known as *Brahmi Chetana*, the seventh state of consciousness, or 'unity consciousness.' Both the second and third quotes above illuminate the transition to this highest state of consciousness. The TM-Sidhi practitioner talks about perceiving objects in terms of "minute particles of energy . . . moving very rapidly at a different rate and pattern for every object, yet unified somehow in a 'unified field.'" And Thomas Traherne describes how "Eternity was manifested in the light of the day, and something infinite behind everything appeared."

In *Brahmi Chetana,* as the individual's unbounded quality of awareness falls upon an object, it discerns and resonates with the unbounded, transcendent value of the object that is otherwise hidden beneath the more manifest values of the object's reality. The most fundamental value of the object's existence is recognized as identical to the most intimate aspect of one's own existence. "In this unified state of consciousness," Maharishi explains, "the experiencer and the object of experience have both been brought to the same level of infinite value and this encompasses the entire phenomenon of perception and action as well."[257]

In this highest state of consciousness, the essential nature of finite existence is contemplated. The unmanifest, infinite field of Being, the source of objective and subjective existence, becomes a living reality on the level of conscious awareness. In this state, everything is experienced in terms of the universal Self, the intimate core of one's own existence. This has been eloquently described in the following manner: "[E]very particle of creation, even the farthest, most distant point of the universe is experienced as a wave in the unbounded ocean of transcendental consciousness, which is one's own Self. . . . In Unity consciousness, the whole field of existence . . . is discovered to be one limitless sea of Cosmic Being."[258] The following accounts give additional perspectives on the experience of unity consciousness:

> [B]it by bit I went off into the greenery of the pastures and into the current of the rivers that I watched go by; and I no longer knew where my soul was, it was so diffuse, universal, spread out. . . . Your mind itself finally lost the notion of particularity which keep it on the alert. It was like an immense harmony engulfing your soul with marvellous palpitations, and you felt in its plenitude an inexpressible comprehension of the unrevealed wholeness of things; the interval between you and the object, like an abyss closing, grew narrower and narrower, until the difference vanished, because you both were bathed in infinity; you penetrated each other equally, and a subtle current passed from you into matter while the life of the elements slowly pervaded you, rising like sap; one degree more, and you would have become nature, or nature become your . . . immortality, boundlessness, infinity, I have all that, I am that! I feel myself to be Substance, I am Thought!
>
> —Gustave Flaubert, French writer [259]

> Just as in a flower, the petals, stem, leaves, and all the parts are interconnected and form a whole—everything I perceive is interconnected, a part of that wholeness. . . . It seems all of creation constitutes the fluctuations of my body and consciousness. These fluctuations have a quality of sameness. The same style of wave

function is in everything. It also seems that every object contains all sizes of waves, all in some kind of synchrony. Yet underlying that, there is no movement or fluctuation.

When I perceive an object, it is as if the Absolute pops at me at zero distance away, yet space is somehow created within me. I touch something and I seem to be caressing all creation. . . . The Absolute as my Self in its purity is a void of empty nothingness. It, or I, becomes lively in rippling fluctuations that seem to be the area where knowledge is. . . . Then that knowledge becomes more expressed as space and time in the relative within me.

—practitioner of the TM and TM-Sidhi programs[260]

Unity consciousness is the pinnacle of human development. In this state, consciousness has come full circle. The gap between the knower and the object of his knowing has been closed. The conceptual distinction between knower, knowing, and known—which form the structure of pure knowledge within the absolute state of existence—is recognized for what it is—*an appearance of diversity only*. The differences of manifest existence dissolve; no matter where the individual's perception falls, the ultimate nature of the subject and the object of his or her experience are recognized as one. Any object is perceived as simply a reverberation of the unbounded ocean of Cosmic Being, which in turn is recognized as nothing but the fluctuations of one's innermost Self.

Health and Enlightenment

The growth of higher states of consciousness represents a transformation which culminates in that state in which the full value of the transcendental, absolute Self is expressed in all the relative values of the individual's existence. This Vedic representation of reality is reflected throughout history, in all cultures at all times. Thinkers, philosophers, sages, and saints have bespoken the reality of a deeper, unbounded and unmanifest dimension of existence. Universally, they have maintained that this reality is reflected at the deepest levels of human consciousness, and the culmination of human growth is the realization of and union with this unbounded transcendent basis of all existence. The 17th century philosopher G.W. Leibniz coined the term *philosophia perrennis*—the perennial philosophy—to signify the universality of this tradition of knowledge.

"The same Ultimate Reality finds expression through all languages throughout time," explains Maharishi.[261] We have seen how differently the experience of higher states of consciousness can be expressed, yet how clearly they all portray the same essential reality. The same holds true for those wise men in each generation who have expressed the experiential aspect of the spiritual traditions of the world—they all echo the truths that are so lucidly expressed in the Vedic tradition. The reality of unity consciousness is clearly depicted in the writings of the Greek philosopher Plotinus, who describes the illuminated human being who can "see all things not in process of becoming, but in Being and see themselves in the other. Each being contains in itself the whole intelligible world. Therefore All is everywhere. Each is there All, and All is each."[262] And Master Eckhart, the German monk, sage, and mystic echoes the same vision. "When a man sees All in all, then a man stands beyond mere understanding," he writes.[263] "As long as I'm this or that, or have this or that, I'm not all things and I have not all things. Become pure till you neither are nor have either this or that; then you are omnipresent and, being neither this nor that, are all things."[264]

Modern science—in the form of quantum physics—echoes the perennial philosophy. We now know that the deepest level of reality is not small building blocks of matter, but a unified field of undifferentiated primal substance. What Maharishi in his restoration of the Vedic Science adds to this discovery is the possibility of experiencing this finest level of reality in one's own consciousness.

The immense dignity of experience associated with the direct apprehension of the common basis of existence, the Ultimate Reality, is beyond expression. All that is important in this process is the continuous refinement of *both* mind and body which results from the repeated experience of pure consciousness. This physiological refinement is described in various ways by those who experience it. One individual talks about "a soft but strong feeling of blissful evenness" present most of the time in both mind and body, "an extremely delightful liveliness throughout the body." In another report, one person notes, "Very often during activity there has been a frictionless flow, that is, the body flows as a sort of superfluid with no resistance—the body feels ethereal and transparent, accompanied with great sweetness." Another person describes how "a lightness of body developed, a buoyancy, a fluidity, and effortlessness of movement . . . as if I could walk without touching the ground."[265]

Time is an important factor in this development. Raising consciousness to higher levels is a constant, steady process. It has nothing to do with imagination or with trying to be in a more 'exalted' mood. Inevitably the imagined reality or the mood subside, and consciousness falls into its usual mode of functioning. To experience that dynamic, delicate level of existence where the unmanifest unified field takes on specific expressions, the nervous system must be keenly sensitive and extremely refined. The development of body and mind goes hand in hand. The path to enlightenment is intimately linked to increasing health and general physiological refinement, and growing health is connected with the increased expression of love, expanded capacity for happiness, achievement, devotion, and purity which accompany the growth of consciousness.

Patients, Maharishi says, are 'candidates for knowledge.' In the Maharishi Vedic Approach to Health, clients partake of a doubly wondrous adventure as the quest for supreme health pays off in spiritual enrichment and unfoldment of all the wonderful possibilities for growth and expansion that each of us carries inside. It is a tribute to the depth of the Vedic insights that the Maharishi Vedic Approach to Health is unique in its emphasis on the importance of the body in the growth of human consciousness. The essence of development of consciousness lies in creating a physiology that is able to sustain the experience of the refined values of mind and consciousness that characterize the state of enlightenment. Thus, the growth toward supreme health becomes a delightful journey of discovering the infinite possibilities of our own inner nature.

RESOURCES

This book presents a comprehensive natural health care system, including its underlying theoretical basis and research conducted on various modalities of this health care system. No one, however, should attempt to treat an illness or disorder simply on this basis. If you are ill, consult a physician.

IN THE UNITED STATES

To locate a physician in your area trained in the Maharishi Vedic Approach to Health and Maharishi Ayur-Veda, or for further information call:

1-800-843-8332 or 1-800-888-5797

Maharishi Amrit Kalash and other Maharishi Ayur-Veda herbal mixtures are available as nutritional food supplements formulated according to Ayurvedic protocol. They are offered by the formulators as dietary supplements and for no other use or purpose.

Call: 1-800-255-8332
Or fax: 719-260-7400
Or write: Maharishi Ayur-Ved Products International, Inc.
            P.O. Box 49667
            Colorado Springs, CO 80949-9667
            USA

IN CANADA

Call: 1-800-461-9685

Or fax: 819-835-9590

Or write: Maharishi Ayur-Veda Products

P.O. Box 9402, 40 Chemin Cochrane

Compton, Quebec J0B 1L0

Canada

IN THE UNITED KINGDOM

Call: 44-1695-51015

Or fax: 44-1695-50917

Or write: Maharishi Ayur-Ved Products

Peel House, Peel Road

West Pimbo

Skelmersdale

Lancashire, WN8 9PT

England

IN EUROPE

Call: 31-475-404060

Or fax: 31-475-404055

Or write: Maharishi Technology Corporation

Tussen de Bruggen #10

NL 6063 NA Vlodrop

The Netherlands

IN AUSTRALIA

Call: 61-3-9467-4633

Or fax: 61-3-9467-4688

Or write: Maharishi Ayur-Veda Products

P.O. Box 81, Bundoora

Victoria 3083 Australia

IN NEW ZEALAND

Call:	64-9-524-5883
Or fax:	64-9-524-5430
Or write:	MAP New Zealand
	9 Adam Street, Greenlane
	Auckland, New Zealand

IN INDIA

Call:	91-761-410325
Or fax:	91-761-315722
Or write:	Maharishi Mahesh Yogi Vedic Vishwa Vidyalaya
	871 Napier Town
	Jabalpur, Madhya Pradesh 482 001, India

Call:	91-11-694-6501/2/3/4
Or fax:	91-11-683-6682
Or write:	Maharishi Ayurved Corporation, Ltd.
	A-14, Mohan Co-op Industrial Estate
	Mathura Road
	New Delhi 110 044, India

Footnotes

1   National Center for Health Statistics (1995). *Health United States, 1994.* Hyatsville, MD: Public Health Service. DHHS Pub. No. (PHS) 95-1232. p. 6.

2   ibid.

3   Institute of Noetic Sciences with William Poole. (1993). *The Heart of Healing.* Atlanta: Turner Publishing.

4   National Center for Health Statistics. (1995). *Health United States, 1994.* Hyatsville, MD: Public Health Service. DHHS Pub. No. (PHS) 95-1232. p. 6.

5   Hoffman, C., Rice, D., and Sung, H.-Y. (1996). Persons with chronic conditions. Their prevalence and costs. *Journal of the American Medical Association,* 276(18): 1473-1479.

6   ibid.

7   Weitz, M. (1982). *Health Shock.* Englewood Cliffs, NJ: Prenctice-Hall. p. v.

8   Blendon, R. J. and Taylor, H. (Spring, 1989). Views on health care: Public opinion in three nations. *Health Affairs,* 8, 150-157.

9   Eisenberg, D. M., Kessler, R. C., Foster, C., Norlock, F. E., Calkins, D. R., and Delbanco, T. L. (1993). Unconventional medicine in the United States. Prevalence, costs, and patterns of use. *New England Journal of Medicine,* 328(4): 246-252.

10 Jonas, W. B. (1993). Evaluating unconventional medical practices. *Journal of NIH Research,* 5: 64-67.

11 Das, S. (1971). The science of Ayurveda. *The Medical Journal of Australia,* 1(4): 224-225.

12 Larry is a composite character with traits from a number of people I know who live their lives under similar conditions.

13 Many readers will recognize the description of Larry's physiological ordeals as a simplified outline of the stress response.

14 As an example, consult the comprehensive collection of contemporary health rating scales and questionnaires in the book *Measuring Health* [McDowell and

Newell (1987) New York: Oxford University Press]. It features not one scale or questionnaire that attempts to measure health in positive terms.

15 *Charaka Samhita* (1992). Dr. Ram Sharma and Vaidya Bhagawan Dass (translators). Varanasi, India: Chaowkhamba Sanskrit Studies Office, Vol. XCIV. p. 233.

16 Health Insurance Association of America. (1995). *Source Book of Health Insurance Data 1994.* Washington, DC. p. 146.

17 In 1991, for example, cardiovascular disease was responsible for almost a million deaths, while cancer took about half a million lives [American Heart Association (1993) *Heart and Stroke Facts: 1994 Statistical Supplement.* Dallas, TX: American Heart Association. p. 1].

18 A number of behavioral factors, such as diet, alcohol use, smoking, drugs, and sexual behavior are among the main factors implicated in the development of chronic diseases. Many psychological and social factors also play a role in predisposing a person to chronic disease.

19 *Work in America.* (1973). Report of a special task force to the Secretary of Health, Education and Welfare. Cambridge: MIT Press.

Jenkins, C. D. (1971). Psychologic and social precursors of coronary disease. *New England Journal of Medicine,* 284: 244-255.

20 The debate about cholesterol has been going on for several years. For a survey of the literature on this topic, the following articles are recommended:

Hulley, S. B., Walsh, J. M. B., and Newman, T. B. (1992). Health policy on blood cholesterol. Time to change directions. *Circulation,* 86(3): 1026-1029.

Oliver, M. F. (1992). Doubts about preventing coronary heart disease. *British Medical Journal,* 304: 303-305.

Davey Smith, G. and Pekkanen, J. (1992). Should there be a moratorium on the use of cholesterol lowering drugs? *British Medical Journal,* 304: 431-434.

21 *Physicians' Desk Reference.* (1995). Mevacor® Tablets (Lovastatin), U.S.P. Montvale, NJ: Medical Economics Data Production Company. p. 1584-1588

22 Rose, G. (1981). Strategy of prevention: lessons from cardiovascular disease. *British Medical Journal,* 282: 1847-1851. Quote on p. 1851.

23 Doctors fail nutrition. *Natural Health*, September/October, 1993. p. 19.

24 ibid.

25   ibid.

26   Dubos, R. (1990). Self-healing: A personal history. In: Ornstein, R. and Swencionis, C. (eds). *The Healing Brain*. New York: Guilford Press.

27   Melmon, K. L. (1971). Preventable drug reactions—Causes and cures. *New England Journal of Medicine*, 284(4): 1361-1368.

28   Weitz, M. (1982). *Health Shock*. Englewood Cliffs, NJ: Prentice-Hall. p. v.

29   Lander, L. (1978). *Defective Medicine*. New York: Farrar, Straus, Giroux. p. 45.

30   Inlander, C. B. (1990). *Medicine on Trial*. New York: Pantheon.

31   ibid, p. 113-114.

32   Moyers, B. (1993). *Healing and the Mind*. New York: Doubleday. p. 90. Interview with Dr. Dean Ornish.

33   Hoffman, C., Rice, D., and Sung, H.-Y. (1996). Persons with chronic conditions. Their prevalence and costs. *Journal of the American Medical Association*, 276(18): 1473-1479.

34   Blendon, R. J. and Taylor, H. (Spring, 1989). Views on health care: Public opinion in three nations. *Health Affairs*, 8: 150-157.

35   *New York Times*, Feb. 18, 1990. p. L1.

36   Kuhn, T. (1970). *The Structure of Scientific Revolutions*. Chicago: University of Chicago Press. p. 111.

37   See, for example, Lemonick, M. D. (July 17, 1995). Future tech is now. *Time*, p. 41.

38   Quoted in: Pietroni, P. (1992). *The Greening of Medicine*. London: Trafalgar.

39   Institute of Noetic Sciences with William Poole. (1993). *The Heart of Healing*. Atlanta: Turner Publishing. p. 54-55.

40   ibid.

41   Moyers, B. (1993). *Healing and the Mind*. New York: Doubleday. Interview with Dr. Dean Ornish, p. 99.

42   Moerman, D. E. (1991). Physiology and symbols: The anthropological implications of the placebo effect. In: Romanucci-Ross, L., Moerman, D. E., and Tancredi, L. R. (eds). *The Anthropology of Medicine: From Culture to Method*. New York: Bergin & Garvey.

43   Researchers are now beginning to realize that some deeper cause may be at play. A common human virus, the cytomegalovirus, may be inhibiting the expression of a gene which normally limits cell growth, causing the rapid regrowth of muscle cells in vessels that have undergone angioplasty. If researchers confirm this theory, they may develop remedies against this particular virus. However, questions remain regarding the deeper levels of causality involved. Since this is a virus common to all human beings, why would it have this effect in vessels that have undergone angioplasty?

Source: Dickstein, L. (July 25, 1994). A viral link to heart disease? *Time*, p. 19.

44   Stringer, M.D., Görög, P. G., Freeman, A., and Kakkar, V. V. (1989). Lipid peroxides and atherosclerosis. *British Medical Journal*, 298: 281-284.

45   Sarafino, E. P. (1990). *Health Psychology: Biopsychosocial Interactions*. New York: Wiley. p. 5-7.

46   Moore, T. J. (September, 1989). The cholesterol myth. *Atlantic Monthly*, p. 37-70.

47   Walton, K. G., Pugh, N. D. C., Gelderloos, P., and Macrae, P. (1995). Stress reduction and preventing hypertension: Preliminary support for a psychoneuroendocrine mechanism. *Journal of Alternative and Complementary Medicine*, 1(3): 263-283.

48   Hammer, S., Dorfman, A., and Wilbur, A. (August, 1985). Zeroing in on the molecular level to conquer cancer. *Science Digest,* p. 31.

49   Thomas, L. (1974). *The Lives of a Cell. Notes of a Biology Watcher.* New York: Bantam Books. p. 38.

50   In: Cousins, N. (1979). *Anatomy of an Illness*. New York: Norton. Foreword.

51   O'Regan, B. (1985). Placebo: The hidden asset in healing. *Investigations. Institute of Noetic Sciences*, 2(1): 1-3.

52   Hurley, T. J. (Summer, 1985). Placebos and healing: A new look at the "sugar pill." *Institute of Noetic Sciences Newsletter*, p. 28-31.

53   Turner, J. A., Deyo, R. A., Loeser, J. D., Von Korff, M., and Fordyce, W. E. (1994). The importance of placebo effects in pain treatment and research. *Journal of the American Medical Association*, 271: 1609-1614.

54   ibid.

55   White, L., Tursky, B., and Schwartz, G. E. (1985). Proposed synthesis of placebo models. In: White, L., Tursky, B., and Schwartz, G. E. (eds). *Placebo: Theory, Research and Mechanisms*. New York: Guilford.

56   Institute of Noetic Sciences with William Poole. (1993). *The Heart of Healing*. Atlanta: Turner Publishing.

57   Moerman, D. E. (1991). Physiology and symbols: The anthropological implications of the placebo effect. In: Romanucci-Ross, L., Moerman, D. E., and Tancredi, L. R. (eds). *The Anthropology of Medicine: From Culture to Method*. New York: Bergin & Garvey. p. 134.

58   Quoted in: Hurley, T. J. (1985). Placebo effects: Unmapped territory of mind/body interactions. *Investigations. Institute of Noetic Sciences*, 2(1): 4-11.

59   White, L., Tursky, B., and Schwartz, G. E. (1985). Proposed synthesis of placebo models. In: White, L., Tursky, B., and Schwartz, G. E. (eds). *Placebo: Theory, Research and Mechanisms*. New York: Guilford.

60   Sullivan, M. D. (1993). Placebo controls and epistemic control in orthodox medicine. *Journal of Medicine and Philosophy*, 18: 213-231.

61   White, L., Tursky, B., and Schwartz, G. E. (1985). Proposed synthesis of placebo models. In: White, L., Tursky, B., and Schwartz, G. E. (eds). *Placebo: Theory, Research and Mechanisms*. New York: Guilford.

62   Roberts, A. H., Kewman, D. G., Mercier, L., and Hovell, M. F. (1993). The power of nonspecific effects in healing: Implications for psychosocial and biological treatments. *Clinical Psychology Review*, 13: 375-391.

63   Turner, J. A., Deyo, R. A., Loeser, J. D., Von Korff, M., and Fordyce, W. E. (1994). The importance of placebo effects in pain treatment and research. *Journal of the American Medical Association*, 271: 1609-1614.

64   Institute of Noetic Sciences with William Poole. (1993). *The Heart of Healing*. Atlanta: Turner Publishing.

65   O'Regan, B. (May, 1987). Healing, remission, and miracle cures. *Institute of Noetic Sciences Special Report*, p. 44-54.

66   O'Regan, B. (November, 1987). Spontaneous remission: Studies of self-healing. Presentation at the Institute of Noetic Sciences conference in Washington, DC. p. 14-15.

67   Quoted in: Institute of Noetic Sciences with William Poole. (1993). *The Heart of Healing*. Atlanta: Turner Publishing. p. 20.

68 Weinstock, C. (1977). Notes on "spontaneous" regression of cancer. *American Society of Psychosomatic Dentistry and Medicine Journal*, 24(4): 106-110.

69 Quoted in: Institute of Noetic Sciences with William Poole. (1993). *The Heart of Healing.* Atlanta: Turner Publishing. p. 174.

70 Horgan, J. (July, 1994). Can science explain consciousness? *Scientific American*, 258: 88-94.

71 Ironson, G., Taylor, C. B., Boltwood, M., Bartzokis, T., Dennis, C., Chesney, M., Spitzer, S., and Segall, G. M. (1992). Effects of anger on left ventricular ejection fraction in coronary artery disease. *The American Journal of Cardiology*, 70: 281-285.

Barefoot, J. C., Dahlstrom, W. G., and Williams, R. B. (1983). Hostility, CHD incidence, and total mortality: A 25-year follow-up study of 255 physicians. *Psychosomatic Medicine*, 45(1): 59-63.

Musante, L., Treiber, F. A., Davis, H., Strong, W. B., and Levy, M. (1992). Hostility: Relationship to lifestyle behaviors and physical risk factors. *Behavioral Medicine*, 18: 21-26.

72 Pelosi, A. J. and Appleby, L. (1992). Psychological influences on cancer and ischaemic heart disease. *British Medical Journal*, 304: 1295-1298.

73 Peterson, C., Seligman, M. E. P., and Vaillant, G. E. (1988). Pessimistic explanatory style is a risk factor for physical illness: A thirty-five year longitudinal study. *Journal of Personality and Social Psychology*, 55: 23-27.

74 Vaillant, G. E. (1979). Natural history of male psychologic health: Effects of mental health on physical health. *The New England Journal of Medicine*, 301(23): 1249-1254.

75 Moyers, B. (1993). *Healing and the Mind.* New York: Doubleday. p. 207.

76 Eccles, J. C. (1986). Do mental events cause neural events analogously to the probability fields of quantum mechanics? *Proceedings of the Royal Society of London*, B227: 411-428.

77 Davies, P. (1988). *The Cosmic Blueprint.* New York: Simon and Schuster. p. 101.

78 Shapiro, R. (1986). *Origins: A Skeptic's Guide to the Creation of Life on Earth.* New York: Summit.

79 Davies, P. (1995). *Are We Alone? Philosophical Implications of the Discovery of Extra-Terrestrial Life.* New York: Basic Books. p. 27.

80   Kauffman, S. (1995). *At Home in the Universe. The Search for Laws of Self-Organization and Complexity.* New York: Oxford University Press.

81   ibid.

82   Sheldrake, R. (1981). *A New Science of Life.* Boston: J. P. Tarcher, Inc.

83   ibid.

84   Gaze, R. M., Chung, S. H., and Keating, M. J. (1972). Development of the retinotectal projection in Xenopus. *Nature,* 236: 133-135.

      Gaze, R. M., Keating, M. J., Szekely, G., and Beazlley, L. (1970). Binocular interaction in the formation of specific intertectal neuronal connections. *Proceedings of the Royal Society of London,* B175: 107-147.

85   Goodwin, B. (1994). *How the Leopard Changed Its Spots. The Evolution of Complexity.* New York: Charles Scribner's Sons. p. 34.

86   Hoyle, F. (1983). *The Intelligent Universe.* New York: Holt, Rinehart and Winston.

87   Scott, A. (1995). *Stairway to the Mind. The Controversial New Science of Consciousness.* New York: Springer Verlag. p. 186.

88   Cohen, J. and Stewart, I. (1994). *The Collapse of Chaos. Discovering Simplicity in a Complex World.* New York: Penguin Viking. p. 441.

89   Weiss, P. A. (1971). *Hierarchically Organized Systems in Theory and Practice.* New York: Hafner Publishing Company. p. 37.

90   Pattee, H. H. (1970). The problem of biological hierarchy. In: Waddington, C. H. (ed). *Towards a Theoretical Biology: Three Drafts.* Edinburgh: Edinburgh University Press.

91   Goodwin, B. (1994). *How the Leopard Changed Its Spots. The Evolution of Complexity.* New York: Charles Scribner's Sons. p. 196.

92   ibid, p. 196.

93   Kauffman, S. (1995). *At Home in the Universe. The Search for Laws of Self-Organization and Complexity.* New York: Oxford University Press. p. vii.

94   ibid, p. 8.

95   Maharishi Mahesh Yogi. (1972). *The Science of Creative Intelligence®: Knowledge and Experience.* [Lessons 1-33]. Videotaped course.

96   Heisenberg, W. (1962). *Physics and Philosophy—The Revolution in Modern Science.* New York: Harper and Row. p. 28.

97   Herbert, N. (1993). *Elementary Mind. Human Consciousness and the New Physics.* New York: Plume. p. 143.

98   Quoted in: Capra, F. (1983). *The Tao of Physics.* New York: Bantam Books. p. 123.

99   Herbert, N. (1985). *Quantum Reality. Beyond the New Physics.* New York: Anchor Press/Doubleday. p. 230.

100 Davies, P. and Gribbin, J. (1992). *The Matter Myth. Dramatic Discoveries That Challenge Our Understanding of Physical Reality.* New York: Simon and Schuster. p. 224.

101 d'Espagnat, B. (1979). The quantum theory and reality. *Scientific American,* 241: 158-181.

102 Quoted in: Herbert, N. (1985). *Quantum Reality. Beyond the New Physics.* New York: Anchor Press/Doubleday. p. 18.

103 Interview in: Davies, P. C. W. and Brown, J. R. (1986). *The Ghost in the Atom. A Discussion of the Mysteries of Quantum Physics.* Cambridge: Cambridge University Press. p. 66.

104 Capra, F. (1983). *The Tao of Physics.* New York: Bantam Books. p. 196-197.

105 Davies, P. and Gribbin, J. (1992). *The Matter Myth. Dramatic Discoveries That Challenge Our Understanding of Physical Reality.* New York: Simon and Schuster. p. 235.

106 Gell-Mann, M. (1994). *The Quark and the Jaguar. Adventures in the Simple and the Complex.* New York: W. H. Freeman.

107 Davies, P. (1992). *The Mind of God. The Scientific Basis for a Rational World.* New York: Simon and Schuster. p. 198.

108 Gribbin, J. and Rees, M. (1989). *Cosmic Coincidences. Dark Matter, Mankind and Anthropic Cosmology.* New York: Bantam Books.

109 Davies, P. (1995). *Are We Alone? Philosophical Implications of the Discovery of Extra-Terrestrial Life.* New York: Basic Books. p. 114.

110 Herbert, N. (1993). *Elementary Mind. Human Consciousness and the New Physics.* New York: Plume. p. 215.

111 Davies, P. C. W. and Brown, J. R. (1986). *The Ghost in the Atom. A Discussion of the Mysteries of Quantum Physics.* Cambridge: Cambridge University Press. p. 61.

112 Wigner, E. (1962). Remarks on the mind-body question. In: Good, J. (ed). *The Scientist Speculates*. London: Heinemann.

113 Jeans, Sir James. (1937). *The Mysterious Universe*. Cambridge: Cambridge University Press. p. 122.

114 The full quotation reads: "Everything we know about Nature is in accord with the idea that the fundamental process of Nature lies outside space-time. . . . but generates events that can be located in space-time."

Quoted in: Davies, P. and Gribbin, J. (1992). *The Matter Myth. Dramatic Discoveries That Challenge Our Understanding of Physical Reality*. New York: Simon and Schuster. p. 295.

115 Maharishi Mahesh Yogi. (1995). *The Science of Being and Art of Living*. New York: Meridian. p. 21. (Original work published in 1963).

116 Stapp, H. (1993). *Mind, Matter, and Quantum Mechanics*. Berlin; New York: Springer-Verlag.

117 The late Nobel Prize winner Roger Sperry makes this comment in his book *Science and Moral Priority*. (1983). New York: Columbia University Press.

118 Crick, F. (1988). *What Mad Pursuit. A Personal View of Scientific Discovery*. New York: Basic Books, Inc. p. 156-157.

119 Quoted in: Davies, P. (1983). *God and the New Physics*. New York: Simon and Schuster. p. 89.

120 See, for example:

Davies, P. (1983). *God and the New Physics*. New York: Simon and Schuster.

Chalmers, D. J. (1995). Facing up to the problem of consciousness. In: Hameroff, S. R., Kaszniak, A. W., and Scott, A. C. (eds). *Toward a Science of Consciousness*. Cambridge: MIT Press.

121 Chalmers, D. J. (1995). Facing up to the problem of consciousness. In: Hameroff, S. R., Kaszniak, A. W., and Scott, A. C. (eds). *Toward a Science of Consciousness*. Cambridge: MIT Press.

122 Maharishi Mahesh Yogi. (1994). *Maharishi Vedic University. Introduction*. Holland: Maharishi Vedic University Press. p. 53.

123 James, W. (1990). *The Varieties of Religious Experience*. New York: Vintage Books. p. 343. (Original work published in 1901).

124 This figure derives from physicists' calculations of the energy-density of the vacuum.

125 Maharishi Mahesh Yogi. (1985). Inaugural address. In: *Maharishi Vedic University Inauguration.* Washington, DC: Age of Enlightenment Press. p. 65-66.

126 Maharishi Mahesh Yogi. (1994). *Vedic Knowledge for Everyone.* Vlodrop, Holland: Maharishi Vedic University Press. p. 335.

127 Maharishi Mahesh Yogi. (February 16, 1992). *Structure of the Constitution of the Universe in Rik Veda.* Videotaped lecture. Vlodrop, Holland.

128 Hagelin, J. S. (1987). Is consciousness the unified field? A field theorist's perspective. *Modern Science and Vedic Science,* 1: 29-87. p. 77.

129 ibid, p. 75.

130 Hagelin, J. S. (1983). *An Introduction to Unified Field Theories.* Fairfield, IA: MIU Press.

131 Maharishi Mahesh Yogi. (1994). *Maharishi Vedic University. Introduction.* Holland: Maharishi Vedic University Press. p. 64.

132 Maharishi Vedic University. (1986). *His Holiness Maharishi Mahesh Yogi: Thirty Years Around the World—Dawn of the Age of Enlightenment.* The Netherlands: Maharishi Vedic University Press. p. 497.

133 *Bhagavad Gita,* 9.8.

134 Wallace, R. K., Fagan, J. B., and Pasco, D. S. (1988). Vedic physiology. *Modern Science and Vedic Science,* 2(1): 3-59.

135 Weiss, P. (ed). (1971). *Hierarchically Organized Systems in Theory and Practice.* New York: Hafner Publishing Company. p. 23.

136 Ingold, T. (1990). An anthropologist looks at biology. (Curl Lecture, 1989). Man (NS), 25: 208-229. Quoted in: Goodwin, B. (1994). *How the Leopard Changed Its Spots. The Evolution of Complexity.* New York: Charles Scribner's Sons. p. 198.

137 Weiss, P. (ed.) (1971). *Hierarchically Organized Systems in Theory and Practice.* New York: Hafner Publishing Company. p. 1-43. p. 7-8.

138 ibid, p. 9-10.

139 Carr, T. (1991). Medicine at the mind-body interface: The approach of Maharishi Ayur-Ved. *International Clinical Nutritional Review,* 11: 190-220.

140 Cutler, R. G. (1985). Dysdifferentiative hypothesis of aging: A review. In: Sohal, R. S., et al. (eds). *Molecular Biology of Aging: Gene Stability and Gene Expression.* New York: Raven Press. p. 307-340.

141 Maharishi Mahesh Yogi. (1967). *On the Bhagavad Gita. A New Translation and Commentary.* Baltimore: Penguin Books. p. 78.

142 Quoted in: Wallace, R. K. (1993). *The Physiology of Consciousness.* Fairfield, IA: Maharishi International University Press.

143 Differences in individuals' physiological response to stress are also dictated to some extent by their health habits, constitutional strength, and hereditary factors. This, however, does not change the basic relationship between a person's interpretation of events and the consequent effects on his or her body, which is the topic of interest in the present context.

144 *Charaka Samhita.* (1992). Dr. Ram Sharma and Vaidya Bhagawan Dass (translators). Varanasi, India: Chaowkhamba Sanskrit Studies Office. Vol. XCIV. p. 41.

145 Dillbeck, M. C. and Orme-Johnson, D. W. (1987). Physiological differences between Transcendental Meditation and rest. *American Psychologist,* 42: 879-881.

146 Wallace, R. K. (1970). Physiological effects of Transcendental Meditation. *Science,* 167: 1751-1754.

Wallace, R. K. and Benson, H. (1972). The physiology of meditation. *Scientific American,* 226: 84-90.

Wallace, R. K., Benson, H., and Wilson, A. F. (1971). A wakeful hypometabolic physiologic state. *American Journal of Physiology,* 221: 795-799.

147 Eppley, K. R., Abrams, A., and Shear, J. (1989). Differential effects of relaxation techniques on trait anxiety: A meta-analysis. *Journal of Clinical Psychology,* 45(6): 957-974.

148 This meta-analysis found that concentration techniques produced no effect on reducing anxiety. The other techniques (including the placebos) had similar effect sizes, ranging from 0.28 to 0.4. TM had an effect size of 0.7, which was statistically significantly greater than the effect sizes of the other techniques.

149 Harantani, T. and Hemmi, T. (1990). Effects of Transcendental Meditation on health behavior of industrial workers. *Japanese Journal of Public Health,* 37(10): 729.

Harantani, T. and Hemmi, T. (1990). Effects of Transcendental Meditation on mental health of industrial workers. *Japanese Journal of Industrial Health,* 32(7): 177.

150 Ottoson, J.-O. (1977). *Transcendental Meditation.* Socialstyrelson, D: nr SN3-9-1194/73.

Suurküla, J. (1989). The Transcendental Meditation technique and the prevention of psychiatric illness. Vasa Hospital, University of Gothenburg, Gothenburg, Sweden, 1977. In: Chalmers, R. A., Clements, G., Schenkluhn, H., and Weinless, M. (eds). *Scientific Research on Maharishi's Transcendental Meditation and TM-Sidhi Program: Collected Papers, Vol. 2.* Vlodrop, The Netherlands: MVU Press. p. 896-897.

151 Stark, M. J. (1992). Dropping out of substance abuse treatment: A clinically oriented review. *Clinical Psychology Review,* 12: 93-116.

152 Alexander, C. N., Robinson, P., and Rainforth, M. V. (1994). Treating and preventing alcohol, nicotine, and drug abuse through Transcendental Meditation: A review and statistical meta-analysis. *Alcoholism Treatment Quarterly,* 11: 13-87.

Review articles:

Clements, G., Krenner, L., and Mölk, W. (1988). The use of the Transcendental Meditation programme in the prevention of drug abuse and in the treatment of drug-addicted persons. *Bulletin on Narcotics,* 40(1): 51-56.

Gelderloos, P., Walton, K. G., Orme-Johnson, D. W., and Alexander, C. N. (1991). Effectiveness of the Transcendental Meditation program in preventing and treating substance misuse: A review. *International Journal of the Addictions,* 26: 293-325.

153 Wallace, R. K., Silver, J., Mills, P. J., Dillbeck, M. C., and Wagoner, D. E. (1983). Systolic blood pressure and long-term practice of the Transcendental Meditation and TM-Sidhi program: Effects of TM on systolic blood pressure. *Psychosomatic Medicine,* 45(1): 41-46.

Chalmers, R. A., Clements, G., Schenkluhn, H., and Weinless, M. (eds). (1989). *Scientific Research on Maharishi's Transcendental Meditation and TM-Sidhi Program: Collected Papers, Vols. 2-4.* Vlodrop, The Netherlands: MVU Press.

Wallace, R. K., Orme-Johnson, D. W., and Dillbeck, M. C. (eds). (1993). *Scientific Research on Maharishi's Transcendental Meditation Program: Collected Papers, Vol. 5.* Fairfield, IA: MIU Press.

154 Schneider, R. H., Alexander, C. N., and Wallace, R. K. (1992). In search of an optimal behavioral treatment for hypertension: A review and focus on Transcendental Meditation. In: Johnson, E. H., Gentry, W. D., and Julius, S. (eds). *Personality, Elevated Blood Pressure, and Essential Hypertension.* Washington, DC: Hemisphere Publishing Corporation. p. 291-312.

Schneider, R. H., Staggers, F., Alexander, C. N., Sheppard, W., Rainforth, M., Kondwani, K., Smith, S., and Gaylord King, C. (1995). A randomized controlled trial of stress reduction for hypertension in older African Americans. *Hypertension,* 26: 820-827.

155 Alexander, C. N., Langer, E. J., Newman, R. I., Chandler, H. M., and Davies, J. L. (1989). Transcendental Meditation, mindfulness, and longevity: An experimental study with the elderly. *Journal of Personality and Social Psychology,* 57(6): 950-964.

156 Cooper, M. J. and Aygen, M. M. (1978). Effect of Transcendental Meditation on serum cholesterol and blood pressure. *Harefuah, the Journal of the Israel Medical Association,* 95(1): 1-2.

Cooper, M. J. and Aygen, M. M. (1979). Transcendental Meditation in the management of hypercholesterolemia. *Journal of Human Stress,* 5(4): 24-27.

157 Orme-Johnson, D. W. (1987). Medical care utilization and the Transcendental Meditation program. *Psychosomatic Medicine,* 49(1): 493-507.

The TM group had 87 percent less hospitalization than the population norm for heart disease and nervous system disorders, 73 percent less for nose, throat, and lung disorders, and 55 percent less for tumors. The large reduction in the incidence of heart disease should be viewed in light of the fact that TM reduces a number of cardiovascular risk factors, such as hypertension, cholesterol, smoking, obesity, and the sensitivity of certain cardiovascular receptors to stress.

158 Herron, R. E., Hillis, S. L., Mandarino, J. V., Orme-Johnson, D. W., and Walton, K. G. (1996). The impact of the Transcendental Meditation program on government payments to physicians in Quebec. *American Journal of Health Promotion,* 10(3): 208-216.

159 Wallace, R. K., Dillbeck, M. C., Jacobe, E., and Harrington, B. (1982). The effects of the Transcendental Meditation and TM-Sidhi programs on the aging process. *International Journal of Neuroscience,* 16(1): 53-58.

160 Barrett-Connor, E., Khaw, K.-T., and Yen, S. S. C. (1986). A prospective study of dehydroepiandrosterone sulfate, mortality, and cardiovascular disease. *New England Journal of Medicine,* 315: 1519-1524.

161 Browney, B., Cameron, E. H. D., Griffiths, K., Gleave, E. N., Forrest, A. P. M., and Campbell, H. (1972). Plasma dehydroepiandrosterone sulphate levels in patients with benign and malignant breast disease. *European Journal of Cancer,* 8: 131.

Wang, D. Y., Bulbrook, R. D., Herian, M., and Hayward, J. L. (1974). Studies on the sulphate esters of dehydroepiandrosterone and androsterone in the blood of women with breast cancer. *European Journal of Cancer,* 19: 477.

162 Deutsch, S., Benjamin, F., Seltzer, V., Tafreshi, M., Kocheril, G., and Frank, A. (1987). The correlation of serum estrogens and androgens with bone density in the late postmenopause. *International Journal of Gynaecology and Obstetrics,* 25: 217.

163 Glaser, J. L., Brind, J. L., Vogelman, J. H., Eisner, M. J., Dillbeck, M. C., Wallace, R. K., Chopra, D., and Orentreich, N. (1992). Elevated serum dehydroepiandrosterone sulfate levels in practitioners of the Transcendental Meditation (TM) and TM-Sidhi programs. *Journal of Behavioral Medicine,* 15(4): 327-341.

164 Alexander, C. N., Rainforth, M. V., and Gelderloos, P. (1991). Transcendental Meditation, self actualization, and psychological health: A conceptual overview and statistical meta-analysis. *Journal of Social Behavior and Personality,* 6(5): 189-247.

165 The statistical effect size for Transcendental Meditation was .88 standard deviation units; for other forms of meditation it was .22 (14 studies) and for relaxation it was .28 (6 studies). Any effect size above .8 is considered significant, whereas effect sizes around .25 are considered similar to the effects of placebo treatments, which in some cases can be as large as .4.

166 Chandler, H. M. (1990). Transcendental Meditation and awakening wisdom: A 10-year longitudinal study of self development. *Dissertation Abstracts International,* 51(10): 5048B.

167 Cranson, R. W., Orme-Johnson, D. W., Dillbeck, M. C., Jones, C. H., Alexander, C. N., and Gackenbach, J. (1991). Transcendental Meditation and improved performance on intelligence-related measures: A longitudinal study. *Personality and Individual Differences,* 12: 1105-1116.

168 Travis, F. (1979). Creative thinking and the Transcendental Meditation technique. *The Journal of Creative Behavior,* 13(3): 169-180.

169 Pelletier, K. R. (1974). Influence of Transcendental Meditation upon auto-kinetic perception. *Perceptual and Motor Skills,* 39: 1031-1034.

170 Turnbull, M. J. and Norris, H. (1982). Effects of Transcendental Meditation on self-identity indices and personality. *British Journal of Psychology,* 73: 57-68.

171 Van Den Berg, W. P. and Mulder, B. (1976). Psychological research on the effects of the Transcendental Meditation technique on a number of personality variables. *Gedrag: Tijdschrift voor Psychologie,* 4: 206-218.

172 Aron, E. N. and Aron, A. (1982). Transcendental Meditation program and marital adjustment. *Psychological Reports,* 51: 887-890.

173 Maharishi Mahesh Yogi. (1967). *On the Bhagavad Gita. A New Translation and Commentary.* Baltimore: Penguin Books. p. 123.

174 Quoted in: Ranganathananda, S. (1991). *Human Being in Depth.* New York: State University of New York Press. p. 130.

175 James, W. (1958). *The Varieties of Religious Experience.* New York: Menor-NAL. (Original work published in 1902).

176 Symonds, J. A. (1895). *A Biography.* London: H. F. Brown.

177 Ionesco, E. (1971). *Present Past Past Present.* (Helen R. Lane, translator). New York: Grove Press.

178 Chew, G. and Needleman, J. (1985). Gentle events. An interview with Geoffrey Chew and Jacob Needleman. *Parabola,* 10: 42-46.

179 For a review of the biochemical and physiological changes associated with the fourth state of consciousness, see: Alexander, C. N., Cranson, R. W., Boyer, R. W., and Orme-Johnson, D. W. (1987). Transcendental consciousness: A fourth state of consciousness beyond sleep, dreaming, and waking. In: Gackenbach, J. *Sleep and Dreams: A Sourcebook.* New York: Garland Publishing, Inc.

180 Quoted in: Radice, B. and Baldick, R. (eds). (1965). *The Upanishads.* Harmondsworth, England: Penguin Books. p. 83.

181 Browning, R. (1906). Paracelsus. Reprinted in: *The Poems and Plays of Robert Browning 1833-1844.* New York: Dutto. (Original work published in 1835).

182 Maharishi Mahesh Yogi. (1995). *The Science of Being and Art of Living.* New York: Meridian. p. 25. (Original work published in 1963).

183 Quoted in: Davies, P. (1983). *God and the New Physics.* New York: Simon and Schuster. p. 89.

184 *III Khanda Upanishad, I.* p. 149 (I).

185 *Caraka Samhita.* (1983). Sharma, P. V. (editor and translator). Delhi, India: Chaukhambha House of Orientalia and Antiquarian Books.

Quoted in: Lonsdorf, N., Butler, V., and Brown, M. (1993). *A Woman's Best Medicine.* New York: Tarcher/Putnam. p. 290.

186 Quoted in: Wallace, R. K. (1993). *The Physiology of Consciousness.* Fairfield, IA: MIU Press. p. 176.

187 Maharishi Mahesh Yogi. (1995). *Maharishi University of Management—Wholeness on the Move.* Vlodrop, Holland: Maharishi Vedic University Press. p. 212-213.

188 Borland, C. and Landrith III, G. (1976). Improved quality of city life through the Transcendental Meditation program: Decreased crime rate. In: Orme-Johnson, D. W. and Farrow, J. T. (eds). (1977). *Scientific Research on the Transcendental Meditation Program: Collected Papers, Vol. 1.* Rheinweiler, W. Germany: MERU Press.

Dillbeck, M. C., Landrith III, G., and Orme-Johnson, D. W. (1981). The Transcendental Meditation program and crime rate change in a sample of forty-eight cities. *Journal of Crime and Justice,* 4: 25-45.

189 Dillbeck, M. C. (1990). Test of a field theory of consciousness and social change: Time-series analysis of participation in the TM-Sidhi program and reduction of violent death in the U.S. *Social Indicators Research,* 22(4): 399-418.

Dillbeck, M. C., Banus, C. B., Polanzi, C., and Landrith, G. S. (1988). Test of a field model of consciousness and social change: The Transcendental Meditation and TM-Sidhi program and decreased urban crime. *Journal of Mind and Behavior,* 9(4): 457-485.

Dillbeck, M. C., Cavanaugh, K. L., Glenn, T., Orme-Johnson, D. W., et al. (1987). Consciousness as a field: The Transcendental Meditation and TM-Sidhi program and changes in social indicators. *Journal of Mind and Behavior,* 8(1): 67-103.

Cavanaugh, K. L., Orme-Johnson, D. W., and Gelderloos, P. (1984). The effect of the Taste of Utopia Assembly on the World index of international stock prices. In: Chalmers, R. A., Clements, G., Schenkluhn, H., and Weinless, M. (eds). *Scientific Research on Maharishi's Transcendental Meditation and TM-Sidhi Programme: Collected Papers, Vol. 4.* Vlodrop, The Netherlands: MVU Press.

190 Orme-Johnson, D. W., Alexander, C. N., Davies, J. L., Chandler, H. M., and Larimore, W. E. (1988). International Peace Project in the Middle East: The effects of the Maharishi Technology of the Unified Field. *Journal of Conflict Resolution,* 32(4): 776-812.

191 Personal communication, May 1992.

192 Maharishi Mahesh Yogi. (1996). *Maharishi Forum of Natural Law and National Law for Doctors.* Second Edition. Delhi, India: Age of Enlightenment Publications. p. 312.

193 Maharishi Mahesh Yogi. (1994). *Vedic Knowledge for Everyone.* Vlodrop, Holland: Maharishi Vedic University Press. p. 327-328.

194 Wald, G. (1994). The cosmology of life and mind. In: Harman, W. (ed). *New Metaphysical Foundations of Modern Science.* Sausalito, CA: Institute of Noetic Sciences. p. 124.

195 Maharishi Mahesh Yogi. (1995). *Maharishi's Vedic Approach to Health.* Vlodrop, Holland: Maharishi Vedic University Press. p. 4-5.

196 Maharishi Mahesh Yogi. (1994). *Vedic Knowledge for Everyone.* Vlodrop, Holland: Maharishi Vedic University Press. p. 333.

197 For a detailed presentation of the parallels between the anatomical and functional structure of the physiology and the structure of the Vedic Literature, see: Nader, T. (1996, in press). *Human Physiology, Expression of Veda and the Vedic Literature.* Vlodrop, The Netherlands: Maharishi Vedic University Press.

198 Nader, T. (1995). *Human Physiology: Expression of Veda and the Vedic Literature.* Vlodrop, The Netherlands: Maharishi Vedic University Press. p. 200-201.

199 Sharma, H. M., Kauffman, E. M., and Stephens, R. E. (1996). Effect of different sounds on growth of human cancer cell lines in vitro. *Alternative Therapies in Clinical Practice,* 3(4): 25-32.

200 *Charaka Samhita.* (1992). Dr. Ram Sharma and Vaidya Bhagawan Dass (translators). Varanasi, India: Chaowkhamba Sanskrit Studies Office. Vol. XCIV. p. 419.

201 The U.S. Senate Select Committee on Nutrition and Human Needs. (1975). *Nutrition and Health: An Evaluation of Nutritional Surveillance in the United States.* Washington, DC: U.S. Government Printing Office.

202 Janiger, O. and Goldberg, P. (1992). *A Different Kind of Healing.* New York: Putnam Publishing Group. p. 102.

203 Fagan, J. (1995). *Genetic Engineering: The Hazards. Vedic Engineering: The Solutions.* Fairfield, IA: Maharishi International University Press.

204 Mayeno, A. N. and Gleich, G. J. (1994). Eosinophilia-myalgia syndrome and tryptophan production: A cautionary tale. *Trends in Biotechnology,* 12: 346-352.

205 Janiger, O. (1993). *A Different Kind of Healing: Doctors Speak Candidly about their Successes with Alternative Medicine.* New York: G. P. Putnam's Sons. p. 73.

206 The National Institute of Nutrition (Canada). (1990). Risks and benefits of vegetarian diets. *Nutrition Today,* 25(2): 27-29.

207 ibid.

208 Dotto, L. (1990). *Losing Sleep. How Your Sleeping Habits Affect Your Life.* New York: William Morrow & Co.

209 Everson, C. A. (1993). Sustained sleep deprivation impairs host defense. *American Journal of Physiology,* 265(5, Part 2): R1148-R1154.

210 Naitoh, P., Kelly, T. L., and Englund, C. (1990). Health effects of sleep deprivation. *Occupational Medicine: State of the Art Reviews,* 5(1): 209-237.

211 Dotto, L. (1990). *Losing Sleep. How Your Sleeping Habits Affect Your Life.* New York: William Morrow & Co.

212 Goldberg, P. and Kaufman, D. (1978). *Natural Sleep. How to Get Your Share.* Emmaus: Rodale Press.

213 *Charaka Samhita* (1992). Dr. Ram Sharma and Vaidya Bhagawan Dass (translators). Varanasi, India: Chaowkhamba Sanskrit Studies Office. Vol. XCIV. Ch. XXI, [26].

214 ibid, [25].

215 Fuson, J. W. (1976). The effect of the Transcendental Meditation program on sleeping and dreaming patterns. Doctoral thesis, Yale Medical School in partial fulfillment of the requirement for the degree of Doctor of Medicine. In: Chalmers, R. A., Clements, G., Schenkluhn, H., and Weinless, M. (eds). *Scientific Research on the Transcendental Meditation and TM-Sidhi Programme: Collected Papers, Vol. 2.* Vlodrop, The Netherlands: Maharishi Vedic University Press.

Miskiman, D. E. (1972). The treatment of insomnia by the Transcendental Meditation program. In: Orme-Johnson, D. W. and Farrow, J. T. (eds). (1976). *Scientific Research on the Transcendental Meditation and TM-Sidhi Programme: Collected Papers, Vol. 1.* Rheinweiler, W. Germany: Maharishi European Research University Press.

216 Sharma, H. M., Nidich, S. I., Sands, D., and Smith, D. E. (1993). Improvement in cardiovascular risk factors through Panchakarma purification procedures. *The Journal of Research and Education in Indian Medicine,* 12(4): 3-13.

Waldschütz, R. (1988). Influence of Maharishi Ayur-Veda purification treatment on physiological and psychological health. *Erfahrungsheilkunde—Acta medica empirica,* 11: 720-729.

Wallace, R. K. (1993). *The Physiology of Consciousness.* Fairfield, IA: Maharishi International University Press.

217 Maharishi Mahesh Yogi. (1996). *Maharishi Forum of Natural Law and National Law for Doctors.* Second Edition. Delhi, India: Age of Enlightenment Publications. p. 33.

218 Sharma, H. M., Dwivedi, C., Satter, B. C., Gudehithlu, K. P., Abou-Issa, H., Malarkey, W., and Tejwani, G. A. (1990). Antineoplastic properties of Maharishi-4 against DMBA-induced mammary tumors in rats. *Pharmacology Biochemistry and Behavior,* 35: 767-773.

Sharma, H. M., Dwivedi, C., Satter, B. C., and Abou-Issa, H. (1991). Antineoplastic properties of Maharishi Amrit Kalash, an Ayurvedic food supplement, against 7, 12-dimethylbenz(a)anthracene-induced mammary tumors in rats. *Journal of Research and Education in Indian Medicine,* 10(3): 1-8.

219 Patel, V. K., Wang, J., Shen, R. N., Sharma, H. M., and Brahmi, Z. (1992). Reduction of metastases of Lewis Lung Carcinoma by an Ayurvedic food supplement in mice. *Nutrition Research,* 12: 51-61.

220 Prasad, K. N., Edwards-Prasad, J., Kentroti, S., Brodie, C., and Vernadakis, A. (1992). Ayurvedic (Science of Life) agents induce differentiation in murine neuroblastoma cells in culture. *Neuropharmacology,* 31: 599-607.

221 Dileepan, K. N., Patel, V., Sharma, H. M., and Stechschulte, D. J. (1990). Priming of splenic lymphocytes after ingestion of an Ayurvedic herbal food supplement: Evidence for an immunomodulatory effect. *Biochemical Archives,* 6: 267-274.

222 Inaba, R., Sugiura, H., and Iwata, H. (1995). Immunomodulatory effects of Maharishi Amrit Kalash 4 and 5 in mice. *Japanese Journal of Hygiene,* 50: 901-905.

223 Inaba, R., Sugiura, H., Iwata, H., Mori, H., and Tanaka, T. (1996). Immunomodulation by Maharishi Amrit Kalash 4 in mice. *Journal of Applied Nutrition,* 48(1/2): 10-21.

224 ibid.

225 Dileepan, K. N., Varghese, S. T., Page, J. C., and Stechschulte, D. J. (1993). Enhanced lymphoproliferative response, macrophage mediated tumor cell killing and nitric oxide production after ingestion of an Ayurvedic drug. *Biochemical Archives,* 9: 365-374.

226 Misra, N. C., Sharma, H. M., Chaturvedi, A., Ramakant, Srivastav, S., Devi, V., Kakkar, P., Vishwanathan, Natu, S. M., and Bogra, J. (1994). Antioxidant adjuvant therapy using a natural herbal mixture (MAK) during intensive chemotherapy: Reduction in toxicity. A prospective study of 62 patients. In: Rao, R. S., Deo, M. G., and Sanghvi, L. D. (eds). *Proceedings of the XVI International Cancer Congress.* Bologna, Italy: Monduzzi Editore. p. 3099-3102.

227 Engineer, F. N., Sharma, H. M., and Dwivedi, C. (1992). Protective effects of M-4 and M-5 on Adriamycin-induced microsomal lipid peroxidation and mortality. *Biochemical Archives,* 8: 267-272.

228 Sharma, H., Guenther, J., Abu-Ghazaleh, A., and Dwivedi, C. (1994). Effects of Ayurvedic food supplement M-4 on cisplatin-induced changes in glutathione and glutathione-S-transferase activity. In: Rao, R. S., Deo, M. G., and Sanghvi, L. D. (eds). *Proceedings of the XVI International Cancer Congress, Vol. 1.* Bologna, Italy: Monduzzi Editore. p. 589-592.

229 Sharma, H. (1993). *Freedom From Disease—How to Control Free Radicals, A Major Cause of Aging and Disease.* Toronto: Veda Publishing.

230 Niwa, Y. and Hanssen, M. (1989). *Protection for Life: How to Boost Your Body's Defences Against Free Radicals and the Ageing Effects Of Pollution and Modern Lifestyles.* Wellingborough: Thorsons Publishers, Ltd.

231 Sharma, H. M., Hanna, A. N., Kauffman, E. M., and Newman, H. A. I. (1992). Inhibition of human low-density lipoprotein oxidation in vitro by Maharishi Ayur-Veda herbal mixtures. *Pharmacology Biochemistry and Behavior,* 43: 1175-1182.

232 Fields, J. Z., Eftekhari, E., Hagen, J. F., Wichlinski, L. J., and Schneider, R. H. (1991). Anti-aging and oxygen free radical (OFR) scavenging effects of an anti-carcinogenic natural product, Maharishi Amrit Kalash (MAK). *Journal of the Federation of American Societies for Experimental Biology,* 5(6): A1735. (Abstract).

Fields, J. Z., Rawal, P. A., Hagen, J. F., Ing, T., Wallace, R. K., Tomlinson, P. F., and Schneider, R. H. (1990). Oxygen free radical (OFR) scavenging effects of an anti-carcinogenic natural product, Maharishi Amrit Kalash (MAK). *Pharmacologist,* 32: A155. (Abstract).

Tomlinson, P. F. and Wallace, R. K. (1991). Superoxide scavenging of two natural products, Maharishi-4 (M-4) and Maharishi-5 (M-5). *Journal of the Federation of American Societies for Experimental Biology,* 5: A1284. (Abstract).

Niwa, Y. (1991). Effect of Maharishi 4 and Maharishi 5 on inflammatory mediators—with special reference to their free radical scavenging effect. *Indian Journal of Clinical Practice,* 1(8): 23-27.

Bondy, S. C., Hernandez, T. M., and Mattia, C. (1994). Antioxidant properties of two Ayurvedic herbal preparations. *Biochemical Archives,* 10: 25-31.

233 Hanna, A. N., Sundaram, V., Falko, J. M., Stephens, R. E., and Sharma, H. M. (1996). Effect of herbal mixtures MAK-4 and MAK-5 on susceptibility of human LDL to oxidation. *Complementary Medicine International,* 3(3): 28-36.

Sundaram, V., Hanna, A. N., Lubow, G. P., Koneru, L., Falko, J. M., and Sharma, H. M. (1997, in press). Inhibition of low-density lipoprotein oxidation by oral herbal mixtures Maharishi Amrit Kalash-4 and Maharishi Amrit Kalash-5 in hyperlipidemic patients. *The American Journal of the Medical Sciences,* 314 (5).

234 Lee, J. Y., Hanna, A. N., Lott, J. A., and Sharma, H. M. (1996). The antioxidant and antiatherogenic effects of MAK-4 in WHHL rabbits. *The Journal of Alternative and Complementary Medicine,* 2(4): 463-478.

235 Sharma, H. M., Feng, Y., and Panganamala, R. V. (1989). Maharishi Amrit Kalash (MAK) prevents human platelet aggregation. *Clinica & Terapia Cardiovascolare,* 8(3): 227-230.

236 Dogra, J., Grover, N., Kumar, P., and Aneja, N. (1994). Indigenous free radical scavenger MAK 4 and 5 in angina pectoris. Is it only a placebo? *Journal of the Association of Physicians of India,* 42: 466-467.

237 Quoted in: Norman, C. W. and Cooper, M. C. (September, 1990). Building for Heaven on Earth. The theory and practice of Maharishi Sthapatya-Ved. *Fairfield Source,* p. 24-29.

238 Lawlor, S. (July/August, 1989). Maharishi Sthapatya Ved—Using the science of building in accord with natural law. *Fairfield Source,* p. 22-25.

239 Tate, N. (1994). *The Sick Building Syndrome: How Indoor Pollution Is Poisoning Your Life and What You Can Do.* Far Hills, NJ: New Horizon Press.

240 Matanoski, G. M. (1991). Electromagnetic field exposure and male-breast cancer. *Lancet,* 337: 737.

Demers, P. A., et al. (1991). Occupational exposure to electromagnetic fields and breast cancer in men. *American Journal of Epidemiology,* 134(4): 340-347.

Tomenius, L. (1986). 50-Hz electromagnetic environment and the incidence of childhood tumours in Stockholm County. *Bioelectromagnetics,* 7: 191-207.

London, S. J., et al. (1991). Exposure to residential electric and magnetic fields and risk of childhood leukemia. *American Journal of Epidemiology,* 134(9): 932.

241 The following account owes much to these two articles by architects who have studied Maharishi Sthapatya Veda:

Lawlor, S. (July/August, 1989). Maharishi Sthapatya Ved—Using the science of building in accord with natural law. *Fairfield Source,* p. 22-25.

Norman, C. W. and Cooper, M. C. (September, 1990). Building for Heaven on Earth. The theory and practice of Maharishi Sthapatya-Ved. *Fairfield Source,* p. 24-29.

242 Quoted in: Norman, C. W. and Cooper, M. C. (September, 1990). Building for Heaven on Earth. The theory and practice of Maharishi Sthapatya-Ved. *Fairfield Source,* p. 29.

243 Davies, P. and Gribbin, J. (1992). *The Matter Myth. Dramatic Discoveries That Challenge Our Understanding of Physical Reality.* New York: Simon and Schuster. p. 138.

244 Nader, T. (1995). *Human Physiology: Expression of Veda and the Vedic Literature.* Vlodrop, The Netherlands: Maharishi Vedic University Press.

245 Maharishi Mahesh Yogi. (1967). *On the Bhagavad Gita. A New Translation and Commentary.* Baltimore: Penguin Books.

246 James, H. (ed.) (1920). *The Letters of William James.* Boston: Atlantic Monthly Press. To W. Lutoslawski, May 6, 1906.

247 Chew, G. and Needleman, J. (1985). Gentle events. An interview with Geoffrey Chew and Jacob Needleman. *Parabola,* 10: 42-46.

248 Quoted in: Maharishi Mahesh Yogi. (1977). *Creating an Ideal Society.* Livingston Manor, NY: Age of Enlightenment Press. p. 82.

249 ibid, p. 80.

250 Quoted in: Huxley, A. (1969). *The Perennial Philosophy.* New York: Harper and Row. p. 66.

251 Maharishi Mahesh Yogi. (1969). *On the Bhagavad Gita. A New Translation and Commentary, Chapters 1-6.* Baltimore: Penguin Books. p. 314.

252 Maharishi Mahesh Yogi. (1972). *The Science of Creative Intelligence: Knowledge and Experience.* [Lessons 1-33]. Videotaped course. Lesson 23.

253 Raines, K. (1975). *The Land Unknown.* New York: George Braziller.

254 Quoted in: Maharishi Mahesh Yogi. (1977). *Creating an Ideal Society.* Livingston Manor, NY: Age of Enlightenment Press. p. 81.

255 Quoted in: Huxley, A. (1969). *The Perennial Philosophy.* New York: Harper and Row. p. 75.

256 Raines, K. (1975). *The Land Unknown.* New York: George Braziller.

257 Maharishi Mahesh Yogi. (1972). *The Science of Creative Intelligence: Knowledge and Experience.* [Lessons 1-33]. Videotaped course. Lesson 23.

258 Maharishi Mahesh Yogi. (1995). *The Science of Being and Art of Living.* New York: Meridian. Foreword by Dr. Bevan Morris, p. xvii. (Original work published in 1963).

259 Jehcott, E. F. N. (1972). *Proust and Rilke: The Literature of Expanded Consciousness.* London: Chatto & Windus.

260 Quoted in: Maharishi Mahesh Yogi. (1977). *Creating an Ideal Society.* Livingston Manor, NY: Age of Enlightenment Press. p. 84-85.

261 Maharishi Mahesh Yogi. (1994). *Vedic Knowledge for Everyone.* Vlodrop, Holland: Maharishi Vedic University Press. p. 228-229.

262 Quoted in: Huxley, A. (1969). *The Perennial Philosophy.* New York: Harper and Row.

263 Quoted in: Huxley, A. (1969). *The Perennial Philosophy.* New York: Harper and Row. p. 57.

264 ibid, p. 76.

265 All quotes in this paragraph are from: Maharishi Mahesh Yogi. (1977). *Creating an Ideal Society.* Livingston Manor, NY: Age of Enlightenment Press. p. 77-85.

INDEX